random 03.27.01
$22.99

Eminent
Canadians

Eminent Canadians

Candid Tales of Then and Now

JOHN FRASER

M&S

Canadian Cataloguing in Publication Data

Fraser, John, 1944-
  Eminent Canadians: candid tales of then and now

Includes bibliographical references.
ISBN 0-7710-3133-5

1. Canada – Biography. 2. Canada – History. I. Title.

FC25.F723 2000   971'.009'9   C00-930072-4
FI005.F73 2000

We acknowledge the financial support of the Government of
Canada through the Book Publishing Industry Development
Program for our publishing activities.

We further acknowledge the support of the Canada Council
for the Arts and the Ontario Arts Council for our
publishing program.

Typeset in Bembo by M&S, Toronto

Printed and bound in Canada

McClelland & Stewart Inc.
The Canadian Publishers
481 University Avnue
Toronto, Ontario
M5G 2E9

1 2 3 4 5 6   04 03 02 01 00 99

For

ROBERT FULFORD
journalist

and

RALPH HEINTZMAN
historian

Contents

Let us now praise famous men,
and our fathers that begat us.

– ECCLESIASTICUS, 44.1

Come let us mock at the great
That had such burdens on the mind
And toiled so hard and late
To leave some monument behind,
Nor thought of the leveling wind. . . .

Mock mockers after that
That would not lift a hand maybe
To help good, wise or great
To bar that foul storm out, for we
Traffic in mockery.

– W. B. YEATS,
Nineteen Hundred and Nineteen

Introduction
My Known Dear Land

From Bruce Hutchison's *The Unknown Country*, published in 1942, in the midst of the Second World War:

> No one knows my country, neither the stranger nor its own sons. My country is hidden in the dark and teeming brain of youth upon the eve of its manhood. My country has not found itself nor felt its power nor learned its true place. It is all visions and doubts and hopes and dreams. It is strength and weakness, despair and joy, and the wild confusions and restless striving of a boy who has passed his boyhood but is not yet a man. . . . For we are young, my brothers, and full of doubt, and we have listened too long to timid men. But now our time is come and we are ready.

So, Uncle Bruce, apparently this won't do any more. Apparently it hasn't been the case for some time. Now, it seems, everyone knows our country, both the pollsters and the pundits, all the politicians and the poets, the press and the New York bond raters. The list just doesn't end. There are the university epidemiologists and the philosophers, the political scientists and the psychologists, and even the bloody botanists. They all know us *only* too well.

They say Canada is the best place in the world to live, but it's also so costly it's driving every bright young thing south of the border. We have created a multicultural haven, but in the process you can allegedly see the sparks flying from a racial tinderbox. We are a model of bilingual and bicultural accommodation, but our leaders seem determined – either by design or through misadventure – to break us up. Through good times and bad we have used our natural resources and limited manpower to create one of the world's best economies, but our entrepreneurial spirit is going to hell in a handbasket, just as an end is in sight to all that ubiquitous hewing of wood and drawing of water.

On and on it goes. We are about to become an extension of the United States, or we already have been part of the United States for decades without formally acknowledging it. A colony we began and a colony we remain, only the mother country has changed. We didn't notice because we kept the royal relics of the former while pocketing the standard of living of the latter. Although we are already part of Great America, we are nevertheless a "kinder and gentler" place that is, paradoxically, fed up with welfare bums and illegal immigrants. I can hear the whinging of the Saturday op-ed "think" pieces telling me even now that "The purblind nationalism of a generation ago seems today . . ." or "For Canada, the economic realities of the emerging global economy . . ." or "Immigration policy in Canada is today in a shambles after the illegal arrival . . ." I've written them all in my day, God forgive me: *mea culpa, mea culpa, mea maxima culpa.* I have even read an op-ed piece about a plan for selling our water in "iceberg packaging" to thirsty Arabs. I think it was published in *The Globe and Mail* the same day or the same week there was an arts-section front page on the National Gallery's big Group of Seven retrospective. Does this all mean we have stepped through the looking-glass and become hewers of water and drawers of wood? Is this how the end comes for Canada? Not with a bang but a pun?

And our leaders! How small and craven and unworthy the media make them seem now, where once they were written up bigger than life. In 1952, Uncle Bruce wrote a book about William Lyon Mackenzie King and called it *The Incredible Canadian*. ("The mystery of William Lyon Mackenzie King is not the mystery of a man. It is the mystery of a people. We do not understand King because we do not understand ourselves.") My father had a copy of it, and now I have it in my library, as I have all his books and his father's books and his grandfather's. They surround me with the passion and the insight of yesteryear that we have either forgotten or snigger at.

It was these old tomes that got me thinking about doing this book. I was struck so often by the contrasts, both good and bad, between then and now that it seemed to me I could try to emulate the *effect* of my library in a single book. We know, for example, that Mackenzie King consulted ghosts rather than polling gurus. If he had been trying to run for office today, we would have exposed that soon enough and laughed him to derision long before his first mandate was over. Were we so wrong to exaggerate our leaders' better qualities then? Are we right to magnify their flaws now? In the great court awaiting all journalists (a lesser court than the one awaiting real estate agents, lawyers, and historians, to be sure, but a severe one all the same), will not the sin that will most shame us and earn us time in purgatory be the effortless way we dismissed – I like the current argot which has reduced the word to "dissed" – the very people who struggled to bring and hold us together? Can we hear the inimitable sounds of the newer Canada in the babble of bitching *a Mari usque ad Mare*, in the grasping smallness of minds of the provincial premiers, on radio talk shows and letters to the editors, in the querulousness of our moral teachers in the pulpits and on ethics committees, in the confusion of our academics as they avoid any coherent definition of our past by sniffing at particulars of scant interest to anyone but themselves?

Oh yes, they all know our country only too well, Uncle Bruce. But we – the famous we that is R.O.C., the "rest of Canada" – we don't. It's changed a lot since *The Unknown Land* was first published, but change doesn't necessarily mean that it's different. We still have not grasped it yet, the full substance of it, in our hands and below our feet and in the air. We have not yet properly measured the pulse of its heart, the flex of its muscles, the pattern of its mind. And, as Uncle Bruce would say, we are getting on, my brothers and sisters, and still we are full of doubt, and still we listen too much to the words of timid men. Has our time come and gone? If, as Sir Wilfrid Laurier once said, the twentieth century belongs to Canada, then our time is obviously gone. Gone with east-west trade, gone with passenger rail, gone with Eaton's, gone with the island ferries to Prince Edward Island and the profits of Canadian Airlines. Gone, gone, gone.

Then again, maybe Laurier was a romantic and "twentieth century" meant something else to him than the nasty hundred years we are only now trying to put to rest. We all screwed up the twentieth century so badly we should try it again in the twenty-first. We should give Laurier, and ourselves, a second chance. If "next year Jerusalem" worked for all the centuries of the Diaspora, then surely "the twentieth century belongs to Canada" deserves some new, reinvigorated life. Why don't we agree that the nineteenth century, with its world wars and heightened nation-alism, didn't end until 1999 and begin the twentieth century right now? It is merely a matter of metaphysics and faith, and if you are a Canadian it is always wise to look favourably upon metaphysics as it helps you pass over all the rough spots and impassable barriers.

But in attempting a Tinkerbell ("If you believe, clap your hands"), let us also be mindful not only of the great folk who pre-ceded us but also of those who tried to hold the fort in our own time. We have been a people who for too long have found our history inconvenient and have cast it aside in some memory hole in order to placate the temper, and often the political correctness, of our own time. Institutions as well as people have held Canada together, by the proverbial hook and crook, yet often the institu-tions themselves have been the source of all the forgetfulness.

My aim in what follows is not to resurrect the dead and kill off the living but to reconcile the present with the past through the expedient of examining the mortal, malleable human beings who came to offices of great influence or power then and now. To this end, I have tried – in structure if little else – to emulate a famous book written shortly after the turn of the twentieth century, Lytton Strachey's *Eminent Victorians*. Strachey had different objec-tives than I have in this book. He was out to skewer the Victorian era that he and his colleagues in "the Bloomsbury Group" so loathed. The book's title was deeply ironic, and within its covers he took the reputations of poor Florence Nightingale, General Charles "Chinese" Gordon, Thomas Arnold, and Henry Cardinal Manning on a mischievous roller-coaster ride from which these titans of their era emerged shrunken and considerably discredited. The good that they had done was largely discounted and the bad much exaggerated: in other words, Strachey had devised the classic formula for the journalistic profile, especially in magazines, that was to dominate the media up to the present time.

Like Strachey, I too feel the pull of the mischievous, but in an alternative direction. I would rather redeem the dismissed and humanize the demonized, although to do so requires – as Strachey discovered in his opposite task – stretching the edges. The "eminent Canadians" in this book are a diverse bunch, but they are deserving of the adjective because they all assumed heavy burdens of office and struggled to live up to the challenges they found. If there is irony here it is in the fact that Canadians are reluctant to honour these struggles with little other than cursory acknowledgement. We have allowed historical figures such as Bishop John Strachan and George Brown to dwindle into obscurity, while their contemporary successors – Bishop Terence Finlay and William Thorsell – have been denied the respect that their predecessors at least enjoyed during their lifetimes. With others, such as the sovereigns (Victoria and Elizabeth II) and the prime ministers (Laurier and Jean Chrétien), the general decline in deference of our own age has led to a climate of insinuation and mockery – so much so that we are in danger of destabilizing institutions that bind our society and country together.

So the motive for this book lies not so much in Strachey's cheeky tome, despite the usefulness of the title and his format of four dramatic biographical essays, but in my own curiosity about Canada's past and how it bears on our future. It seems to me that as the texture of Canada, and indeed the very complexion of Canadians, continues to change dramatically, it is more important than ever to come to terms with our past. I'm sure that's one of the key reasons why there has finally been a resurgence of interest in history after several decades of uncaring ignorance. The short answer to Professor Jack Granatstein's recent and usefully provocative book – *Who Killed Canadian History?* – is you, me, and everyone else.

What follows is an attempt, however humble, to redress some of the excesses of my own profession of journalism, allied to the efforts of today's Canadian historians and teachers to redress their own past failings. I don't believe we can make intelligent decisions, or read the news sensibly, without understanding our past and seeing how the past is connected with the present. My own belief, which is certainly to the fore in this book, is that more people strive for their best intentions than succumb to their worst. I do not deny the worst, or even evade it, but I reject the notion that bad intentions define a human being more precisely than the good ones. The best historians know this; the worst journalists never give it a second thought.

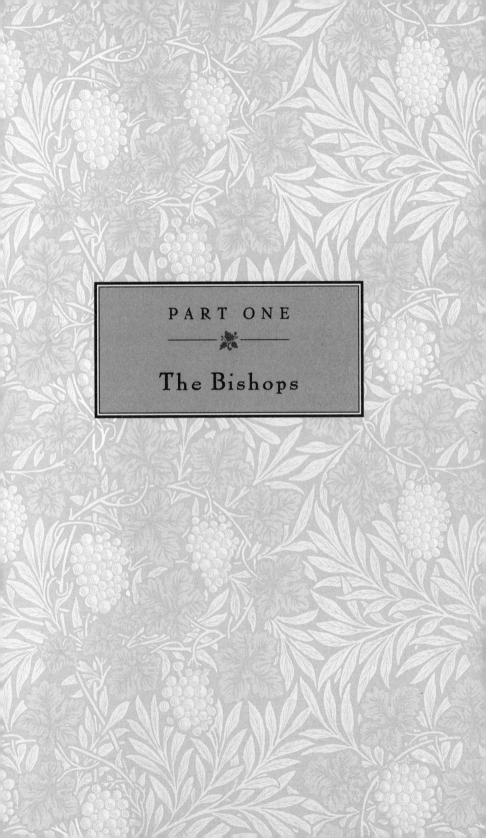

PART ONE

The Bishops

I

Even before the liturgical dancers had started leaping and the theological clowns had put on their knowing grimaces, it had seemed silly. Right up to the morning of the day in 1989 when it happened, it seemed silly. For some, but by no means everyone or even most, it was still silly when it was mercifully concluded.

The idea was to fill the entire SkyDome – all 60,000 seats. Fill it with signed-up communicants from the 215 Anglican parishes in Toronto on the 150th anniversary of their diocese. *Figures, figures, figures. The media like figures.* Just get them down there, line them up, put them in their seats, and let everyone take a look at themselves. Wow! *So that's what a diocese looks like!*

Then bring over the Archbishop of Canterbury (or if he can't make it, which he couldn't, get the Archbishop of York . . . *anyone* from the Mother Church). Bring in the five "area bishops," all three hundred full-time clergy, and another three hundred-plus clergy in retirement or visiting or studying at the city's two great theological colleges (Trinity and Wycliffe). The interdenominational colleagues were invited, of course, not forgetting our Judeo-Christian comrades from the synagogues (though possibly forgetting our Mormon, Muslim, Hindu, Taoist, and Christian Scientist brothers and sisters, yet perhaps some sort of informal word could be got, even to them). And don't forget the serried ranks of *ecclesia anglicana*: the suffragans, the deans and the rural archdeacons, the canons prebendary and residential, the curates and the lesser deacons, the sacristans and crucifers and vergers and sextons, the altos and basses and trebles and sopranos (in cassocks and surplices). Yes, the liturgical dancers and theological clowns too. *And the counter-tenors. For God's sake, don't forget the counter-tenors.* March them all in and have a concelebration of the Holy Eucharist at the largest altar ever seen in Toronto, or at least the largest since the Pope was here: certainly the largest *Protestant* altar, well not all that Protestant actually (mind you, with all those female priests, not all that Catholic either). Anyway, for sure the largest *Anglican* altar.

I had already encountered the clowns. Red noses, fuzzy hair, big feet – the whole show. Honestly! They carry within them the notion of "the foolishness of God" – simplicity, humour, pathos, tragedy through a smile and a simile. Someone in the cheap seats pointed out the obvious: *why draw attention to all the clowns who are already in holy orders?*

The liturgical dancers, however, were something new, at least to me. As befitted the gargantuan cavity they were trying to fill, the dancers' movements and gestures were . . . large. Very large. Each step seemed to be a leap, or a *galumph*. And as they lunged meaningfully forward, these *galumphs* seemed to land the dancers in a cubist variation of the balletic fifth position, their toes turned out as their arms took on the shapes of Pharaonic pyramid decorations. Back again in the cheap seats, someone described the whole procession as looking like a lost scene from the fictitious film *The Return to Nefertiti's Tomb*.

It wasn't the tenth Bishop of Toronto, the Right Reverend Terence Finlay, who said it, of course. He was nowhere near the cheap seats. He did laugh when he heard the line, though, and to give him his due, he hadn't really been so keen on this Anglican phantasmagoria. It had been his predecessor's idea. That predecessor – the Most Reverend Lewis Garnsworthy, the ninth bishop – wasn't just a bishop either; he was also the metropolitan bishop of an entire ecclesiastical province of dioceses and thus an archbishop. Archbishop Garnsworthy never thought small. When Bill Davis, the premier of Ontario, extended public support to the Roman Catholic high-school system (it already had public funding for the primary levels), His Grace likened him to Adolf Hitler. Just to make the point extra strong.

If Bishop Finlay was less imperial and intemperate than Archbishop Garnsworthy, he had nevertheless at his own enthrone-ment at St. James' Cathedral a few months earlier given permission to the youths of his diocese to carry helium balloons in the first processional down the main aisle of the nave. So even if he was thought to be unkeen to march in the old archbishop's parade, pre-sumably he didn't find the hijinks utterly abhorrent. What he was on record about was more serious, and it was simply that he hoped all the anniversary proceedings did not smack of triumphalism. Christ's message may be one of triumph over despair, but his church's obligation was to proclaim it in humility and with awe.

For a man who not only believed fervently in the traditional Anglican "middle way" and, moreover, who would in a few months' time stage a widely reported overnight protest on behalf of the poor and the homeless outside the provincial legislature building at Queen's Park, this Gothic ecclesiastical Disneyanna at the SkyDome was simply missing the point. Terry Finlay had not been put on this earth to rumble temple dancers or debate with clowns. When this kindly, decent son of a kindly, decent clergyman had first embraced his vocation, it was clear to many that he had come to continue the beleaguered notion of a Christ-filled life in an orderly but confused society at the end of the second millennium. That was a tall enough order in itself and if the task could be done at all, it could certainly be done without clowns and dancers. On the other hand, he was undoubtedly too kind to tell the clowns that they lacked a sustainable vocation and, in the end, he thanked them for their "special ministry." That's the sort of guff modern Anglican bishops have to say from time to time, and Terry Finlay was the very model of a modern, mitred Anglican.

To be fair, the day the Anglicans exchanged "The Peace of Christ" with each other at the SkyDome turned out to be more than a vaguely memorable moment of excess. The triumphalism was there all right, the sheer numbers ensured that, and there was silliness, but beyond the dancers and the clowns there was simplicity and grace. The concelebration worked too, at least for the faithful.

Yet, in retrospect, it is clear there was something else lurking around the premises, something spooky and maybe even malevolent. As in Scrooge's Christmastide, spectral visitors had come calling. In this case, they were spectral visitors from Episcopal Past and Episcopal Future.

Episcopal Future, Bishop Finlay's scorching encounter with contemporary mores about sexuality, was about to lurch out from one of his trim suburban parishes. A frivolous hint of the looming confrontation came, once again, from the cheap seats where I sat when a gay friend, observing some of the more outlandish priestly and secular outfits in the opening procession, commented that the annual gay pride parade had nothing to match it.

The other spectre, Episcopal Past, was the old century literally chomping at the bit. Through the haze of incense, it was just possible for the mind's eye to make out at the tail end of the grand procession a handsome black barouche with a liveried coachman driving four fine horses. Inside was the first Bishop of Toronto, John Strachan, the sixth son of an unpretentious Scottish quarryman. He wore a frock coat over his ecclesiastical bib and collar, and his bandy legs were swathed in gaiters, buttoned from top to bottom. Beside him was his chaplain, clutching a fair copy of the bishop's sermon and keeping an eye on his vestments and episcopal ornaments (cross and crozier, ring and sterling communion vessels) in their velvet-lined, cherry-wood travel box. Across from them was his verger, in charge of the bishop's purse and lesser luggage, his travelling port decanter and crystal glasses in their fitted mahogany case with brass hinges, and his special stock of linen handkerchiefs.

If Bishop Strachan had caught sight of the clowns or dancers, he would probably have dismissed them as *agents provocateurs* from the mayor's office. Or one of The Rev. Egerton Ryerson's damn fool ideas. In any event, he didn't let on he'd noticed. With one of his trademark whistles, deployed alike to register astonishment and feigned disinterest, he set to counting priests. When he first came to Toronto, or York as it was still called in June 1812, there was only one and it was him.

II

He was his mother's favourite. The final child usually is. Something about a last fling. And for a favourite in a family not exactly poor, but certainly not at all well off, his special mandate came at a cost. John Strachan, his mother, Elizabeth, decreed, "must be made a gentleman." That meant a grammar school in Aberdeen and an outlay of cash. Strachan's father is described as agreeing to this plan with reluctance. What choice did he have? *These mothers!* These Scottish mothers from the eighteenth century: how they circumnavigated the hardships of their lives, the cruelty of the land clearances, the deaths of so many of their children, the repeated defeats of their husbands' endeavours, the utter privation of opportunity. They simply transferred their blighted ambitions to their offspring, or at least the most favoured amongst their offspring. No, there wasn't any choice for John Strachan. At least one of Elizabeth's six children would be given the chance to step out of a circle that was not so much vicious as it was unavoidable. Unavoidable without a superhuman effort anyway. The only thing to be said for the eighteenth century in the highlands of Scotland in March 1799, when John Strachan made his decision to come to Canada via New York, was that there were only nine months of it left.

It seems symbolic now. On the very last day of the old century, December 31, 1799, at the age of twenty-two, Strachan reached Kingston, Ontario, and – at an annual salary of eighty pounds sterling – began teaching the very children – offspring of the Loyalists, merchants, and other settlers – who would grow up to run most of the affairs of the nascent colony. The sum and substance of the origins of the famous Family Compact – that allegedly nefarious, insidious, corrupt, and undemocratic oligarchy so loathed and resented by William Lyon Mackenzie and Egerton Ryerson and Jesse Ketchum and all proper-minded reformers and progressives – were to be found here in Strachan's first classroom in Kingston, and later in Cornwall, and, definitively, in York.

And what messianic wiles did the young Scottish teacher deploy to so bedazzle his youthful charges that they would later do his unquestioned bidding on any issue he resolved to either uphold or attack? It didn't seem to matter if the issue was the noxious question of the Clergy Reserves, those special allotments of Crown land given over to "the Protestant church," which Strachan would define exclusively as the "Protestant Church of England in Upper Canada." Or the "outrageous prerogatives" of the legislative executive council. Or the role of state-funded education. This "meddling little priest," as one of his greatest enemies labelled him even before he was consecrated into the episcopacy by the Archbishop of Canterbury, this "evil" bishop simply deployed a new teaching concept to fix the bond between him and his pupils for all the time they were to share in Upper Canada. He spent his energy teaching the older students and then made them teach the younger ones under his guidance. That's all, but it was at a time before the Church Lads' Brigade, before the International Scout Movement, before the pedagogical concept of responsibility, before children were thought of as human beings. He did it because he understood that power dispersed is based on power accrued. He also did it because, frankly, he wasn't that keen on teaching little boys and knew that their peers could do a better job.

Finally, he did it because although he was in many ways a typical early-nineteenth-century man, he was way ahead of his time in understanding that survival in this tenuous colony depended on the resilience and self-esteem of the first generation of leaders brought up in the new land, along with any sense of patriotic identity he could inculcate.

And let us be under no illusion about that tenuousness. Seven months of winter was its own annual assault. But in 1812, the year Strachan arrived in York to take charge of the new Church of England parish of St. James' Church, the United States Congress declared war on Great Britain. The Americans weren't fools. Angry at British attacks on their merchant navy, they had noticed that their former colonial rulers were preoccupied in Europe with Napoleon, against whom the bulk of their troops were deployed. There were spin doctors in the Washington of 1812, believe me, even if they were called by other names, and they saw in the unde-fended border of Britain's nearest colony a plum so ripe for picking, they could almost taste it in the newly built White House.

III

The hatred that the Rector of York and first Bishop of Toronto felt for Americans, born of two parts experience and three parts paranoia, was raw and not very pretty. It was one of the sign-ificant bequests John Strachan left his Anglo-Canadian countrymen, many of whom passed it on undiluted to this day. The fear and loathing sits there like a toad atop Strachan's nobler bequests, such as one of the liveliest dioceses in the worldwide Anglican Communion and two of the country's greatest seats of learning: McGill University in Montreal and the University of Toronto.

Often when the anti-Americanism surfaces in Strachan's story, it leaves an unpleasant whiff precisely because it seems to be in the same class as his intolerance of other Christian denominations. On these two subjects his personal cosmology was brutally simple: Americans and American sympathizers were traitors to the Crown; anyone in Upper Canada not married by the Church of England in Canada was not married. And A equalled B in both cases.

His national patriotism ran parallel to his denominational prejudice. He hated Americans and suspected them all of being Methodists: if someone in Upper Canada was an American, Strachan assumed they were Methodist; if they were Methodist, well then they were probably American or, at the very least, American sympathizers (which amounted to the same thing). The hatred gave a harsh, shiny glow to his patriotism because in puffing up the animosity, he seemed to be imbuing his definition of the alternative – honest, reliable, modest, sturdy, monarchical Canada – with almost metaphysical cogency and sanctity. For the future, this patriotism became an easy but unproductive cul-de-sac for English-speaking Canadians to travel down because the effort of finding other ways of self-protective accommodation with the United States were usually so difficult. Too often in our history when we needed flinty resolve and clever strategies, we embraced Strachan's darkest suspicions and lost the speedy, adaptable initiative a small man needs when he is next to a lumbering giant.

And Strachan's enmity could be very fierce. He hated the Americans openly, almost as much as he quietly stored up resentment against members of the Mountain family of Montreal: Montreal and too damn many other places. And that was hardly the half of it. The Mountains were neither Methodist nor American. In fact, they were English and Anglican, and not just English and Anglican but the definitive English-Anglican family. The great progenitor of this tribe in Upper and Lower Canada, the Right Reverend Jacob Jehoshaphat Mountain, was already ensconced as Bishop of Quebec when Strachan arrived in Kingston.

Jacob Jehoshaphat Mountain: what a mouthful for an honest Scot to say. Though an eternity away and tucked into the forbidding fastness of the Upper Canadian wilderness, in 1812 the far parish of York was still part of the vast diocese ruled by Bishop Mountain in Montreal. And then there was his infernal family: the Brother (the Reverend Elias Mountain); the Son (the Reverend Deacon George Jehoshaphat Mountain, eventually to become the first rector of York and the third Bishop of Quebec); and the Older Nephew (the Reverend Canon Salter Jehoshaphat Mountain).

The first Bishop Mountain, Jacob Jehoshaphat, the man responsible for holding back Strachan's advancement in the church for so long (while his own son, George Jehoshaphat, soared ahead), was dismissed slyly by the new Rector of York as being "too English" for the raw ways of Canada. He was an "elegant" preacher. Yes, yes, yes. And he had very fine manners. Oh yes, Bishop Mountain had lovely manners, no doubt about that. But to what avail was such delicacy? To what effect such sensitivity in the rough-and-tumble byways of the real Canada? For what purpose was his widely dispersed flock edified by edicts on the correct manner of consuming the sacraments when it was a backwoods miracle if a priest could get within fifty miles of a remote settlement? It would have amused Strachan's sense of ironical justice to learn that one day francophone language police in Montreal would insist that the street named after Bishop Mountain be renamed Rue Montagne. A perfect conclusion for the whole lot of these refined gentlemen.

The resentment Strachan steadfastly maintained for the Mountains had all to do with personality and career and present necessity. His hatred of the Americans, however, was visceral and metaphysical. It was grounded in the seminal experience of being invaded by the Americans and Strachan's courage in the face of the enemy. All of this, happening in 1813, is what gives his anti-Americanism its most effective cogency. It also explains why he was always on a collision course with those Canadians who had a far higher opinion of the great American experiment than he was constitutionally capable of. There was a context for his darkest suspicions: American troops once set his hometown on fire and looted the residences and commercial premises of his friends and neighbours.

When he arrived in York in June 1812 to take up the post of Rector at St. James', he had already been trying to warn his fellow colonists about the looming menace from the south. As early as 1809 he had served notice that war was coming and that Upper Canada was particularly vulnerable to invasion because of the sparseness of its settlements, their proximity to the border, and the large number of "probable traitors" – Americans who had drifted north in search of land but felt no allegiance to the Crown and were often at odds with the first generation of Loyalists who had fled the revolution.

There were various outlets for his harangues and polemics. He published discourses under his own name, which were reasonably judicious, and – within the context of the times and setting – uncontroversial, sometimes veering towards the unctuous and sycophantic (*vide* "A Discourse on the Character of King George the Third," 1810). When he wanted to stoop a little and join battle with bare knuckles, he could hack with the best of gutter journalists and wrote under a pseudonym in journals generally published in places other than York, which was prudent. His style here was pugilistic and often enough menacing. I imagine the effect was a bit like reading a jointly written column by today's Terence Corcoran of *The National Post* (for anger and contemptuous irritation) and Peter Worthington of *The Sun* newspapers (for patriotism and feistiness).

And then there were Strachan's sermons. When the situation called for it, he could rise to considerable eloquence. Unlike Bishop Mountain, he did not get detoured into the niceties of ecclesiastical or liturgical etiquette. He would launch out on a broad polemic and stick to it. Subtleties were for lawyers and other pedants. In what was perhaps his first sermon at St. James', he lacerated the United States for finding common cause with a despot such as Napoleon and described his concept of a "just" war. He preached with the assumption that in his congregation there would be some – possibly quite a few – whose sympathies might lie more with the troops of the Union than with the colonial militia. Given his true feelings on this touchy subject, his judiciousness is impressive:

A great consolation which will support us during the present unhappy times is the conviction that, on our part, the war is just. We were at peace and war has been declared against us; we have been invaded and attacked, so that we are constantly acting on the defensive, that is, we are repelling injury. Now the justice of our cause is of the greatest advantage to us; it is, indeed, half the victory....

In a free country like this, where differences of opinion concerning public affairs may be sincerely maintained, great danger arises lest a few designing men should take advantage of any party spirit that may exist, to promote their machinations, and induce by specious pretences the adoption of the most pernicious measures, under the cloak of securing their liberties, and maintaining their independence. In order to avoid any thing like this, let us carefully eschew all those questions on which we are known to differ; let us instead make a joint sacrifice of all the heats and animosities which those differences may have engendered; and since we are all anxious to defend our country against the common enemy by word and deed, let our only contention be, who shall outstrip the other in this race of glory.

He was addressing people fearful for their homes and lives, and from all reports this cogent martial talk reassured and armed them for the looming conflict. But he was far more than an effective pulpit orator. As chaplain to the local militia, Strachan took an intense interest in its preparedness and strategy. His support for Gen. Isaac Brock, commander-in-chief of the severely limited colonial forces (barely fifteen hundred regular soldiers for the whole of Upper Canada), was total. In an interesting counterpoise to his sermon on the sanctity of defensiveness, he praised Brock for going on the offensive once war had been declared and while others waited tremulously for the Americans to act. In this regard, he was very much an eighteenth-century parson. But this too: his natural courage in the face of harsh reality still has the power to arouse admiration. He knew, for example, that if the Americans came in any number, the meagre militia forces at York would be slaughtered. They hadn't a hope of defending the town.

When the time of testing finally came on April 26, 1813, and two thousand American troops arrived at the harbour of York, the militia disappeared along with what able-bodied men remained in town. There was to be no foolish wasting of lives when the population was still so sparse. It was left then to the women, children, a few Indians, and the Reverend John Strachan to attend to the safety of the small capital of Upper Canada. As he did during other pivotal moments in his long career when ordinary people were at grave risk, he summoned from within himself a far broader humanity than we have generally given him credit for. In this regard, he was the bravest of men and a real priest, ministering to the fearful and the deprived with a quiet, sturdy faith in a divinity beyond his full comprehension, but with a conviction that God's people had a duty to attend to their own destinies.

Years later, right up to Confederation in 1867, as long as there were people alive in Toronto who knew directly or had heard from their parents how Strachan had conducted himself during this and a second invasion four months later, the priest's bravery was always acknowledged. Never did a man busy himself so much with the myriad details of, in wartime, his seemingly irrelevant office. As American troops spread out through York, snooping into government offices and private homes, eyeing the younger women, blowing up artillery depots, and burning public buildings, there too was the Reverend John Strachan: tending to the sick (and admonishing a looter); leading a church service (and lecturing the commander of the Americans to respect the terms of capitulation he himself negotiated); visiting the old and infirm (and checking out the numbers of troops left aboard the fourteen invading American vessels); rescuing a widow's commandeered cow (and sending messages on the enemy's progress to "absent friends" beyond the town limits).

When the Americans came again in the summer, he even lectured their commander, Comdr. Isaac Chauncey, about his troops' behaviour during the previous invasion and presented a list of looted items he, John Strachan, wanted to see returned to their rightful owners.

No, they didn't forget his role in the war, nor did he. Out of this conflict, the Scottish-born priest became a Canadian patriot – or, at least, an Upper Canadian English-speaking patriot. One of the small militia corps in General Brock's command was entirely manned by Strachan's students or former students, including those who later became the prosperous, resourceful people who turned their generous portion of the globe into the envy of the world: William and Sam Jarvis, Archibald McLean, George Ridout, Robert Stanton, and John Beverley Robinson. These were all the Reverend John Strachan's boys. They fought with him for King and country; they saved their land from the invader; they grew famous and rich and started families that are now dispersed everywhere in Canada under dozens of different surnames, high and low.

They also formed a solid core of support for the priest as he rose in the hierarchy and in local government. Together, in the way of the world, they came to be seen as a compact group of conservatives and enemies of progress, which – in part – they probably were. Yet of all the new people in Upper Canada, they retained the strongest emotional links to the land. They were the ones who made the original land treaties with the Indians, not the later "pro-gressives" – good people such as Egerton Ryerson or Robert Baldwin – who never seemed to give a primary, let alone a sec-ondary, thought to aboriginal territorial legitimacy. John Strachan knew. It was only with the help of the Indians under Tecumseh that General Brock had managed to repel the Americans. There were some who felt, even up to his dying days, that the old bishop preferred the company of a heathen to one of those damn Methodistical Americans, always spouting "liberty and democ-racy" and forever waiting to annex the whole bloody country.

IV

In 1995, when by good fortune I came to preside over the affairs of Massey College in Toronto, I found myself at a tribute dinner sitting next to Emmett, Cardinal Carter. I told him about the small interdenominational chapel at the college and asked him if he thought it would be possible to find a Roman Catholic priest to say mass there.

"Oh, Mr. Fraser," said the old cardinal-archbishop with such a woeful countenance that my heart nearly went out to him. "Oh, Mr. Fraser, in this day and age, I'm sure you can find a Catholic priest who will do just about *anything*."

R.C., Anglican, United, Presbyterian: they're all doing every-thing these days, and it's hard to find a regular sort of cleric to tend to normal pastoral care. At the Church of St. Clement (Eglinton) in North Toronto, where Terence Finlay was rector for nearly five years between 1982 and 1986, there were certainly good priests before and after him, but no one who experienced his ministry there will ever say that there was anyone better. It is my own parish, so I can report personally that given the denominational profile and geographic location of St. Clement's, he was an almost perfect priest.

Time warms the best of memories and freezes all the rest, so I'm sure I exaggerate when I recall the special excitement of going to St. Clement's in Finlay's days. But not much. His sermons were not necessarily profound, but they were always deeply felt and he had a way – still does – of getting across the struggle he goes through on thorny problems. He was a man burdened with contemporary issues and acquainted with the complexity of modern life. A period of prolonged querulousness during the early part of his episcopacy, when he was locked in seemingly mortal combat with The Gay Issue, was the dark side of a trait that at St. Clement's had seemed mostly felicitous: a generosity in sharing the process of decision-making and empathetic patience (but not necessarily tolerance) in hearing out the endless tangles people get themselves into.

St. Clement's is situated more or less where John Strachan's male parishioners retreated when the Americans invaded. What then was virgin forest, traced by the nearby extensive ravine system that is such a distinguishing feature of Toronto, is now a series of middle-class homes, private schools, churches, and up-market shops. The architectural style of the church is ersatz Gothic, serviceable enough in its modest way but I think it is perfectly safe to say that no one will ever point to the grace of its soaring flying buttresses, the splendour of its nave, or the beauty of its stained-glass windows and other furnishings. Yet, come wind and weather, it is as warm and snug a redoubt as you can find during the bleak Toronto winter. As for summer, few know what it is like because most of the congregation are gone to cottage country in Muskoka or Georgian Bay.

Uniquely, of all the parish churches in the diocese of Toronto, a traveller in time and space from thirty years ago could perch herself on one of the rafters of the nave in St. Clement's and think nothing much had changed. There are still hordes of children going to the largest Anglican Sunday-school program in the city and possibly the country (over six hundred enrolled some years). There are still Girl Guides and Boy Scouts, senior and junior choirs, Altar Guild and church orchestra, Bible study groups and amateur dramatic societies, youth groups and a branch of Alcoholics Anonymous, military church parades every autumn and at least three Christmas Eve services to accommodate the seasonal hordes, support for Third World projects and inner-city needs, Scottish dancing and badminton clinics. In contrast to many of the desiccated parishes where it is now sometimes difficult to attract a congregation bigger than the assembled clergy and servers at the altar, St. Clement's is bustling with activity and brimming over with people. And prosperous too: it didn't get its nickname – "St. Clement's-and-all-Stockbrokers" – for nothing.

Yet if that time-traveller was coming from thirty or so years ago, she would certainly be clutching a copy of Pierre Berton's celebrated 1965 screed, *The Comfortable Pew*, which was commissioned by the Anglican Church of Canada to much howling from its conservative wing. Looking down from the rafters, our time-traveller likely would see St. Clement's full of precisely the pews described in the title. Parishioners are still prosperous and plentiful, still mostly white, heterosexual, and generally respectful of established hierarchies in church, in schools, in business, in family life, and — notwithstanding election-time grumbles — in politics. Hierarchical respect was one of the major bugbears in Berton's indictment of the institutional church emerging from "the complacent Fifties."

"The national creed of North America involves the worship of status and conformity," Berton began a chapter entitled "The Ecclesiastical Caste System." He quoted an anonymous Anglican priest who told him that "the whole system of getting clergy is actually geared to conformity. At the beginning you're shipped to a small rural parish. If you adapt, you're moved to a larger community. If you continue to adapt, you are moved to a metropolitan suburb and maybe eventually you attain a bishopric. The key word is 'adapt.' The fellow who is expected to provide leadership is the fellow expected to conform."

His mordant description of the ideal pastor of 1965 reads like some sort of churchy Babbitt:

> The best thing, it seems, that can be said of a clergyman today is that he is a regular guy, "one of the boys," "just like you or me." In spite of the prophetic tradition of the Bible, the Church encourages this attitude. Personal opinions, tendencies to radical criticism, a sense of irony, all distinctive personal traits, it seems, must be submerged so that the minister in no way stands out from his flock. Not only must his own personal tastes and views be sacrificed to those of the mass denominator, so also must those of his wife and children. The worst things that could be said of a minister today is that he is "different," an agitator, a disturber, an eccentric, an oddball, a radical.

There you go! Talk about an opening gambit for the rest of the 1960s. Berton was at his prime here as a journalist with his nose to the wind and a deft turn of phrase: even in this excerpt you can see him quite clearly, can't you, spotting the still-forming mood of the public, giving it coherent form and direction. It's the art of being ahead of the crowd, but not too far ahead. Just a half-pace ahead so that people can recognize the path and follow and think that you are a genius. Within a few years, the new joint Anglican and United Church hymnal would be stirring up any remaining comfortable pews with zingers such as "Sing We a Song of High Revolt" that includes this immortal fourth verse:

> He calls us to revolt and fight
> with him for what is just and right,
> to sing and live Magnificat
> in crowded street and walkup flat.

Or the ornate, giddy silliness of:

> Now thank we God for bodies strong, vitality and zest,
> for strength to meet the day's demands, the urge to give our
>   best,
> for all the body's appetites which can fulfillment find,
> and for the sacrament of sex that recreates our kind.

And not forgetting my all-time favourite:

> God of concrete, God of steel,
> God of piston and of wheel,

God of pylon, God of steam,
God of girder and of beam,
God of atom, God of mine:
all of the world of power is thine.

And so on and so on. Thus it was that with Berton's goading, as well as with the willing compliance of those for whom his text rang true, the Canadian branch of a church that had once worshipped God with the soaring language of Thomas Cranmer, and enticed John Donne and George Herbert in the seventeenth century and T. S. Eliot and C. S. Lewis in the twentieth to approach a metaphysical understanding of life through imagery that still has the power to seize the soul, this very same church decided to eschew all that and embrace concepts and imagery so banal that whatever comfort lingered belligerently in any pew seemed a blessing, best kept secret.

At St. Clement's, the congregation has gone along with many of the liturgical and language changes, but a succession of wise rectors has carefully retained the *Book of Common Prayer* for many services. That discriminating strategy was developed by Terry Finlay, who inched his appreciative parish along the way of church reform. Not for him the overturning of the fixed altar in the side chapel or the banishment of formal matins. He had his finger on the pulse of a complicated community longing for leadership and inherently conservative, even if it didn't want to fall too far behind progressive reform. He gave the leadership that this mixed-up jumble of spiritual and social ambitions needed and he gave it effortlessly with a smile or a serious look of involvement. And endless consultation.

The pews of St. Clement's retain wonderful secrets that are almost impossible to convey to outsiders. How many times over the past twenty-five years have I talked to priests and concerned lay people who recoiled almost in horror when they heard I worship at St. Clement's. In their minds, St. Clement's is to devotional worship what Kraft's shiny processed slices are to cheese. The whole notion of a large, vibrating parish is considered vulgar and against the mainstream of decline, where necessity has produced a generation of priests who have accommodated shrinking – not expanding – congregations: our numbers may be small, they always seem to intimate, but our worship is pure; our cause may be belea-guered, but our sincerity and suffering is beyond rebuke.

No thanks. I like a large crowd around me at church, a choir that can sing descants, a pipe organ that swells elegantly in a grand crescendo, and a priest who's a regular gal – or guy. It is a curious development in the mainstream Protestant churches that dysfunc-tional priests seem somehow holier than anyone else and that dwindling congregations are a sign of purer faith. In this light, St. Clement's was an aberration in Finlay's time because under his stewardship the congregation swelled in numbers, the Sunday-school program expanded, and the scope of the church's opera-tions and variety of its endeavours took on the dimensions of a small diocese. People who didn't like bustle with their religion didn't like St. Clement's. There was also a strong prejudice in favour of families, simply because the surrounding neighbourhood was filled with young couples and their vigorous offspring, many of whom started turning up at St. Clement's for the same reason my own family did: we wanted to do something together that was different from what we did throughout the rest of the week. It made a big difference, too, if there was a good priest.

So what makes a good priest at the end of the second millennium since the birth of Christ? Someone whose struggle to reach and sustain a sturdy faith is transparent. Someone who brings people together and dissipates factions, the bane of many churches. Someone who keeps his hands off children. Someone who can listen with patience to points of view quite different from her own. Someone who can laugh and cry. Someone who can communicate well, by word and deed. Someone whose humility does not diminish his dignity. Someone who has struggled to understand Bible scholarship, learned her church history, and understands that pastoral care is something more than pop psychology. Someone, in short, who makes a difference.

On all these fronts, the Rector of St. Clement's came out on top, or near the top. If there was a complaint – and there are always complaints under any form of leadership, secular or ecclesiastical – it came from a minority who felt that the Rector, while sympathetic enough, was out of touch with the complexities of life in the big city in the 1980s.

Let us reflect for a moment, as one might say in a sermon. We are talking relationships now. This is the end of the twentieth century and relationships – the definition of them, the lack of them, the longing for them, the whys and wherefores of them – are the passionate focus of many people. St. Clement's had its own fair share of happily married couples, single people, divorced people, lesbians, people in loveless marriages, closet gays and open gays, stressed-out families, and rock-solid companions. They were all there, kneeling and praying and singing beside each other, no one quite sure what was driving his or her neighbour into those pews, but liking the community and hoping, praying, *longing* for a certain relationship to last, to begin, to improve, to cease, to ease the pain of living, to share the joy of being alive.

I remember one Palm Sunday during Terry Finlay's regime when my wife, Elizabeth MacCallum, was singing in the choir for the eleven o'clock service of matins. Loathing matins as I do, I had snuck out of the service and was roaming around the familiar building and found myself approaching a small reception room. I first heard the desolate sobbing about twenty yards away and it stopped me in my tracks. Gasping sobs, a high howling into the blank universe and a despair that stabbed my own heart. Gingerly I approached the doorway and caught a glimpse of the poor woman inside. As soon as I saw her, I knew what the problem was. Her husband was having an affair with another member of the congregation, whom I also knew, and it had spiralled utterly out of control because the estranged spouse on the other side had also become sexually involved with a very important member of the parish community.

Before I heard the sobbing, which brought the emotional tragedy of betrayal close to home, I had thought the bits of gossip about all this rather amusing. I said to my wife, who was then a director and producer for *The Nature of Things* (the Canadian Broadcasting Corporation's signature science program), that life was continuing very strange. I at *The Globe and Mail* and she at the CBC both worked at institutions where common-law marriages were frequent and where, one would have thought reasonably enough, there was considerable stress and transience to relationships. We went to church, or so I told close friends, because that was where relationships were hallowed under God's law and we thought it was good to be around people who took their vows seriously. *But what was this?* Sobbing in the vestry, hanky-panky in the choir room, remorse in the nave, forgiveness at the altar, and – I hoped – salvation at the grave. "I'm going to write a little Harlequin novel about my experiences at St. Clement's," Finlay said to me one day after what was no doubt a rough session of sorting couples out, "and I'm just going to call it *North Toronto Pastor*. It'll be a real page-turner, I promise you."

Well, so far as I could observe, he did sort that one out. One couple left the church, another separated, and the ex-husband was handed on to another parish. Yukky enough stuff, but someone had to bring in some coherent humanity to the situation and help people to help themselves. Somehow Finlay did it, and as I never heard a single bitter word about him from any of the affected parties, I made the assumption that the angels had been on his side.

And then there was my married friend who phoned me up one day to say he really needed to talk to me about the mess his life was in and did I mind being "a listening ear." I didn't say, "Yes, I damn well do mind, so get yourself a priest or a psychiatrist," because that's not what friends are supposed to say. The real trouble was I could guess the problems only too well. My poor chum was married and I was pretty sure he was gay and should never have married. He was also having a difficult time trying to figure out where God fit in to the nightmare of his life. This was all hopelessly complicated by the fact that my dear, desperate friend was also about to become a priest, so on my luncheon menu that day was (1) a crisis of marriage, (2) a crisis of faith, and (3) a crisis of sexuality. This was a bad bill of fare and all I wanted was a club sandwich with extra mayonnaise.

I am a good strategist, but I am not terrific with pastoral care. My concept of dealing with emotional problems is to employ stiffeners for the upper lip. I was such a beast to my friend at this lunch that I think I even hurled Martin Luther King's famous line to him, ludicrously out of context ("Undeserved suffering ennobles the soul"), and recommended that he take counselling from his pastor, our rector.

"I can't," my poor friend moaned. "He's kind, but he's on another planet."

Yet even here where he was thought to be unsympathetic to the central dilemma, Finlay must have done something right because, years later, when his own great trouble ensued with The Gay Issue, this man – now priested, comfortable with his homosexuality, and forever struggling with celibacy – became a quiet ally of the beleaguered bishop and defended him within the gay and gay-sympathetic community of his church, a community that was far bigger and more mainstream than the bishop had ever before realized. Finlay may have come from "another planet," but he had credit in a bank in Mars that helped to assuage some of the conflict and pain waiting to waylay him.

He also had credit in another, and closer, relationship. As the son of a clergyman and an astute observer of relationships, he understood how appalling was the life usually accorded ministers' spouses in the Anglican Church. Consequently, the relationship he had with Alice-Jean Finlay and their two daughters set the kind of example that simply made everyone at St. Clement's struggling to live decent, loyal family lives feel good about themselves. It was just as well, for in the ordeal that lay ahead, his best ally was Alice-Jean, who became his shield and buckler, his solace and the real source of his courage. It turns out there are rewards for monogamy and faithfulness that can lighten the corners of even the darkest days.

But all this is jumping ahead. In the goodness of time and, no doubt, as a reward for the careful and sensitive work he had done, Terence Finlay was elected the tenth Bishop of Toronto and

ninth successor to John Strachan. His enthronement at St. James'
Cathedral – the third building Bishop Strachan had been
required to erect on the ashes of its predecessors – was a splendid
event. As the bishop-elect processed down the central aisle, surrounded by a congregation drawn from junctures of his life, he
could be forgiven any sense of elation the soaring organ and
choir may have induced.

His triumphantly ascending curriculum vitae all seems so
inevitable now: bachelor of theology from the University of
Western Ontario and master of arts from Cambridge; ordained
deacon in 1961 and priest the next year; chaplain at Sir Wilfrid
Laurier University; dean of residence at Renison College,
University of Waterloo; Rector at All Saints, Waterloo; Incumbent
at St. Aiden's, London, Ontario; Rector of St. John the Evangelist,
London; Rector of Grace Church, Brantford; Archdeacon of
Brant; Incumbent at St. Clement's (Eglinton), Toronto; Consecrated
Bishop in 1986 and Appointed Area Bishop of Trent-Durham;
elected Bishop Coadjutor of Toronto in 1987; and – in the goodness of time – installed as the tenth Bishop of Toronto on January 6,
1989. I suppose "Archbishop and Primate of All-Canada" could be
added to this CV to conclude it properly (appointments in heaven
itself can wait), but if you talk to Anglicans in the know, they will
tell you that the Primate's job is a bit of a step down from the bishopric of Toronto. Judging from the splendour of his enthronement
in St. James' Cathedral, you would have thought that only a king
of England at his coronation in Westminster Abbey could summon
more pomp and circumstance.

Still, he was warned.

Waiting to embrace him was his predecessor, old Archbishop
Garnsworthy, bent over from the vicissitudes of age, the side effects

of a recent stroke, and the ordeals of office. At the end of processional, with the organ's trumpet fanfares still echoing in his ears,
the frail prelate leaned on Finlay's strong shoulders and whispered
hoarsely in his ear, "Enjoy this moment, Bishop. It's all downhill
from here."

V

The picture of John Strachan that comes through the mist of
pre-Confederation Canada has generally been one of an
officious elitist and a meddling political priest. If he himself was
not above nudging historical facts to suit his own definition of the
way things were, or should be, or better be, a long list of detractors
– you could start with Egerton Ryerson and conclude, for the
moment, with Pierre Berton – have ensured that the most
significant figure in English-speaking Canada during its earliest
years has been aggressively and effectively caricatured and thus
sidelined except within the memory of those who love his church
and know the specifics of his contributions.

Berton's picture is a convenient summary of the process. In
The Invasion of Canada, for example, almost the first reference to
Strachan – the sixth son of a quarryman – is as an "aristocrat,"
and this theme is picked up in *Flames Across the Border*, the second
volume of Berton's history of the 1812–14 war, where Strachan is

portrayed as being fanatically obsessed with power. You have to keep in mind that the real fanatic of the age, William Lyon Mackenzie, has generally been served up to us as an idealized democrat ahead of his time, rather than the intemperate and malignant nincompoop that he truly was. In this preference for the dysfunctional rabble-rouser over the efficient leader, the romantic over the pragmatic, and the melodramatic asshole over the wise counsellor, we have formed a history that dooms us to consistently depressing assessments of our political culture, whatever it may have been or is at the moment. John Strachan helped to build a country, and we pay him little regard; William Lyon Mackenzie tried to destroy the careful if precarious construction, and we turn him into a secular saint.

If you like playing this game of historical manipulation and enjoy seeing how it is done, consider the following facts. *Item*: In 1807, Strachan married his beloved wife, Ann Wood McGill. *Item*: McGill was the widow of Andrew McGill of Cornwall, who was the brother of the legendary fur merchant, James McGill. *Item*: It was Strachan who was responsible (though a largely forgotten fact) for persuading James McGill to leave enough funds in his will to found the great university in Montreal named after him. *Item*: Throughout his teaching career, Strachan pushed the brightest of his charges to accept responsibility for the governance of the fragile colony, and everyone else was taught to respect the Crown, love the land, and nurture enterprise. *Item*: As soon as he spied a likely lad who showed great promise, he pushed him hard to excel, as there was such a dearth of good public servants. The first to receive this treatment was John Beverley Robinson, who esteemed Strachan for the rest of his life. *Item*: Any advancement he got for

himself, Strachan usually had to plead for, sometimes – for someone who contributed so much – in almost embarrassing terms.
Item: Whether it was his rectory in York, his doctoral degree from
the University of Aberdeen, or even his bishopric, *nothing* ever
seemed to come to Strachan on a silver platter. *Item*: He was constantly in debt and money lenders were always on his trail, pressing
him hard – so hard that his debts stayed with him till death and he
was never able to retire.

Here's Pierre Berton in *Flames Across the Border* on some of
these same facts in a brief (but calculatingly conclusive) character
sketch of Strachan, "caught out" at just the moment he first heard
of the arrival of the invading Americans in 1813. Forget for now
that the bulk of Strachan's illustrious career still lies ahead of him.
Forget that he has been in York for only a year. Forget that British
forces faded away after the arrival of the American invaders and it
was left to the new Rector of York to stand up to the enemy and
extract whatever promises of good behaviour he could. Forget his
native wit and Scottish cunning. Berton has already introduced
Strachan as a jingoistic warmonger and Tory loudmouth, although
he can't quite obliterate the image of the priest being the only
prominent citizen of York to mitigate the effects of the invading
troops:

> John Strachan is up at four and astride his horse, galloping
> westward toward the garrison. The American fleet has come
> into view, and Strachan cannot stand to be on the perimeter of
> action. He must be at the centre, for it is power he seeks – he
> makes no bones about that – and as the events of the next few
> days will show, he knows how to seize it. Not for nothing has
> he educated the sons of the elite, first in Cornwall, now at

York. His avowed plan is to place these young men in positions of influence. The weak lower house – the House of Assembly – the only elected body in the province, is composed, in his view, of "ignorant clowns." He blames that on "the spirit of levelling that seems to pervade the province," a dangerous Yankee idea. But when he gets his pupils into the assembly, then "I shall have more in my power." Already his chief protege, John Beverley Robinson, a solemn twenty-one-year-old of good Loyalist stock who fought at Queenston, has been made acting attorney general.

Strachan understands the road to power, knows how to cultivate the aristocracy, how to make the most of opportunity. He has married into power: his pretty little wife, Ann, is the widow of Andrew McGill, brother of James, one of Montreal's leading fur merchants whose name will one day be enshrined on a famous university. The McGill connection has opened doors to Montreal's ruling merchant class. A Doctor of Divinity degree, for which Strachan has actively lobbied, adds to his stature. Strachan, the elitist, knows how to make the most of his fellow elitists, for although "there are no distinctions of rank in this country no people are so fond of them. If a fellow gets a commission in the militia however low he will not speak to you under the title of Captain." But everyone speaks to the Reverend Doctor Strachan.

This is rich stuff, and in its own guileful way rather fun. I love the deployment of adjectives that put everyone in his or her place: Ann McGill is "little," and John Beverley Robinson is "solemn." I love the whole concept of an aristocracy in Upper Canada at this time: it's a bit like looking today for the Duke of York in Bramalea.

Ignoring the crucial role he played as a founder of McGill, Strachan is instead portrayed as "actively" lobbying for an honorary degree when, in fact, the actual lobbying was done by close friends at the University of Aberdeen. And then there's all this influence with the powerful in Montreal. To what effect, one wants to ask? Perhaps family connections may, for a while, have helped his eldest son find employment years later, but his eldest son also dwindled into near bankruptcy, so it's hard to see where this power was being deployed. It certainly didn't speed up his own ecclesiastical preferment. He had to "actively lobby" (I borrow from Mr. Berton's terminology) for his non-paying bishopric and even here he had years of frustration trying to circumvent the Mountain family, who really did have solid connections to the Montreal power-brokers. (How could they not? Every week the Mountains forgave them all their sins!) Instead of procuring any financial relief for himself, he persuaded his "Montreal connections" to support a great university. For years in York, all his connections and power could not bring about his most fervent dream – a university – and when he finally did get it going and became its first president, was he not forced out within a few years, which led to a second start with what is now Trinity College within the University of Toronto? Here we are, then, in the dark heart of the notorious Family Compact oligarchy: family, wealth, privilege, land, access to the highest echelons of government, control over political ridings, preferment for offspring, secret understandings, and ominous dealings. And the evil result of all this pernicious collusion and conjunction of influence is . . . McGill University? The University of Toronto? Trinity College?

It is much more useful to take a look at Strachan's enemies than forage about like this in the embers of the Family Compact and all the attendant paranoia. The Family Compact as a political entity ruled Upper Canada for a while; it was instrumental in rallying the colony in the face of American expansionism and bullying; it laid the roots for subsequent economic prosperity although it seemed hard-hearted and vanquished of useful policy when faced with recession; it got arrogant in office; it lost power. The same could be said of the first post-Confederation administration of Sir John A. Macdonald or the Trudeau years. There's not a lot more that's truly intriguing about the business. But enemies! You could learn to love a man by his enemies just as easily as you could learn to despise him. There is an ideological divide here, a Left/Right if you like, although Strachan was not so much the doyen of "The Tory Establishment" as he was the establisher of the Establishment, and there's a difference. In nurturing and defending his people during wartime and peace, the Rector of York won a position for himself that was willingly accorded him by most reasonable people in Upper Canada. Long after the Family Compact had dwindled into history and after the Clergy Reserves* question was decisively settled contrary to his lifelong campaigns and hopes, John Strachan was still Bishop of Toronto. But in his prime, outside

---

* The Clergy Reserves bedevilled the early history of Canada almost up to Confederation. The name refers to the land set aside in Upper and Lower Canada in the Constitution Act of 1791 "for the support and maintenance of the Protestant clergy." This was not small potatoes as it amounted to somewhere between a seventh and an eighth of all Crown land in the two vast colonial provinces. Muscular Anglicans, ever proprietorial, tended to talk about them a bit like Mr. Thwackum in Henry Fielding's *Tom Jones*: "When I talk about religion, Sir, I don't mean any religion but the Christian religion, and not just the Christian religion, but the Church of England." John Strachan was a muscular enough Anglican, but he was also a prior Presbyterian, and when really pushed to the wall he did not object to the Presbyterians or the Roman Catholics getting their hands on the Clergy Reserves. He was not so forbearing with the Methodists. Clearly, other Protestant groups resented any suggestion that the Reserves were exclusively for the Church of England. In time, the whole notion of Clergy Reserves became hotly contested, not just by Methodists, but by land developers and government officials who found them "a consternation and a damn nuisance."

of church affairs, he did wield real power through his position on the executive council of the legislature. Like all people in such positions, he was to learn that you can make enemies simply by waking up in the morning and going to work.

In enduring for so long, however, in becoming a myth in his own time, he easily outlived most of his political enemies. Yet, one way or another, he also made peace with most of them. He loathed Methodists, as we already know, but he was not by any stretch of the imagination a blind denominational bigot. His Anglicanism was traditional establishment centrism that often strikes non-Anglicans as arrogant. And the trappings embellish the misunderstanding, although Strachan certainly grew splendidly into all his Trollopian roles. If he felt there was no question that his church was the "appropriate" vehicle for upholding civility, careful governance, and the pious acceptance of Christian fate, he nevertheless ultimately understood that the evolving colony and province – and particularly its educational institutions – were not going to conform to his ideal. If he always fought briskly and to the limit, he also knew when he was defeated and how to retreat. Despite his vigorous campaign to keep the Clergy Reserves exclusively for the Anglicans, a fight he ultimately lost with stubborn grace, he consorted and liked Presbyterians, Lutherans, and Roman Catholics. He was, in essence, the kind of forbearing Anglican parson who upset and unsettled the sterner denominations. Years later, when he was on one of his ceaseless rounds of the diocese, sometimes baptizing and confirming thousands, a sanctimonious worthy gentleman snitched on the bishop's local incumbent because he "drank his liquor straight from the bottle." Strachan assured the worthy gentleman that he would admonish the foolish priest at once. "It's wasteful to consume liquor by the bottle," he said. "He should purchase it as I do – by the barrel."

Also – and, for me, this is a crucial test in evaluating the character of any historical or publicly prominent figure – he could differentiate amongst his enemies between scoundrels, mad men, and men of honour. God particularly knows how much the Reverend Egerton Ryerson got under the first Bishop of Toronto's skin. For one thing, he was part of the infernal cabal of dissenters who "plotted" to steal the Clergy Reserves or to secularize his beloved King's College. But Ryerson was also a patriot and a man who believed fervently in the emancipation of the mind through education. At this intellectual intersection, at least, there was a rough bond. Once, in 1842, after years of harsh words to and about each other, they found themselves in the same coach heading for Kingston. Both men must have been somewhat chagrined, but in *Story of My Life*, Ryerson reported that they did not argue at all, "nor could I desire to meet with a more affable and agreeable man than the Bishop." And Ryerson was not just any Methodist: he was *the* Methodist.

Strachan's greatest foe, of course, was William Lyon Mackenzie, who successfully got the Rector of York and Bishop of Toronto labelled an oligarch and whose repeated assaults on the pernicious Family Compact in his newspaper, *The Colonial Advocate*, have been grist for Strachan's detractors ever since. There's no question that Mackenzie caused Strachan real grief, and the priest saw him as the harbinger of the growing restlessness in the colony that was perversely attracted to American political concepts. Strachan had an abiding belief that Upper Canada would remain loyal to the Crown and its duly elected government, but he also believed only fools or mystics took such things for granted. From such convictions came his fierce resolve that Britain should do nothing to undermine the forces of loyalty in the colony, nor promote the ambitions of the spoilers and wreckers, the radicals and social tinkerers. To Strachan, Mackenzie was a dangerous clown who had little concept of the forces he was seeking to unleash. A government, any government, that allowed such a knave free licence to foment rebellion was endorsing its own demise.

The bishop was relentless in pursuing Mackenzie until he broke out into ill-advised and poorly prepared revolt and had to flee to safety in the United States. There is nothing in the story of John Strachan and William Lyon Mackenzie to dissuade supporters of either side on the correctness of their views. They were classic foes in a New World setting. Had Strachan not existed, Mackenzie would have found someone else to symbolize his warped political ambition; had Mackenzie not existed, Strachan would have attracted the animosity of another dysfunctional rebel: they are set pieces on a board game – bishop and knave. Far more intriguing, and telling, was Strachan's earlier struggles against another fellow Scot, Robert Gourlay.

Gourlay was born in Scotland in 1778, less than a month before Strachan. The Gourlays were far better off. He was the third child of four and his father was, by all accounts, a substantial landlord and an armchair political radical who approved of the French Revolution. He had a gentleman's education, afforded far more easily than Strachan's was, and followed up his master's degree with two years of training in agricultural science. I suspect that as a young man, Robert Fleming Gourlay was very attractive – both emotionally and physically – to women and men. Although I can't find any useful physical descriptions, it is clear he was a spellbinding talker until he would go over the top and start scaring people. He was, initially at least, the sort of romantic figure that the age was producing, and his early espousal of the plight of the rural poor gives him the shining patina of social reformer.

If you were concocting a stew of influences and impulses to create the kind of egotistical radical who causes, or has the potential to cause, far more trouble and damage than the problems he is decrying, the complex and ultimately tragic personality of Robert Gourlay has all the necessary ingredients. As a younger son, he stood to inherit nothing from his father, a perennial source of easily understood bitterness. On the other hand, in 1807, he married a young woman named Jean Henderson who had a bit of a dowry and the hope of inheriting some valuable land in the apparently prosperous new colony of Upper Canada. Word of prosperity often increases in inverse proportion to the distance from reality. Untamed land in Upper Canada was only valuable if it was appropriately located and there was significant immigration. Since neither the British Isles nor mainland Europe was yet supplying many immigrants, the colony had come to depend on American newcomers, which, considering the looming volatile political situation, was a mixed benefit.

Before this inheritance came to his wife, Gourlay managed one of his father's farms for nearly a decade. But when this didn't generate sufficient funds for his growing family (there were four children in quick succession), he became, in 1809, a tenant of the Duke of Somerset. Close proximity to the high aristocracy did not in any way mitigate Gourlay's political views. As a kind of appendix to his academic studies, and at the behest of the Board of Agriculture, he had carried out a statistical survey and studied the conditions of farm labourers in northern England. So there was substance to the man, and he had practical experience of the abuses he later decried. This was a dreamer, not a fool; but he was also a rebel and never understood that what the fledgling society he stumbled into needed most were builders.

Heaven knows, he provided more than enough advance notice of his coming clashes with the government in Upper Canada and specifically with the Rector of York. Any number of pie-eyed revolutionary concepts were available in published documents that eventually made their way into the files of the Upper Canada administration. These were polemics published in Great Britain to a highly specialized readership. Amongst other pertinent things, Gourlay was on the record as damning the "kept clergy . . . those whitewashers of iniquity." And that was one of the less intemperate things he said in these incendiary diatribes. Their inconsistency of argument and lack of logic prefigured a mind that became so egotistical and disordered that it utterly destroyed him. But this is pushing his story too fast. It is important to appreciate that even before he set out to take a look at the nearly 900 acres his wife inherited in the Niagara area in 1817, he was a man who was as convinced about the ultimate goodness of mankind as he was about the incorrigible evil of anyone and everyone in government because of the deep flaws in mankind. In other words, he was a classic "nutter," but a very dangerous one because, while he lacked metaphysical logic and coherence, he had a semblance of pseudo-scientific skills to weave his mischief.

In Canada, we encounter him first at the home of his Niagara-area cousin, Thomas Clark. Clark was one of those rural grandees who loved sounding off about the arrogance of a far-away government, although if he ever got his hands on the government controls there would be new definitions of arrogance. It's rather fun to think of Gourlay during his first six weeks in Canada as he is described surviving the sweltering heat, swatting mosquitoes, and imbibing all of Clark's political bile. Three years after the successful conclusion of hostilities with the United States, the colony was troubled. Prohibitions against land sales to Americans made both Clark's and Gourlay's acres virtually worthless. Compensation for war damage was slow to come and, generally, there was a bit of a recession. With each swat of a mosquito you can almost sense the radical temperature rising.

Gourlay would have cut quite a figure in the backwoods of Upper Canada. If he held all government in contempt, what he reserved for "the grubby and contemptible vermin of little York" is easy to fathom. After arriving in Quebec and moving to Clark's, he had only intended to stay a few months in the Canadas, sell his wife's acres for a handsome sum, and bring the loot back home to get on with the revolution in the British Isles. "I am quite a radical," he later wrote in defence of himself, "and I am known in both England and Scotland because of my peculiar opinions, and these opinions are by many misunderstood." It is this kind of brutal honesty coupled with his sincere concern for the poor and the bizarre and self-destructive things he does that make Robert Gourlay such a tragically intriguing figure. That was John Strachan's view too and their clashes were about to begin because Gourlay had decided to grace Upper Canada with the fruits of his labours and the benefit of his wisdom.

That summer of hot chatter in the Niagara area produced a new resolve in Gourlay. He walked now with a sense of destiny. After all, he was a man who by his own account had stood up to the "second peer of England" and was unlikely to be cowed by any hicks from the colonies. Without any particularly compelling vision of what he would do with it, he circulated one of his specialties: a survey questionnaire for landowners in the colony. He'd done this sort of thing in Britain without particular incident. In Upper Canada, it was a sensation, and of the thirty-one seemingly innocuous questions, the last caused the most stir: "What, in your opinion, retards the improvement of your township in particular, or the province in general; and what would most contribute to the same?"

Through his Niagara relations and new friends, he got the questionnaire distributed with copies of the *Upper Canada Gazette*, perhaps the first of many controversial insertions in Canadian newspapers – and no less effective to the cause of the progenitor! This was in February 1818. From here on, things happened in quick succession. Gourlay's questionnaire had a dramatic effect in two different settings: it excited all those angry with the government, from settlers sympathetic to the United States to those who wanted immigration from the States opened again to drive up the price of land; and it also drew the attention of the beleaguered colonial administration to real trouble on the immediate horizon. John Strachan, on the executive council, was the first to sniff the brewing trouble. The governor and the rest of the administration were lethargic and loathe to respond to what they initially dismissed as a minor nuisance. Procrastination would probably solve a problem that might go away with the next boat back to Scotland. Or the one after.

The Rector of York, however, understood human nature well enough to appreciate that an outspoken radical galvanizing public opinion during a period of internal discontent was major trouble. In a letter Strachan wrote to a friend after the Gourlay affair seemed somewhat settled, he argued that "a character like Mr. Gourlay in a quiet colony like this where there has been little or no spirit of inquiry and very little knowledge may do much harm by exciting uneasiness, irritation and unreasonable hopes." That wasn't the half of it. The administration didn't start waking up until a new governor had arrived, and Gourlay decided to directly challenge the whole apparatus of administration in Upper Canada. He also fixed on Strachan his most venomous hatred: this "monstrous little fool of a parson," he called him, and when his cousin Thomas Clark remonstrated with him to moderate his attacks, he stormed that he saw no reason to hold back when dealing with a priest who should "stop dabbling in politics and get himself to a penitentiary."

Gourlay's descent into near rebellion, providing for some historians a little foretaste of William Lyon Mackenzie's similar and more serious foray in 1837, sped up at this point. He made so many enemies and wrapped himself up in such seditious libels that all his allies soon fell away and he was left quite alone, as alone as he left his wife and children back in Britain (the letters from his wife, facing the creditors, are heart-rending). Against Strachan's strong advice, Gourlay was arrested under dubious legislation. The rector felt the ordinary laws of libel could handle the Gourlay situation perfectly and he understood very well the process and uses of secular martyrdom. In the end, Gourlay was simply expelled and banished from Upper Canada, told in effect to attend to his own affairs. The business left him permanently affected and for years, back in Britain, he sought redress for imaginary affronts. He was once arrested for accosting a member of parliament in Westminister who he felt was not properly attending to his business. He even wrote an absurd (for him) polemic denouncing Mackenzie, of all people, after the rebellion for "betraying the Crown."

That, in summary, is Robert Gourlay's story. I've coloured it from my own palette, but it's an orthodox accounting from the known documents and largely borrowed from the excellent essay on Gourlay by Professor S. F. Wise in Volume IX of the *Dictionary of Canadian Biography*. Yet, what is so intriguing about the whole business is the response of John Strachan. This was a period in which he exercised considerable power and Gourlay singled him out as the most sinister figure in the government and, indeed, the entire colony. So far as I can determine, the Rector of York's response was one in which, given the times and the particular circumstances, was measured, restrained, and with a dash of Christian charity. All of this -- particularly the Christian charity – probably drove poor Gourlay up the wall, but there you go. Strachan himself was initially chagrined to find himself so centred in Gourlay's heated animosities. He realized too late that he had confided his earliest views on the fellow Scot to an untrustworthy acquaintance who had passed the word along to Gourlay so that any chance he might have had of personally mitigating Gourlay's gathering extremism was lost right from the beginning.

Before he came to accept that the man had a disordered mind that was sinking further into a tragic abyss, Strachan realized that he better get busy answering some of Gourlay's complaints about the colonial administration because he appreciated better than anyone else that he was making successful points. He always felt that if you didn't defend yourself, you deserved whatever happened to you. To quietly accept the calumnies of your enemies, or the misinterpretation of your actions by outside observers, meant that you were weak, or lacked resolve – in either case, hardly deserving of the privilege of governance and leadership. Typically, he was all over everywhere all at once. Pseudonymous articles in Kingston, pamphlets in York, books in England, sermons in the pulpit and in religious periodicals: wherever he could, he proselytized. In recognizing that there was "sullen discontent" amongst the population, he sought to rally loyalists who needed to understand better the narrow choices government had.

As for Robert Gourlay himself, Strachan argued forcefully against any undue or special harassment. His view was that if Gourlay had broken the ordinary laws of the land, the ordinary consequences were his to face. Despite the personal attacks, Gourlay was an object of considerable pity to Strachan. He appreciated his fiery nature even as he deplored its inevitable wastefulness, but "from his youth [he] has been restless and turbulent" and, thanks to this, Robert Gourlay, not John Strachan, was the author of his own miseries.

It was a response that speaks well of Strachan, just as a decade and half later, in 1832, he stood out in even clearer focus during a terrible outbreak of cholera in Toronto, where one in twelve was to die in quick order from the highly contagious disease. The killer sickness had come in the ships that brought immigrants from the north of England. The disease was at its height in the hot and humid summertime, claiming dozens of victims every day. I don't know whether we can properly summon up the fear an epidemic like this caused in those days. It was, however, understood at the time how serious the risk of contagion was, and sensible, uncontaminated people got as far away from the source of contagion as possible. Even as recently as the 1950s and the last polio epidemic in Ontario, family doctors were advising patients with cottages to stay out of the city until the weather turned dramatically colder.

In the cholera epidemic, Strachan predictably did just the opposite. He stayed in town and did useful things such as spearheading the creation of the Society for the Relief of the Orphan, Widow, and the Fatherless. He raised funds. He turned over St. James' Church on King Street for use as a hospital when the one hospital was filled. He stayed with the dying and rocked them in his flinty heart to their death. When even the undertakers and grave-diggers disappeared, he organized what had to be done. He and his young son, George, often lifted the corpses into their coffins and there were times when they dug the graves too.

Those that survived the pestilence (it came back again two years later) and remembered what Strachan had done never again doubted that he was as brave a man of God as there ever was, as well as a consummately political parson. For himself, he said later he never once felt he had any choice. "I have absolute faith in God," he wrote. "He is using me and giving me added strength for my task. Even when I breathe the foul air in the hospital where several poor souls are dying around me, my trust in God enables me to carry through my tasks."

His courage during the cholera epidemics of 1832 and 1834 was memorialized in two sterling silver gifts: one, a handsome epergne, was from his former students in Cornwall; the other, a vase, was from the citizens of York. On it was engraved: "Memorial of their respect and gratitude for his fearless and humane devotions to his pastoral duties during seasons of great danger and distress from the visitation of an appalling pestilence."

And to make sure posterity understood that whatever his detractors might say about his Scottish Presbyterian roots he was a true Anglican, John Strachan was careful to note that the vase was worth 100 pounds, but the epergne – from his "boys" – was worth 230 guineas.

VI

Terry Finlay never made and never will make enemies the way John Strachan did. Of all the bishops who succeeded Strachan, the only one who came even remotely close in character was Finlay's predecessor, Lewis Garnsworthy, who was as political as could be, as gruff as a billy goat, but whose expansive and welcoming heart warmed those who got near to him. Like Bishop Strachan, Archbishop Garnsworthy lost his biggest and most outrageous cause. Strachan's defeat came when the non-conformist ascendency in Upper Canada killed the notion of the all-Anglican Clergy Reserves.

Garnsworthy lost out a century and a half later when the Roman Catholic ascendency in Ontario enfranchised at public expense Catholic high schools over his much-proclaimed "dead body." Both prelates howled like Lear on the heath prior to their final defeats, but they also struggled to survive the aftermath. Strachan, who had a stronger constitution, did a better job of it than Garnsworthy, which was why the old archbishop was such a spent force when Finlay took over the diocese.

From the beginning it was clear the new man was not going to be the kind of paternalist Archbishop Garnsworthy aspired to be, or John Strachan was by nature. The new man, in fact, was going to be as opposite to all his predecessors as could be. Not for him the isolated, gut-inspired decision in which the consequences are usually pondered after they have occurred. Judging from the administrative and governing processes Finlay sought to put in place, his episcopacy was going to be reasonable, considered, collegial, prayerful, and – above all – it would manifest the implicit hope of the gospel message of redemption and resurrection. There had been too many media farces, too much manufactured controversy during Garnsworthy's sojourn, and it was a time for all farces and needless controversy to cease.

A telling tale: two lesbian deacons once approached Garnsworthy to seek his permission and blessing for an in vitro fertilization of one of their eggs, the said egg to be united with anonymously donated sperm. The sperm donor was variously reported to be a patriarch of the Greek Orthodox Church, a born-again Pentecostal, and a defrocked Anglican archdeacon – all, certainly, delightfully malicious speculation. On the Anglican cocktail-party circuit, there was a lot of dark humour when word was first heard of this extraordinary encounter. Here was a scene, after all, worthy of some churchly variant of "Yes, Prime Minister." We could just call it "Amen, Archbishop" and fill in the dialogue and drama for the deacons, the new-age sexuality, the ancient episcopal office, this crusty old codger with a pectoral cross around his neck and his mitre just handy, and . . . and . . . and then reality breaks in. *What do these two actually want to do?*

The comedy ends with the old archbishop ceremoniously turning off his hearing aid, having officially taken in nothing, and then ushering "the girls" into the office of an assistant, who has news for them of their new separate ministries: one in the remote fastness of the Haliburton Highlands and the other in darkest Bramalea. This is fantasy, of course. All the public and the church got to see was Archbishop Garnsworthy solemnly declaring to the media that he never discussed private pastoral meetings between himself and his clergy. He didn't even discuss them, or so he claimed, with the long-suffering Mrs. Garnsworthy. Whether that infamous egg and its hoped-for sperm ever got together remains almost as much of a mystery as the ancient bond "betwixt Holy Mother Church and the saints triumphant." The incident of the lesbian deacons did serve notice, however, that the times were changing. Boy, were they ever changing!

In whatever dim corridors Anglican bishops in Canada gather to whisper their anxieties, it was known by the end of the 1980s that at least one among them was going to be tested on the issue of homosexuality and holy orders. It would be a challenge from their own clergy, the like of which no bishop had ever previously experienced. How did they know this? Well, the sometimes suicidal but markedly less hypocritical United Church had nearly destroyed itself on the issue of gay ministry a few years earlier, and some spaces in the empty pews of some Anglican churches were being filled by the aggrieved from Methodism's faltering heir. For any future equitable solution to the dilemma of gay priests, however, this new intake was a mixed blessing since these angry converts from the United Church were militantly opposed to any expression of homosexuality and were battle-hardened to an alarming degree, alarming to Thomas Cranmer's denominational successors in any event. Their voices were of a harshness that was new to latter-day Anglicanism and added to an emerging minority of the "zero tolerant."

In the Anglican Church, whenever the battle lines are drawn, deferral is usually the preferred solution. If not always the best, certainly it's the traditional option for this unique branch of Christendom that saw a reflection of itself early on in the fictional

Vicar of Bray, he who changed his ideological and theological principles with all the forethought of a well-oiled weather vane.

Most likely, the challenge would come in Vancouver or Toronto, where the bulk of known or suspected gay clergy were gathered. In what numbers? There are no enumerations in this area, and one is left listening to that insider's educated guess (over 25 per cent) only to have this expert's opinion undermine it (under 10 per cent). What we know for sure was that there was one very troubled gay priest in the diocese of Toronto in the early summer of 1991 in the person of the usually cheery Rev. Jim Ferry, whose unfortunately apt surname added only the first Trollopian dimension to a saga that was, at the same time, inherently tragic.

We know Ferry was troubled because he and a trusted warden at the pleasant parish of St. Philip's in the Toronto commuter town of Unionville had requested an interview with their bishop to tell him of the priest's problems.

Problem number one: Ferry was a homosexual, which in itself was not a problem since the church had come far enough into the new age to acknowledge that sexual instincts could not be denied, although they could be – and for gays, must be – foresworn. For Ferry, however, homosexuality had become an almighty problem because his parishioners didn't know about it and he had come to the agonizing conclusion that he could no longer foreswear it.

Problem number two: Well, not quite all of his parishioners were unaware of his sexual disposition. A couple of agitated and nasty sleuths, either on a hunch or because they had probed more deeply into Ferry's life than he himself knew, were threatening to expose his "lifestyle" to the bishop if he didn't resign from St. Philip's.

Problem number three: Father Ferry, or Reverend Ferry, or Mr. Ferry – you can call an Anglican priest almost anything depending on the kind of Anglicanism he or she embraces (Father is "high" and Catholic, Reverend is "low" and Protestant, and Mr. is middle of the road) – was maintaining "a loving relationship" with another male. The relationship was discreet, however, and the two men were not living together. The same could be said of other gay priests who were prepared to live with a wink and a lie, again with numbers unknown.

These were the ostensible problems and they came together at an explosive time for the newish bishop, who was trying to establish a more collegial way of governing his sprawling diocese and yet make sure his clergy understood that beyond his stated goals of reaching out to the poor and championing their cause, he still had time for some old-fashioned religion and obedience. The Anglican Church was not the United Church: there were bishops and a whole hierarchical chain that bonded each member of the denomination, clergy or layperson, to an historic and structural concept of the universal church. Yet it wasn't the Roman Catholic Church either, with its far broader international clout and a panoply of power centred in Rome that, while it alienated some, also retained the power to inspire awe and obedience in millions.

Anglicans hover somewhere in between. Sometimes the hovering is adroit; at other times it produces sheer misery. A few years ago, at the time of the debate in the Church of England about whether women should and could be ordained as priests, there was a picture of the then Archbishop of Canterbury, Dr. Robert Runcie, on the front page of *The Times*. The look on his face was one of palpable horror, a variant of Francis Bacon's terrifying portrait of a pope caught in a cage. The palms of Archbishop Runcie's hands were wearily pushed up against his sagging cheeks and his eyes were drooped in an aspect so doleful he had the air of an abused and abandoned basset hound. In the cutline below, *The Times* wrote a sentence of such pure Anglicanism, it has never left my memory: "The Archbishop of Canterbury, Dr. Runcie, on the day he argued at Church House that there was no convincing biblical or theological bar to the priesting of women, but advised his colleagues to defer any decision on the controversial issue." If ever there was a motto for contemporary Anglicanism, it is here in this vignette: *Defer and survive*. (For purists, the Latin would be: *Procastino vivere*.)

In the diocese of Toronto, there remains endless speculation about the consequences of that first meeting between Ferry, his warden, and their bishop. Both sides agree it was not unfriendly. Now, however, well over half a decade past all the early anger and accusations, no one can really be relied upon to remember exactly what it was like beyond the fact that there was no rancour and that the whiff of deferral was in the air. Initially, it appears, the right sort of warning bell did go off in Bishop Finlay's head, exactly the way it used to sound when he was a confident parish priest at St. Clement's, where collegiality was all well and good but the rector's word was final – where the rector ministered not just to the church but also to the individual. The bishop asked his priest if he was aware of the bishops' current statements on the matter of homosexuality and celibacy, so warning was certainly given. But the implicit threat from this warning was honeyed over by the pastoral concern of the bishop.

As far as Ferry was concerned, he left Finlay's office with an admonition straight from the heart, and a pretty expansive heart at that: "Nobody is going to push me into a hasty decision," the bishop said. "I'm going to need some time to think and pray about this. The homophobes in the parish will probably complain . . . but you tell them to just cool it down, the bishop is praying." In subsequent media interviews, the bishop allowed that he *did* spend a lot of time praying. The bishop also remembers his priest saying that, contrary to the current rules of the game, he had a male lover and didn't want to hide it any more. "I can't live a lie any longer" were Ferry's precise words. At least that's what others reported him saying. In his own account, Ferry claims a more expansive apologia: "I love someone. Why should I be celibate? The time has come, Terry, when I simply have to stand up and tell you who I am. The conspiracy of silence in the church is killing me, and I can't live with it any longer."

In the Anglican Church, with its centuries of encrusted social and political compromise, that sort of dangerous statement clearly constitutes extremism. *Can't live a lie any longer?* Good God! What on earth did the man think he was doing when he was first ordained and subscribed to every one of the Thirty-Nine Articles of Religion straight from the religious wars of the sixteenth and seventeenth centuries?

In retrospect, we can see plainly that Finlay made his first mistake right here. In a later interview for a feature article in *Saturday Night* when I was the magazine's editor, he said he would never forget Ferry's words about no longer living a lie "as long as I live." I don't mean to make utter sport of this, but it is at precisely this juncture that he should have been wearing Archbishop Garnsworthy's metaphorical hearing aid and turned the damned thing off. If Ferry had then shouted, the bishop should have fainted. There may be truth in the charge that the priest wanted to turn the affair into a millennial issue, but as best as I can determine such a conviction emerged in the subsequent turmoil when this decent, honest, but not very strategic priest uncharacteristically became radicalized. His initial motivation was clearly a cry for help and a plea for support from his decent, honest bishop.

Let's pause for a moment to contemplate the spectacle of two sincere Christians, both of whom had simultaneously decided they could not live with deception. In an earlier age, such fidelity to conscience might have led to the stake for one and conversion to Rome and a cardinal's hat for the other. Had I been their "provincial" and spiritual leader, however, I would have packed the pair of them off to a remote monastic retreat in which Trappist-like vows of silence were strictly enforced and their hands, when not cupped in prayer, separated curds from whey and smartly marketed them in little boxes of balsa wood. This could have been the start of a nice line of products under the generic title of "Bishop's Choice."

Alas, my appointment as archbishop never materialized and this bishop took very seriously his responsibility to enforce the special guidelines promulgated by the Canadian House of Bishops for homosexual clergy. The guidelines were concocted in the late 1970s and reaffirmed twice in the time leading up to the Ferry crisis. On one level, they were a breakthrough in that they acknowledged that priests who were physically attracted to their own sex nevertheless had gifts to give God in valid vocations. Having made this step with a bit of a shudder, of course, the bishops could go no further. At least not for the moment. They ruled that the only valid physical response to the condition of homosexuality was to do nothing whatsoever about it, save pray for deliverance from temptation. Gay priests were to lead strictly celibate lives, as the only sexual activity the church would or could sanction remained between a man and a woman in holy wedlock. Despite the seeming finality of some of the wording, it was nevertheless implicit in the deployment of these guidelines that they could and would be revised again. Why else go to the bother of repeatedly having them reaffirmed? The hint of change to come was both a clever dodge to avoid direct confrontation and an encouragement to rebels and pacesetters to push the church in a certain direction.

A more political and less honest bishop than Finlay would never have forgotten this. A more hypocritical and less sincere bishop would, after the first interview, have telephoned Ferry's warden and talked of his abiding concern and pity for the poor priest. A more strategic and less Christian bishop would then have checked the vacancies at one of his little clergy retreats and enrolled his suffering priest for a good half-year of rest and contemplation, at the diocese's expense. Or maybe a year and a half of study at the Anglican mission in Bangladesh, or anything at all for however long it took for everything to blow over. First and foremost and at the very least, a definitive Anglican bishop would never have gone on holidays without deferring all decisions to the indefinite future.

Instead – perhaps smarting from past charges of procrastination, perhaps wanting to look strong, perhaps annoyed at this direct challenge to his authority, perhaps wanting merely to clear off his desk before taking his exhausted episcopal frame on a well-earned vacation – this politically straightforward, decent, and honest bishop made exactly the worst possible decision. When Ferry returned to speak to Finlay two weeks later, he realized almost at once that the bishop was no longer his pastor but his judge. Clearly, the bishop had taken collegial advice from fellow prelates and the diocese's legalists.

Normally, procrastination is not seen as a worthy human endeavour. In the Anglican Church, however, it is often God's way because all the inactivity lends wider licence to worship, and throughout its history this has meant people with divergent and strong consciences have been able to live safely under one denominational roof. Whether the bread and wine are the real or representational symbols of Christ's body and blood seems not to be the life-and-death issue today that it was in the past; whether a priest can say a blessing over a same-sex couple who want to consecrate their union, on the other hand, is exactly the sort of contemporary issue in need of the historic balm of obfuscation. The ages of the church can still be discerned by its greater and lesser heresies and controversies.

Finlay asked Ferry all the wrong questions and Ferry gave all the wrong answers: are you having a relationship with another man? (*yes*); will you give it up? (*no*). By the time the second meeting ended, it was clear to the priest that his goose was cooked. In the aftermath, some pointed out that Ferry was originally from the United Church, which explained his lack of deference to episcopal authority. There might be some truth in that, but if so there was also an issue that was not going to go away simply because a priest could be bullied back into the closet with his cassocks and surpluses. Under advice, Finlay invoked – uncharacteristically – the full panoply of his power. He "inhibited" Ferry from performing any priestly functions in his parish and removed him from the post. Moreover, he sent a brother bishop – the area bishop within the vast diocese – to the parish to read the inhibition, a bishop moreover who was suspected of harbouring strong anti-homosexual views.

The result of all this was an inadvertent outing for the luckless Ferry and, from the priest's perspective, an appalling betrayal of pastoral trust. The very use of the word "inhibit" was a shock to many Anglicans who didn't have a clue about this ancient power of bishops and found it dramatically at odds with the entire image of "community worship" and "shared ministry" that the touchy-feely post-1970s church had been so assiduously trying to project. As for the poor, feckless priest, Ferry was so traumatized by this speedy sequence of events – Finlay was off on his holidays, or so it seemed, before the ink had dried on his controversial inhibition – that it took him a few days to gather his wits and resources.

It did not take long for Ferry to find allies. Gay activists and human-rights advocates latched onto the story as soon as it got about (through a local weekly newspaper in Richmond Hill). By the time the bishop returned to work, his own trial by fire was ready to begin, attended by the national and international media breathing hard outside his office. Curiously, it was through the device of an ancient church court proceeding – which both parties agreed to and where Finlay's actions were actually exonerated – that the bishop was undone. To understand such a conundrum, we have to look at the revolution that was happening among the homosexual population at large, at shifting attitudes of the Anglican laity towards homosexuality, and at both the historic role and the ambivalent, declining influence of the church.

This was a pivotal moment for my own peripheral involvement in the business. Bishop Finlay had been my priest at St. Clement's and I esteemed him. I am resisting saying that I loved him, in the sense that one loves someone one looks up to, because our acquaintanceship got cut short when I was posted to Europe for *The Globe and Mail* in 1983. Nevertheless, the affection was and remains strong and, initially, I even wondered what else the bishop could have done considering how aggressive Jim Ferry's need for public confession seemed to be, at least to an observer coming after the facts. From the most direct angle, it seemed a simple matter: either the bishop upheld his guidelines or those guidelines were a nonsense and his own position irretrievably damaged. No doubt, this was the view that was urged upon him by his advisers, and if you are presiding over an important organization, you disregard considered advice from your colleagues at tremendous personal and institutional risk. Yet this institution was the church and what was needed, it is now clear in hindsight, was not Vatican-like promulgations and demands for adherence to orthodoxy but Christly forbearance.

With these sorts of ambivalent thoughts rattling around in my brain, I agreed to sit on an informal panel of advisers to the bishop to help him get out of the mess. To use his own phrase, he had "a monkey on his back" and it wasn't clear how to shoo the beast off. In time, alas, the monkey seemed to grow to the size of a gorilla. Finlay was in great danger of being a one-issue bishop and shortending his episcopacy in a welter of legal recriminations and rejection by a large number of gay and gay-sympathetic Anglicans, whose numbers and influence were greater than even they themselves realized.

Within a week of joining the advisers, I found myself in a looming conflict of interest. A senior editor at *Saturday Night* came to me with a proposal for a feature on the crisis by one of the country's top writers, Margaret Canon, who also went to St. Clement's – just to keep the pot bubbling nicely. I couldn't exactly deny that the story was powerful and intriguing, so I found myself having to hightail it from the advisers' group and, no doubt, adding a bit more to the bishop's burden. Compounding all this, at the time my wife was the Canadian correspondent for *The Church Times*, the official Anglican newspaper in England, and was assigned to cover the Bishop's Court hearing into the propriety of the bishop's actions, so we both moved from being former parishioners and friends of Terry Finlay into the camp of perceived media persecutors. Whenever and wherever personal interests and friendships cross professional scrutiny, it is a profoundly uncomfortable and conflicting moment for journalists – or at least it should be if journalists are being honest with themselves. Looking back, I wince a little realizing that these were early days yet.

For me, things came close to home when Finlay's successor at St. Clement's, the Reverend Canon Dr. Douglas Stoute (now Dean of St. James' Cathedral), set about creating a parish-wide series of "encounters" with the expressed aim of examining "faith and sexuality." Since my family was and remains active members of the parish, this meant that we were all for it. To do the beleaguered bishop justice, the Faith and Sexuality Dialogue taken up by a number of Toronto-area parishes came at his instigation and was his attempt at damage control and to lower the anti-homosexual climate that had heated up as a direct result of the inhibition of Father Ferry.

The bishop may also have discovered that many of his allies in this struggle weren't exactly the sort of people he wanted to encourage, and those who ended up so downhearted were often enough people he cared for deeply. It was close to an inconsolable time for a good man laid low by his best intentions, but it did set in train a perceptible change in attitude among some of the faithful for whom a serious consideration of what it meant to live openly as a homosexual at the end of the twentieth century had never been undertaken. That included me.

After the first "encounter" at St. Clement's, I had to do a simple stock-taking. Who in my own life and circle did I know to be openly gay or suspected was a closet gay? The enumeration came as a shock. Three members in my family circle, for starters. At least two of the ten godparents of my daughters. Four friends from school days. A beloved music teacher from my past. A creepy counsellor at a boys' camp. Colleagues at *The Globe and Mail*, where I worked for the better part of two decades. At least five priests – Anglican, United, and Roman Catholic – who, at various times in my life, have been enormously helpful and kind to me when I was in need of both help and kindness. Admired artists in music, ballet, and theatre from my days as an arts critic and writer. Parliamentarian friends (in both the Senate and the Commons) from a compact but instructive period as a newspaper bureau chief in Ottawa. Inspiring acquaintances at my church. Colleagues from *Saturday Night*. Wonderful, but sometimes worried, young scholars at Massey College, where I was a Senior Fellow.

In my life, I realized, I have been amazingly fortunate to find warm and brilliant friends and colleagues and acquaintances, many of whom are gay, yet I had never really thought that much about them as sexual beings. In fact, I didn't like to think about *anyone* – gay or straight – as a sexual being, or at least not exclusively so, and that brought me and some of the other participants at St. Clement's to the first dilemma when dealing seriously with contemporary homosexuality.

This is a crucial point in the heterosexual world because it is tied so closely to attitudes and, in truth, it is at the root of the church's dilemma because the church – or certainly the Anglican Church – is endlessly caught up in societal values. I realized in the early examination of the issue of faith and sexuality that if I thought of anyone as a sexual being, I stopped thinking of them as a human being, or at least I marginalized their humanity to the cul-de-sac of sexuality. What all this was rooted in, I probably don't want to know, but if I thought of someone as a homosexual, it was essentially a negative thought, caught up with boyhood memories of over-friendly teachers and the aforementioned camp counsellor whose violence towards boys only came to light decades after he had caused incalculable injuries.

To me, such marauding males were monsters, walking around with permanently erect penises and trying to stick them into places they weren't wanted. By the same token, after I discovered that a trusted family friend had tried to attack my sister, I saw him in a similar guise – almost as if there were three sexes: men and women and monsters. Occasionally, a woman fits into the monster category – Karla Homolka, for example – but for the most part it is men who hanker criminally after both sexes.

Like many, I can make an easy and clear distinction between a monster heterosexual and a normal man. Despite having many gay friends, however, I can now recognize that I had negative, if some-what inchoate, attitudes towards homosexuality in which – at the very least – the burden of abnormality was for gays, not me, to transcend. Also, once I started going to these damn faith and sex-uality encounters, I found myself having to think about the mechanics of gay sex, which I found profoundly unsettling. I'm talking rear entry here, the orifice of choice. A few years ago, a close male friend of mine in Ottawa told me about an older couple both our parents knew well. The couple had several sons, one of whom was gay. This son, along with several homosexual friends, spent a riotous weekend at the family cottage in the Kawartha Lakes and neglected to clean up, leaving the old couple to discover sheets stained with feces and sperm, and various bits of erotic paraphernalia. Not surprisingly, all of this made the parents' hair stand on end. Word of this spread to family and friends and a wave of anger washed over everyone.

This story is an example of the nausea homosexual sex can arouse in heterosexual males. In fact, as I came to realize when I rethought the story years later, sheets can be made fairly disgusting by heterosexual couples too. The real issues here were: the family's dysfunction, which prevented any caring discussion of the issue in the first place; the laziness and thoughtlessness of the "orgy" participants; and, most crucially, the exposure of the no-man's land between morality and civility, the territory to which heterosexual society traditionally consigns homosexuals. It is territory plagued with tragedy and grievous misunderstandings. It is the territory St. Paul traversed so negatively when he damned homosexuals while probably repressing his own strong attraction to close younger colleagues such as the gentle Timothy or the solemn Luke. It is territory where the church has been terrified to take more than a few hesitant steps in a journey it must eventually complete if it is to minister unto the whole people of God.

The faith and sexuality encounters at our church – as you can tell – were disturbing, but creatively so. I learned to transcend whatever attitudes I had from the contemplation of gay sexual mechanics by the simple and obvious expedient of remembering how important all my gay friends were to me. And with that remembrance, a terrible insight: considering society's historically negative attitudes to homosexuals, considering the horribly high suicide rate among homosexual teenagers, considering the church's two millennia demonization of homosexuality, considering the continuing gay bashing, considering the decimation of the gay population by AIDS-related deaths, and considering a hundred other slings and arrows of outrageous fortune all homosexual men and lesbian women are heir to, who – in God's name – would ever *choose* to be gay?

Forget for the moment the evolving scientific dialogue on whether there is a genetic component to homosexuality. Even in the more forbearing climate of today's North America and Western Europe, it is not exactly a joy to be gay. To "come out" still takes great courage; to "out" a closet gay is still a major threat. It was only a hundred years ago that Oscar Wilde went to prison for buggery. In Canada, the law permitting sexual acts between consenting adults of the same sex was only created in the late 1960s by a minister of justice – Pierre Trudeau – who is still with us.

We are discussing, then, barely one generation of increased tolerance for a behavioural and instinctive phenomenon that is as old as the hills. At Massey College in the University of Toronto, where I preside, it is a point of pride that we try to create each year a model community in which the only rigid and guiding rule is mutual courtesy. This makes it a particularly friendly place for people who might, for whatever reason, feel marginalized by their sexuality. Because they are also a collection of the brightest young graduate minds in the country, there is usually more than enough confidence to withstand the brickbats of the world.

Yet I am sure I would not have as deep a feeling of satisfaction and contentment at encouraging this aspect of total tolerance at the college had it not been for Terry Finlay's unintended but monumental blunder with Jim Ferry. I believe it was a blunder that shook the bishop to his core, one which he has not fully solved yet although as I write it appears the Anglican Church is heading towards an historic understanding of a positive homosexual dimension in society and the church. Quietly and without quite saying so, much of the drive for these gradual but quickening changes are coming from Finlay's initiatives, either made on his own or in conjunction with the bishops in other dioceses where the gay issue gets livelier by the day.

There are many gay priests in Toronto. Although – as I wrote earlier – it can't be proven statistically, the sense is that there are unprecedented numbers of gay priests in both the Anglican and Roman Catholic churches. The initial actions precipitated by Finlay against Ferry caused agony for both sexually active and celibate gays in the church, but especially for gay priests. Why? The reasons are complex and often very personal, but what drives most people to the church these days when there is no longer any social cachet to attendance is – beyond sheer faith – a heightened sense of metaphor in life, a strong streak of spiritual curiosity, and a profound humility and sense of humanity's equal capacity for good and evil. Above all this, it is to share community in a world where community often seems riven.

Here is the crucible of the gay priest's special insight into spirituality. With first-hand knowledge of how irrational and cruel people can be when confronted by the anger and hate aroused by homosexuality; with a special understanding of undeserved suffering; and with a commitment to finding a way through the moral, theological, and philosophical morass they have all had to face throughout their mature intellectual life, gay priests have such unusual, meaningful, and – in certain aspects – Christ-like vocations that they constitute a force for good far more significant than most people, inside or outside the church, yet realize. It is almost, but not quite, on par with the powerful new gifts brought to the Church by female priests.

Although Jim Ferry found the pace of reform and recognition agonizingly slow, his personal and professional crisis was set before remarkable changes in attitudes towards gays in general in Canadian society. *The Globe and Mail* became an active and dramatically friendly observer and commentator on the gay scene and the extension of gay rights. Whether by design or the inadvertent influence leadership always has, *The Globe*'s editor-in-chief, William Thorsell, presided over significant changes in coverage of gay issues, and Ferry's bizarre church trial received more scrutiny and better detailing in the newspaper than 90 per cent of the cases that come before the Supreme Court of Canada.

Generally speaking, Canadian society seemed to become progressively more tolerant of homosexuality. There have been notable exceptions, and the fierce reaction against the United Church's policy of ordaining active homosexuals shows that the old volatility and hostility is still there. But a strange thing happened over the past quarter-century. It became impolite to tell queer jokes and embarrassing to mock gays. The common argot expanded to accommodate details of gay relationships to the point that members of some straight couples, describing their relationships to strangers, had to be careful to make sure the word "partner" or "friend" was properly understood.

An important part of the reason for this, I think, is the AIDS epidemic, which is hugely ironic. The religious and political right in the United States got it wrong. There was a righteous feeling in fundamentalist America, which spilled over to some extent into Canada, that AIDS was a God-inspired plague on sodomites and drug users. I saw an amusing twist on this once when I lived in New York for several weeks completing interviews for a book on Mikhail Baryshnikov and the American Ballet Theatre. In the arts community of New York the emotion over AIDS throughout the 1980s was intense. Staying with friends at their house in Greenwich Village, I headed for Lincoln Center one day down Grove Street, which was plastered with small signs every few yards proclaiming:

LESBIAN BLOOD DONOR DRIVE
Please give as much as you can.
Our blood is the only safe blood.

This being New York, by the time I had reached the subway station in Jefferson Square, there were other signs, one of which admonished readers to "come clean to Jesus" at a nearby mission hostel. Then it dawned on me! The ladies of the lesbian blood donor drive were right. As they exchanged no body fluids, their blood really was the only safe blood. The Bible doesn't even mention their activities. And if all that is the case, and AIDS really is a God-given plague on arch sinners, perhaps someone very much like strident feminist Andrea Dworkin is waiting to judge us in the hereafter. If I were a male fundamentalist preacher, like the Reverend Jimmy Fallwell, that would make me very nervous.

By some people's logic, AIDS should have sent every homosexual running back to the closet ashamed, under the threat of damnation and begging for forgiveness. But it didn't. The inexplicable unfairness of AIDS, the comprehensiveness of its terrible net, and the layered tales of tragedy that left few people untouched or unaffected served to end any remaining attitudes of neutrality towards homosexuality. Neutrality had tended to favour the bigots since so few men, even if they sympathized, wanted to be identified as friendly to the gay cause. But as the times changed, it became increasingly unfashionable to be anti-homosexual.

Unfashionable, but still possible. Very possible. There are many practising Anglicans who feel how "the gay problem" is resolved is the make-or-break issue in the church, even more so than abortion or female bishops. In the Church of England, for example, the Archbishop of Canterbury – the Anglican spiritual leader – has come out strongly against accepting sexually active homosexuals in the priesthood and has resisted any calls for some sort of church recognition of same-sex unions. The issue is still mightily fraught as a subsequent showdown at the Lambeth Conference of the worldwide Anglican Communion proved a few months after the Archbishop's statement.

Finlay clearly realizes this and having once stuck his neck out, with disastrous results, he has been proceeding cautiously to lead his flock beyond mere damage control to a solution that seems to be heading towards church-sanctioned blessings of gay relationships. This logically, and in time, will lead to church-sanctioned sexual relations between ordained priests and their chosen partners. No matter how carefully this decision is arrived at, there will be howling as loud – or possibly louder – as greeted Father Ferry's forced outing. It's one of those horrid dilemmas where there is only grief stored up on either side of the equation, but decisions still have to be made. No one could be blamed for wanting to stick his head in the nearest bucket of sand.

My own view is that blessing same-sex unions is inevitable and will be the right decision for two important reasons. The first is obvious: the church will be siding with the outcast, which is what it should always be striving to do despite so many centuries of contrary activity. Secondly, blessing same-sex unions is the one chance the church has to get a jump ahead of emerging societal tolerance and formally redirect gay consciences and sensibilities towards the moral centre. In supporting homosexual couples, the church – however weakened it may be as a moral force in today's affluent Western society – would be placing behavioural demands set against the example of Christ's life and teaching. In effect, the church comes to accept what gay priests already know: that homosexual relationships are hard as hell to maintain, just like – but different in specifics, obviously – heterosexual relationships. The church has historically busied itself in bringing moral support and metaphysical succour to most relationships in the scope of human experience. In fact, it likes to preside over all our great moments: birth, coming of age, marriage, and death. To continue denying that support and succour to some of the most attuned and sensitive minds of every generation is cruel, sinful, and – ultimately – foolishly destructive of the church's ideals.

The route to this kind of thinking is never easy, no matter how it is made. For the tenth Bishop of Toronto, it has been particularly rough at times. I'll give two examples only, but knowing Terry Finlay for the caring, decent man that he is, I imagine small events less dramatic than these have also pained him grievously. A letter published in *The Globe and Mail* by Prof. Douglas Chambers of Trinity College (what goes around comes around, as John Strachan never said) needs no comment, so terrible are its narrow but succinct parameters. Only a bit of background is required. On November 8, 1990, the Reverend Warren Eling was found naked and murdered and chained to a bedstead in Montreal after a clearly dangerous evening of sado-masochistic sex. Eling had been a respected priest at the downtown Toronto parish of St. Anne's on Gladstone Avenue, and was a well-known and popular figure in certain circles of the church (especially anywhere church music or liturgical practice were taken seriously).

Some time on the night of Nov. 8, Rev. Warren Eling was murdered in the rectory of his parish, St. James the Apostle in Montreal. He was strangled. Warren Eling was my first boyfriend more than 30 years ago, and his death has continued to outrage me ever since I first heard about it. My outrage is against the evidence of continuing homophobic violence that it represents: the death throes of a murderous patriarchy wreaking its random vengeance on gays now as it did on women in Montreal five years ago.

My anger though is for the underlying causes, the causes behind the causes, that led to Warren's death. The police are after the killer, probably a piece of rough trade who picked Warren up in a bar and lured him home to his death. What will they find if they do find anyone? A killer, yes, but an agent of something that probably even he does not consciously understand.

The Bishop of Toronto has spoken of this as an act of "mindless violence." It is nothing of the kind. This violence, this killing, like the violence in our society, is promulgated: by the media, by the state, by the churches themselves.

"Hatred is not a family value," read the bumper stickers, but everywhere it is legitimated by the ravings of the popular press now legally prevented from inciting racial hatred (though not sexual hatred) and by Sunday-morning TV. The denunciation of alternative sexuality is the accreditation of violence. It escapes culpability (and the rigours of the human rights code – even the law) under the cloak of religion. And such "respectable" denominations as the Anglican Church have done nothing to dissociate themselves from it.

A man who urges another to a crime is an accessory before the fact, but a church that harries its gay clergy out of the chancel, out of the church itself, is no less guilty. It condemns them to a life devoid of secure loving relationships, one of furtive secrecies, of complicity in the hypocrisy of sexual denial. It is the "final cause" of what happened (and goes on happening in less overt ways) on the night of Nov. 8.

Warren Eling left the Diocese of Toronto in the wake of the Jim Ferry case: the case of a priest in a stable and loving relationship who had been "outed" by one of his congregation and, thus, dismissed by his bishop. That case was *Kristalnacht* for any Anglican priest known to be gay, no matter how "respectable." At any moment, the jackboots of denunciation might be at the door. Warren went to Montreal, far from most of his friends and the community he knew, depressed and increasingly desperate – in the literal sense of "without hope." He went to his death. . . . It will not do for bishops to deplore the consequences of the hatred – sexual as well as racial – that their own churches have promulgated overtly and covertly. The bishops have had a hand in this death. A torrent of denunciatory rhetoric is not a substitute for thoughtful examination of why this "fine priest and good man" is no longer alive, let alone a bishop. . . .

In 1637, Edward King, a promising young priest forced out of England by a ruthless and uncompromising church, was shipwrecked at sea on his way to Ireland. In his memory, Milton wrote the finest elegy in the language, *Lycidas*, and he was in no doubt as to the cause of Kings's death: not the sea, not the wind, not the rock ... but the bishops. "Blind mouths that scare themselves know how to hold a sheephook," he called them. I wish I could write as powerfully for Warren.

> Professor Douglas Chambers,
> Trinity College,
> University of Toronto.

There are charges here that are patently unfair – Eling's fears of an anti-gay campaign were to a great extent unwarranted – but it is always hard, in retrospect, to recreate a mood of the times. Like Jews throughout most of their history, gays have a heightened sense of imminent danger. And Professor Chambers is certainly correct in claiming that the Ferry case sent a devastating message to all gay priests in the diocese. This was probably not Finlay's intention (although it might have been that of others who were advising him), but it was inevitable nevertheless.

Just as devastating but in a different way was a couple of quiet encounters and correspondence between Finlay and a young medical student at my college. The student is a devout Anglican, gay, sexually active, and one of the most idealistic young men I have ever encountered. If I could turn the clock back on Finlay's life thirty or so years, I expect the young Finlay was like this young student in most respects, except for his sexual orientation.

When the young man, I'll call him Robert, came to me with the suggestion that he could bring some help to the bishop as he tried to dig himself out of the morass he was in during the early post-Ferry days, I thought it was worth his while. The bishop definitely needed a helping hand. Gay activists were disrupting services he presided at and he was under attack, one way or another, in the media, within the church, and within his own conscience. A helping hand from such a fine young man might, at the very least, provide a glimmer of light in the enveloping gloom.

It was not to be, or at least not so far as Robert and I could see. Robert first wrote the bishop a very friendly letter requesting an interview on the issue of gay relationships. He wrote as an Anglican to his chief pastor, as an active member of a downtown parish, and in the spirit of friendly debate. The letter was received as such, and off into the vortex of Bishop Finlay's almighty nightmare – which even fools stayed clear of – went this angel from Massey College. My heart went out to both of them.

When he came back, Robert said he was very encouraged. The bishop had been gracious and forthcoming and Robert had left the meeting with a far greater understanding of the problems a contemporary church leader faced. Even accepting the narrowness of the bishop's options, Robert was impressed with Bishop Finlay's efforts to deal with all his problems in the most humane way possible. During the course of their discussions on same-sex unions, the bishop mused at what would happen if he were asked by a local parish if it could perform such a blessing – an act that is laughingly simple to do yet is also entirely caught up with all the dire politics of contemporary controversy. The bishop said this because he knew he was coming to Robert's parish within the month and because that parish was well known for the number of gay parishioners in its pews. He told Robert, however, not to bring the issue up himself as he, the bishop, would do it at the appropriate moment in the meeting.

When I was told of these events, I could see Robert felt he might be at the centre of a small miracle. If the Bishop of Toronto gave formal, or even informal, approval to a local priest for the granting of a blessing to a gay union, then a hugely important step forward would be taken. He was such an optimist, I felt like a curmudgeon for cautioning him not to get his hopes up too high. The meeting came and, not surprisingly, the bishop smiled past young Robert, empathized like mad with everyone, but failed to fulfill what the young man took to be an implicit promise.

To call his subsequent disappointment "abject" understates the case, and he wrote a letter to the bishop that, for someone like Robert, probably was excruciating to pen. He so longed to admire Finlay, to see him past the error of the Ferry decision. And, most crucially, he wanted to see the church he loved accept him for what he was: a sinner yearning for redemption like all the others, of course, but also a generous young man whose basic instincts were not evil, fulfilled or not. He's still waiting.

VII

"Sex is like money," my late father once told me in what passed for the only discussion I ever had with him on the procreative act. It was typical of my father's philosophy: a bit of a joke and also pithy. "If you've got it, it's hardly worth a second thought. If you haven't got it, you can't think of anything else."

Bishop John Strachan was a happily married man to the estimable Ann McGill and together they had numerous children whom they adored. So far as we are able to tell, he never had to give sex a second thought. Money was a different matter. Much of his correspondence and many of his actions later in life, at least as they affected his personal life, had little to do with anything but money because the first Bishop of Toronto was a chronic debtor. If he was not exactly hounded by his creditors, he was nevertheless never far from their concerned eye.

The ubiquitous James Street – "the richest man in Upper Canada" – at one point was owed close to eight thousand pounds sterling by Strachan. It was an astronomical sum. Think of two maxed-out Visa cards, each with $15,000 credit limits; an executive loan option of up to $25,000 at the bank; a full American Express card with credit up to $20,000; a house mortgage of $150,000; and personal loans from friends of close to $40,000 and you are approaching the neighbourhood of an eight thousand pound debt in the 1840s. His own salary at this period was only a thousand pounds.

Strachan was a generous man, which was part of his problem. He supported his sons and daughter when called upon to do so, especially the impecunious Alexander, whose succession of business failures was a notable drain on his father's financial resources. If a priest's stipend could not sustain him and a large family in a parish, the bishop was always there with a helping hand. He loved the clergy under his charge and he would always defend them, even the slothful ones, even the drunkards. To all of them, if a bit of cash would ease their state, he gave it, regardless of whether he actually had any. Mr. Street – the shadowy source of loans at 8 per cent – may have been the second most important Anglican in the diocese.

The bishop also liked to live well and made no bones about it. This was partly due, no doubt, to the relative poverty of his own boyhood home. He also felt a bishop of the established church – although he never had succeeded in proving that the Church of England was the established church in the colony – should disport himself with a certain style. He lived not in a house but a bishop's palace, bought on a loan. He had a large staff, a smart carriage and impressive horses, and his table was famous for its fine food and drink. The wrinkle here was that when he was consecrated Bishop of Toronto by the Archbishop of Canterbury in 1839, he became the only bishop in the church to reach high office with no salary whatsoever. He had to retain his office of Rector of St. James' Church (now Cathedral) in order to have any income. Within a year of his consecration, the pleading letters to the British government begin, but it was not for several years when he was well into his sixties that Bishop Strachan finally received a salary of 1,250 pounds.

He was not without material resources. Adroit purchases of land had brought him some capital assets that were always in a state of being sold or traded to fend off dire financial embarrassment. Like most Upper Canadians, he speculated wildly in land and stocks and, like most of them, he also lost scads of money.

There was no way he could retire. He couldn't afford to. If he couldn't exist properly on his bishop's salary he certainly couldn't afford to have it cut to pension size. Curiously, considering the high esteem he was held in by all those with whom he didn't come into conflict, no one seems to have offered to get him out of his financial quagmire. He was left to fret quite alone and, as my father said, the lack of money concentrates the mind.

How amazing then was his record as a pastoral bishop. Within a few months of his consecration, he made his first episcopal visits, ranging over his diocese in three monumental trips that became an annual pattern. By steamboat to Niagara and from there to St. Catharines, Grimsby and thence along Lake Erie's shoreline. He would return home for a couple of weeks and then head up north along Yonge Street all the way to Penetanguishene, and then back to Toronto to prepare for the long, arduous pastoral visit along the shores of Lake Ontario to plummy parishes such as Port Hope and Cornwall on the St. Lawrence.

The pace was too much for many of the chaplains and vergers who accompanied him, but he always seemed invigorated by his travels until his bones became too old and sore. He never minimized the physical ordeal of these famous episcopal sorties.

"I found the roads in many places dangerous and almost impracticable," he once wrote. "A rough, strong farmer's wagon is the only vehicle that dares attempt them, and even that occasionally breaks down. And to be prepared for such accidents, we carry with us an axe, a hammer and nails, with ropes, etc. Sometimes we scarcely make a mile per hour, through the fallen trees, roots, and mudholes which lie in our way. Nor is such travelling cheap; and as for accommodation, it is painfully unpleasant, and this, notwithstanding the generous hospitality of the clergy and laity, whenever they have an opportunity. The time consumed is perhaps the thing most to be lamented. We seldom travel further in a day than you may do by a railroad in under an hour, and more often scarcely half the distance. I say nothing much about the fatigue of these journeys, the jolting on the log-carriages, exposure for months to a summer

Canadian sun, and the autumn rains, etc. etc. because these are all incident to the discharge of duty, and neither a proper subject of dissatisfaction nor complaint."

He was appreciated by his clergy because he supported them in nearly all controversies. And he was quite familiar with controversy himself. In truth, he seemed to revel in it and in argument happily exceeded the bounds of what more sober souls thought judicious. As G. M. Craig's wonderful essay on Bishop Strachan in the *Dictionary of Canadian Biography* makes clear, he was a man much misunderstood by history, but not by his clergy, laity, and all his friends.

"Strachan's Toryism," wrote Craig, "was so out of fashion in his day, and increasingly since, that there is some danger of its being misunderstood. . . . He believed in rational religion, opposed 'enthusiasm' and superstition, and devoted much of his life to education at all levels. Nor was it [his Toryism] synonymous with colonial subserviency or with rural conservatism. Strachan strongly resented uninformed interference in Canadian affairs by the British parliament or by Downing Street bureaucrats. He was a vigorous advocate of such projects as canals and banks, and sought generally to advance the economic improvement of British North America."

That he was a pain in the neck to his enemies is clear. And there were a sufficient number of them to ensure that he comes down to us largely as a pain; not nearly enough redress has been allowed. Much of the discomfort he caused can be directly experienced from his correspondence to his family and his fellow clergy. He lived to such a great age – he died of understandable exhaustion in his ninetieth year, still in high office – that contemporary accounts from his last twenty years seem to predominate in the historical record, but even here, as Craig points out, "his native wit and humour took on a certain mellowness." A wonderful mellowness, in fact, for although he could thunder at his priests if they personally irked him – especially at Synod ("Sit down, you fool, you're talking nonsense!" he shouted at a rural canon mid-utterance on one irritated occasion) – he always defended them against attacks by outsiders or agitated parishioners. A deputation of "concerned laymen" once approached him to complain bitterly about their aged rector and demanded that the bishop remove him (the rector in question was two years younger than Strachan, so the complaint was maladroit, to say the least). Amongst the charges against the poor fellow, in addition to his age, were complaints that his dialogue was "too prosy" and that he repeated one particular sermon "far too frequently."

"When did he preach it last?" demanded Bishop Strachan.

"Why, just Sunday last, my lord," came the swift answer.

"What was it about then?" asked Strachan.

None of the deputation could say exactly. One thought he knew, but was contradicted by the other, who nevertheless was himself confused.

"Well," pushed on the bishop, who I can see relishing every moment of the encounter, "at least tell me what the text was."

When no answer came, save silence, he turned to the deputation in suppressed triumph:

"Go back to your rector and ask him to preach it again next Sunday."

John Strachan was a classic progenitor who found it hard to give up his creation, but whose creativity was monumental. The largest and most important Anglican diocese in North America is only one of his bequests. Two of the best universities in Canada – McGill and

Toronto — began as a gleam in his eye. The establishment of Upper Canada, the fierce opposition to the forced union of Upper and Lower Canada, and the final resolution of Confederation, which he championed right up to its establishment on July 1, 1867, are constituent parts of his towering achievement. In a lesser-known achievement that has only recently been seen in a new light, the sense of dignity and entitlement he invariably and quite naturally gave to the aboriginal parishes and communicants in his charge was one of the very few examples of farsightedness in the sad story of race relations between whites and Indians in Ontario during the nineteenth century.

Strachan died on November 1, 1867, exactly four months after the creation of the federal Canadian state. On the morning of his state funeral a week later, most of the principal streets of downtown Toronto were closed so the horsedrawn hearse could be seen by all. Photographs taken of the intersection of King and Yonge streets show all of the buildings draped in black mourning cloth. There were bitter, early-winter winds. Mounted members of local calvary regiments lined the south side of King Street and thousands of people vied for prime spots all along the route to St. James' Cathedral. The mounted 13th Hussars preceded the hearse, along with the chief officers of all the regiments lining the streets. In succession then, the tangible representatives of John Strachan's life marched his body to glory: the students and professors of the University of Toronto and Trinity College; members of the loyal societies (St. George's, St. Andrew's, St. Patrick's); the boys of Upper Canada College, and the staff of the Normal School. And behind them came Strachan's clergy from all over Ontario, drawn alike by the historical moment and the richest panoply of Anglican liturgy yet seen in the province. Immediately in front of the hearse strode the new bishop, Alexander Bethune, and on either side the official pallbearers: the lieutenant-governor, the chief justice, the president of University College, the vice chancellor of the new province of Ontario, the mayor of Toronto, and the archdeacons of Toronto and Niagara. *The Globe*, George Brown's Liberal newspaper and no friend of Strachan in many of his most sacred battles (particularly the Clergy Reserves fight), understood the moment perfectly:

"We have been cut away from the founding spirit of this place and it is up to us to build half so well as he has built."

VIII

I n August 1998, all the bishops and archbishops of the world-wide Anglican Communion travelled to London and Canterbury to take part in the decanal Lambeth Conference. It would mark the first time the new female bishops, mostly from North America, would be seen en masse, if twelve doughty women in full canonicals could be thought of as "en masse."

All the expected issues came to the fore: the increasing distance from the high fervour of the ecumenical movement of the 1960s and early 1970s; the growing suspicion of the conservative papacy of the Roman Catholic Church; the continuing rift between the "declining" church in the affluent West and the spreading influence of the growing church in Africa and Asia; and so on. Curiously, debates on the specific nature of Christ's divinity – which divides the affluent Western church from the Third World church along a perilous fault line where metaphor clashes with fundamentalism – did not raise temperatures nearly as much as the most divisive issue – homosexuality.

On one level, there was never any suspense. It was known to all knowledgeable observers that the bishops of Africa and Asia abhorred any substantial move towards ecclesiastical recognition of gay sex – the blessing of homosexual unions being even more contentious than the issue of gay priests – and would fight it right up to and including notions of schism. Here was rich irony. The Church of England spread throughout the world on the trade winds that first took the entrepreneurs of empire to far-off lands. It was the church of empire and, to its credit, it long ago recognized where it had to make amends and mostly did so. Nevertheless the notion that the leaders of the Western church would one day bend in weak submission to the sense of outraged morality of African and Asian bishops is a development worth more than a footnote in the history of the world.

In a final resolution, approved by 526 bishops to 70 (with 45 abstentions), the church worked out a compromise. Conservative African prelates would allow gays to be priests, but only if they vowed to remain celibate. Dr. George Carey, the Archbishop of Canterbury, reaffirmed traditional church teaching ("I see no room in Holy Scripture for any sexual activity outside of matrimony," Dr. Carey was quoted by Reuter's as saying) and added the familiar, almost welcome Anglican fudge that always accompanies a failure of the spirit: "The dialogue continues amongst us. We need to respect one another and not impugn the motives of one another."

One suspects this was too much for the arch-liberal American Episcopal bishop, James Spong, who allowed himself a politically incorrect moment of observation about the African church, which, he said, was illuminated less by Christian principles than by "tribal animism" and – by implication – superstition. As the howling rose, Bishop Spong made a partial apology, but he seemed pleased with the fuss he had churned up.

Back in Toronto, the bishop embraced collegiality. The diocese of New Westminster became the first in the Canadian church to support the blessing of same-sex unions, and this was done to enliven the upcoming General Synod, which preceded Lambeth. It didn't enliven it that much and, in the end, its bishop also demurred.

To this day, Jim Ferry waits beyond the courts of the Lord, but not quite out of the reach of his bishop, who still agonizes over the hard choices he feels were forced on him. At the end of 1998, the *Anglican Journal* reported that four Anglican clergy, including Ferry, who had been prevented from functioning in the ordained ministry because they were involved in openly acknowledged homosexual relationships, were being allowed to become more involved in the pastoral and liturgical life of their home parish, Holy Trinity in Toronto. All four, the church newspaper reported, had been "inhibited" at some point, and Bishop Finlay had requested that they seek his permission each time they were asked to participate in a leadership role in an occasional service.

The Canadian church, with John Strachan's once mighty diocese in the lead, continues to defer the issue and sails on through rough water as gently as possible into the fading sunset.

Annals of the Diocese of Toronto. Published in 1848 by the Society for Promoting Christian Knowledge.

The Comfortable Pew: A critical look at the Church in the New Age, by Pierre Berton. Published in 1965 by McClelland & Stewart.

Dictionary of Canadian Biography, Volume IX (1861 to 1870). Published in 1976 by the University of Toronto Press.

The Fighting Bishop, by Thomas B. Robertson. Published in 1926 by the Graphic Press.

First Bishop of Toronto, by Henry Scadding. Published in 1868 by W. C. Chewett.

A History of the University of Trinity College, Toronto 1852-1952, edited by T. A. Reed. Published in 1952 by the University of Toronto Press.

"Hot Under the Collar," by Margaret Canon. *Saturday Night*, Volume 107, issue no. 8, October 1992.

In the Courts of the Lord: A Gay Minister's Story, by James Ferry. Published in 1993 by Key Porter Books.

The Invasion of Canada and *Flames Across the Border*, by Pierre Berton. Published between 1980 and 1981 by McClelland & Stewart.

John Strachan, by W. Stewart Wallace. Published in 1930 by The Ryerson Press.

John Toronto: A Biography of Bishop Strachan, by Sylvia Boorman. Published in 1969 by Clarke, Irwin & Company.

Landmarks of Toronto, by John Ross Robertson. Published in 1908 by *The Evening Telegram.*

Memoir of the Right Reverend John Strachan, by Alexander Bethune. Published in 1870 by Henry Rowsell.

Story of My Life, by Egerton Ryerson. Published in 1883 by William Briggs.

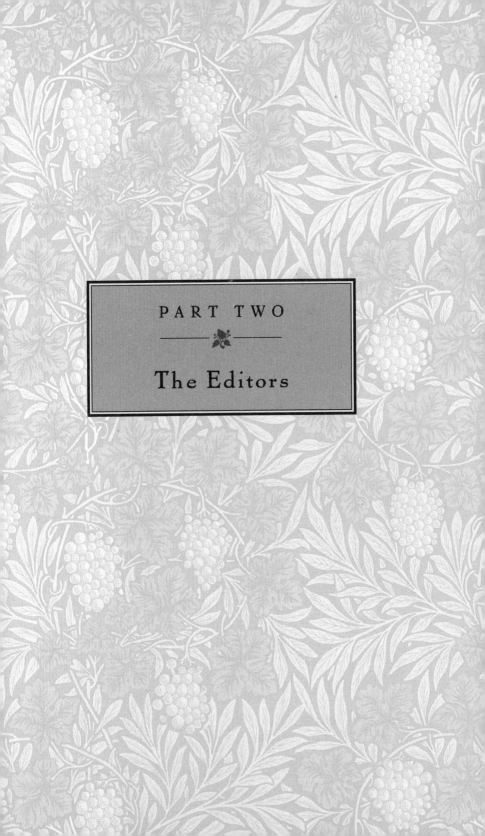

PART TWO

The Editors

I

The year that John Strachan died was a very good year for George Brown, another Scottish immigrant who — forty years after the young clergyman — found his way to Canada via the United States. The founder, owner, and editor of *The Globe* newspaper, Brown was, in the words of the first Governor General of the new Dominion of Canada, Lord Charles Stanley Monck, "*the* man whose conduct in 1864 had rendered the project of union feasible."

This is not some genial and inconsequential Victorian hack we are contemplating, then, but a nation-builder, the founder of the most important newspaper in Canada, one of the key figures in the creation of the Liberal party of Canada — a "natural governing party," if that overworked phrase still has any useful meaning — and a man famous in his own day for his passionate oratory. It was Brown who evoked some of the noblest sentiments in the Canadian historical lexicon, with his eyes fixed resolutely on the West and the North, and more than anyone else he was responsible for taking the fusion of these two defining points on the Canadian compass (the North-West) and implanting it deeply inside the early Canadian consciousness. It was Brown who, for English-speaking Canada, formalized in language that spoke directly to his era the often inchoate longing of "a new people" searching for some sense of geographical cohesion in face of the volatile neighbour to the south (that darker, less altruistic but ever-alluring point on the Canadian compass). That and a real chance of material security and a future for themselves and their families free of the taint of class and religious denomination, but resolutely under a tamed and reformed monarchy.

This was a complex man because he was also a prig and a damn bigot, but I'll get to that later. For the moment, it is sufficient to celebrate the George Brown of 1867, the year of Confederation, when hope was fresh and ambition wild. Or was it the other way around? It is very hard to tell sometimes. Certainly Confederation had come almost as a surprise to the very people who wished for it most ardently. Any living Canadian who has followed the ups and downs of federal-provincial constitutional conferences over the past thirty years will have something of an understanding of the years of frustration leading up to 1867. In the 1840s, there had been so much hope – not unlike that experienced by those who cast all their expectations on the Meech Lake or Charlottetown conferences – and these were all dashed. Dashed for Brown, too, who started seeing dark hands at work in the politics of his chosen land, but who persevered anyway and eventually triumphed.

On Thursday, July 1, 1999, George Brown's newspaper, re-named *The Globe and Mail* after a marriage of economic convenience in 1936 between *The Globe* and *The Mail and Empire*, published the following lead editorial either by or under the authority of Brown's thirteenth successor, editor-in-chief William Thorsell:

When George Brown arrived in Canada in 1843, it was an oddity of a place, a quarrelsome community of English and French settlers that had been thrown together two years earlier into a political union with responsible government under a powerful governor general. It was a constitutional recipe doomed to failure, and George Brown would end up as a prime architect of its demise in 1867. But that was 23 years after he founded *The Globe* in 1844.

In 1843, writes J. M. S. Careless in *Brown of the Globe*, "Canada was little more than a narrow straggling band of settlement stretched out for a thousand miles along the grand St. Lawrence water system, from rugged Gaspé in the east to the fertile western peninsula that lay beyond Lake Huron and Lake Erie."

Beyond the province of Canada to the west, the Hudson's Bay Company prevailed over the Prairies and north, where Fort Edmonton was already 48 years old. A separate British colony existed on the Pacific coast, and the Empire was well established to the east through Halifax and up into Newfoundland. Many of the aboriginal nations had yet to sign treaties with the new colonial power (indeed some have yet to do so).

By 1859, the "united" province of Canada had become a fractious, bitterly partisan place, with deep divisions between Catholic French and protestant British. Once a stout defender of a unitary province, George Brown was now campaigning in a Reform party convention for the redivision of Canada into

Quebec and Ontario, and the addition to these provinces of the other British colonies in a new federation:

"I do hope there is not one Canadian in this assembly who does not look forward with high hopes to the day when these northern countries shall stand out among the nations of the world as one great confederation! What true Canadian can witness the tide of immigration now commencing to flow into the vast territories of the North West without longing to share in the first settlement of that great and fertile country, and making our own country the highway of traffic to the Pacific?"

The simple dissolution of Canada into two separate colonies would not do. Redivision in the context of a new, more diverse nationality would be the recipe for a Canada that would "stand out among the nations of the world."

Here lies the key to the core value of Canada as we know it 140 years later. Canada was never a "nation-state" in the 19th-century sense. It failed miserably in that role during those fractious years of "unity" between 1841 and 1867, when Confederation finally rescued the citizens of Canada from the overly intimate embrace of two distinctive peoples. Canada never possessed the cultural homogeneity that sustained the nation-states of Europe, Australia, New Zealand and, yes, the United States. From the moments of its birth, Canada had a complex, divided personality shared between French settlers and United Empire Loyalists fleeing the American Revolution. The addition of British colonists to the east and west, and of aboriginals in various states of treaty with the Crown, only contributed to the germane diversity of the place. . . .

That's only half the editorial. It continues on for six paragraphs more or less in the same vein as it ponders the course of the nation during the subsequent 140 years. Then it returns to the newspaper's founder:

> This is the last Dominion Day (or Canada Day) of the 20th century and of the second millennium. Canada's history makes it uncannily suited to the realities of the 21st century, which requires mankind to balance its diversity with its common interests, common nature and shared future. On July 1, 1867, George Brown wished in *The Globe* "that the people who now or shall hereafter inhabit the Dominion of Canada . . . who shall populate the northern part of the continent from the Atlantic to the Pacific, shall, under wise and just government, reap the fruits of well-directed enterprise, honest industry and religious principle . . . in the blessings of health, happiness, peace and prosperity. SO MOTE IT BE [*sic*]."
> And so, mostly, it is. And so, Mr. Brown, we carry on.

On the same page, the newspaper's long-serving and militantly sensible political columnist, Jeffrey Simpson, had his own take on Canada Day:

> The Canadian federal system, a bit of a crazy quilt of laws, rules, conventions and exceptions, adjusts itself to events, pressures and fiscal realities. The premiers scream at Ottawa, and Ottawa sometimes takes provinces for granted, but Canadians by and large demonstrate the good sense not to pay much attention to these ritualistic, tiresome squabbles. The political

system is a leftover from the 19th century – first-past-the-post elections, the anachronistic monarchy, the barnacle of the Senate, votes of confidence on just about everything, and strict party discipline. But apart from populist elements in the Reform Party and the cottage industry of academic political scientists, nobody seems to mind.

Even the political style of the Chrétien government hearkens back to an older time. Not for Jean Chrétien the visions and ambitions of Pierre Trudeau and Brian Mulroney, who insisted that Canadians had to change their ways of doing business and organizing their affairs. For Mr. Chrétien, Canada is "No. 1," problems should be solved one at a time, and the less the government appears in the face of Canadians, the better he (and they) like it. Mackenzie King would approve.

Quebec is restless, as it always has been and always will be. Restlessness is the psychology of a permanent minority within Canada and North America with an abiding and justifiable pride, a fierce attachment to its language and cultural heritage, a prickly sense of distinctiveness and a shrewd sense of its political interests. . . .

A time-traveller coming from George Brown's great year of grace, 1867, to the day of this millennial editorial would be left fairly well convinced that what Brown had been so instrumental in creating had worn pretty well.

On the other hand, if the same time-traveller had landed here in the midst of the 1970 invocation of the War Measures Act or during any of the subsequent federal-provincial constitutional wrangles that caused such alternating hope and despair, the emotional landscape of the nation might not have seemed quite so benign. It's worth making this obvious point to reinforce the notion that what the Fathers of Confederation hobbled together has had more staying power than generations of timorous Canadians dared to believe. As a system – however amended, potted, or ana-chronistic – Brown's vision of a federated Canada has endured longer than the constitutional arrangements of most of the countries of Europe and Asia.

It is entirely probable that during the next almighty crisis Canada faces, and it will be over Quebec's anxiety and come within most of our lifetimes, in two years' time or twenty, we will be able to cast our minds back to the certitude of Thorsell's editorial and Simpson's column and remember that 1967 was not "the last good year in Canada," as Pierre Berton once put it. The year 1999 under Prime Minister Jean Chrétien's much-maligned Liberal government leadership may yet glisten and beckon with its own distinctive aspirations and contentment as 1867 still does through its formative genius and more fulsome rhetoric.

II

George Brown was the elder son, but not the eldest child. When he was born in 1818 in Edinburgh, his family was moderately well off, just above the lower middle class with a few pretensions to a higher class through his mother's side (she was the daughter of "George Mackenzie, gentleman, of Stornoway on the

Isle of Lewis"). Brown enjoyed relative prosperity for much of his early years and then, when his father's business took a calamitous turn, he knew overnight shame and desperation. It may be pop psychology, but in my book these are classic formative ingredients in the making of a rebel or — if a measure of civility, however grudging, is also a factor, and it is in the case of George Brown — at the very least a reformer with a big chip on his shoulder.

He adored his father, that's clear. Peter Brown was a successful businessman in wholesale goods in Edinburgh, as well as a collector of municipal assessments, and was thus able to ensure that his elder son, his pride and glory, was able to attend the best schools — or those that were within his financial and class range. It never does to underestimate the importance of class in Britain, whatever the British tell you. I think much of George Brown's particular Anglo-Canadian mystique — a dislike of class, an impatience with sectarian disputes (within Protestantism, at least), an abhorrence of titles and the lesser folderol of high office, a quiet but determined accumulation of savings, a hatred of all but material privilege, a loathing of colourful popinjays and other high-flyers in politics, a rock-bottom faith in due process and the inevitability of justice — can be traced back to his dislike of the class strictures of the Old World, even though he was always proud of his Scottish roots and connections. Such a dichotomy sits very well on the old Anglo-Canadian spirit.

Heaven knows, his father would have been belching out a reformist line even from the moment George emerged from his mother's womb, but the son's rebellion did not take the form of going up against his father, rather; the two of them decided to take on the Establishment. Peter Brown, according to J. M. S. Careless's luminous two-volume study of the son and the related extensive sketch of George Brown's life in the *Dictionary of Canadian Biography*, was a convinced Whig-Liberal and evangelical Presbyterian who, for a farthing, would rail away at Tory or aristocratic privileges wherever he found them, and moreover was one who wore the liberal economic theories of Adam Smith like his own clothes. This was a father who didn't believe in a middle ground and who strode confidently on the sunny uplands of moral certitude. Time and again throughout his active life, if there were a radical position or solution to embrace as well as a moderate or compromise one, Peter Brown would invariably embrace the radical.

Such a father can cut a mighty swath in a son's mind, especially an ambitious son. It doesn't take much imagination to guess at the emotional upset it caused not just the father but especially the adoring and uncritical son when Peter Brown's business affairs turned murky. As a municipal collector of assessments for the City of Edinburgh, Brown *père* somehow mixed the then vast sum of £2,800 sterling in public funds with his own accounts. Although no charges were laid, the turmoil this revelation caused must have been devastating. To Peter's credit, he set about taking drastic measures to restore the funds and his honour. In 1837, "drastic" in Scotland usually meant North America, and off father and son went, the cheapest direct fare being to New York City, then as now a place of fevered energy, high hopes, low life, huge successes, and catastrophic failures.

The trip over was ghastly and they arrived sick as dogs, but like most of those sturdy eighteenth- and nineteenth-century Scots who made of North America one vast territory of unbridled opportunity, Brown & Son soon set up business in Manhattan with a dry goods shop. They were doing sufficiently well to bring out the rest of the family in 1838, a little more than a year after their inauspicious arrival and the necessity of starting from the very bottom. But a life restricted to the exchange of cash or credit for bolts of cotton, kegs of nails, hemp cords, candle wax, and sundry other goods was not for Peter and George Brown. They had much greater game to hunt, and they knew it from the moment they set foot in the New World.

Peter Brown was soon pontificating – if a fervent "free church" Presbyterian can be described as being thus occupied – in a small weekly newspaper aimed at recent British immigrants to New York. We know he connected with his readers because the little paper grew like Topsy and the volume of his overblown journalism increased proportionately. It's a bit of a disease in this journalism business, especially if you get positive feedback. It has been sardonically observed that it does not take very much to bribe or otherwise suborn a journalist: all you have to do is take him seriously. Peter and George Brown, it was clear from all accounts, intended to be taken seriously. Very seriously.

Barely a couple of years into his new life, Brown *père* published a little polemic between hard covers entitled *The Fame and Glory of England Vindicated* and with it the relative fame and glory of the father and son began. In fact, there was no stopping them! The book was a hit, at least amongst newly arrived immigrants in the United States and in the British colonies to the north. None of this, obviously, discouraged Peter from following a new career path out of dry goods and into hot prose. By 1842, his son and trusted partner had already made several trips north to the newly joined colonies formerly known as Upper and Lower Canada and he quickly came into contact with both Presbyterian soul-mates and reform-minded politicians in Toronto, Kingston, and Montreal.

In short order an invitation was sent to Peter, via George, to come north and set up his presses and his Presbyterian vitriol in Canada. Perhaps "vitriol" is unfair, considering the tenor of the times, but "Presbyterian" is the key clue here. Like all immigrant groups that have ever come to Canada, right up to the most recent arrivals from Somalia or Kosovo, old, unresolved battles are invariably brought to the new land.

In Queen Victoria's kilted domain, an almighty battle raged on the status of the established Church of Scotland and its breakaway brethren who had regrouped under the banner of the Free Church of Scotland. The reverberations in the New World from this battle and the subsequent local identification with the dispute were every bit as vociferous and rancorous as in the Old Country. It is a truly curious phenomenon that after the union of England and Scotland in the reign of James I (England) and VI (Scotland), there eventually emerged *two* state churches in the land: the Anglican Church of England and the Presbyterian Church of Scotland. Being state and established churches, the sovereign was (and still is) titular head of both and an aspect of the great sport of disestablishmentarianism came into its own (along with its alphabetically extended dialectic partner: antidisestablishmentarianism).

Peter and George Brown, if they believed in anything in those earliest days in the New World, believed with a zeal we can scarcely comprehend today in the separation of church and state. Fighting the good fight for the Browns began on home turf when they took sides in the great Presbyterian ecclesiastical rift, with the anti-state-church Browns backing the Free Church 200 per cent. Well, if you read their new little weekly *Banner*, perhaps 300 per cent is closer to the effective truth. In the emerging Canada, this loathing of established churches had already involved John Strachan in the fight against the Church of England in Canada for the Clergy Reserves. Far more ominously, it moved George into a position of extreme anti-Catholicism that still stains his record, however considerable and noble his other achievements and however inward-looking the Roman Catholic Church was in those days.

When the Browns finally moved north from New York to Toronto for good, George's natural bent at sturdy polemics and political meddling resulted in the launch first of the *Banner* and then, in 1844, of *The Globe*. Right from its earliest editions, *The Globe* carried the reform-minded zealotry and high seriousness of its founder-editor to its increasingly wide audience. As a newspaper journalist, I find it thrilling to read Careless's adoring account of *The Globe*'s early success:

> [*The Globe*] was really George Brown's from the start. He was above all to make it the most powerful newspaper in British America. He did so through his strong and stirring editorials, by pushing always for the latest and most detailed news reports (so that the *Globe* would be read, reluctantly, even by political enemies), and by seeking constantly to increase circulation through providing even better press facilities. He introduced the new Hoe rotary press to Upper Canada before his paper was even three months old, and the greater production this permitted enabled the *Globe* to set up a book and job printing office also. In 1845 he established the *Western Globe*, to serve Reformers in the rising southwest regions of the province, with its own sub-office in London to which material from the Toronto edition was regularly conveyed by road. The Toronto *Globe* itself advanced from weekly to semi-weekly; by 1849 it had triweekly issues, reflecting its expanding

circulation, and a weekly edition specifically intended for the countryside was added. It was a further sign of success of Brown's "forward policy" that the *Globe* in 1853 became daily, printed by a steam press. By that time his paper had already become a province-wide institution, and soon would claim – with few to deny it – the largest circulation in British North America.

By this time, Brown *fils* was in the thick of colonial politics and had proclaimed himself a reformer, a champion of representation by population, and an opponent of arbitrary rule. He and *The Globe* took on a succession of governor generals, who have been handed down to us in his own handcrafted "progressive" view of contemporary politics as desiccated, aristocratic, and reactionary bottom-feeders. In reality I suspect they were orthodox representatives of their time and political class and had to grit their teeth occasionally at jumped-up grandees such as Comrade Brown, who could make their administrative life such a misery. Brown could make his own life a misery as well and some of his scrapes form the matrix of our enduring political fixations.

Take the business of the union of Canada West (Ontario) and Canada East (Quebec) in 1848 for starters. This shotgun marriage of the old divisions of Upper and Lower Canada was an attempt by the colonial authorities to undermine the population advantage enjoyed at the time by Quebec. By forcing equality between the more numerous inhabitants of Canada East and the hot-to-trot but sparsely populated Canada West, the authorities hoped first to undermine and then vanquish French culture by a patently unfair "equality" in the number of legislative seats allowed Canada East and West. English Canadians forget their history about six minutes after it happens and can't understand why French Canadians, like the Bourbons, forget and forgive nothing as they drag their entire past (and then some) along with them like so much dead-weight luggage. Well, here's as good a place as any to start understanding the dilemma.

Everyone in Canada West thought it was just dandy to have equal representation until a decade or so after union when census reports started showing that the population in Canada West was outstripping Canada East. The manipulation of the francophone numerical superiority had backfired in the face of Protestant Canada West, which had feared and assumed that papist fecundity would always keep Quebec more numerous. In fact, Canada West — as it is still — was the principal beneficiary of immigration, and this started having a dramatic effect in Brown's day. By the time the population numbers game started looking like a bad deal to Canada West and the salvation of Canada East (with all the attendant and inevitable political groupings imaginable), George Brown had worked himself up into an almighty lather about the wickedness of equal representation. In Canada East, they remembered all too well how the system had been conceived, and now embraced what had once been loathed with newborn passion. It was this embrace that convinced Brown "equal rep" was truly evil and "rep by pop" was the only answer. He threw everything into the fight, but when he discovered that the Roman Catholic Church enthusiastically supported the status quo, he dwindled for far too long into being the most intemperate and powerful anti-Catholic in the land.

We are very close to the dark part of Brown's heart here. In ways that are caught up with both the tenor of the times and a particular human nature, this great Father of Confederation embraced denominational rancour with such vigour and venom that it still has the power to shock. This is despite all the apologies made for it by the forces of historical objectivity, despite the provocation of the church itself, and despite his own subsequent mellowing. At its peak, Brown's anti-Catholicism was raw and ugly and you will rarely read reminders of it in *The Globe and Mail*, just as you will fail to read reminders of the vicious anti-Semitic past of *Le Devoir* in today's *Le Devoir*. It does not fit the historical self-image of either of these leading newspapers. Nor is it much ameliorated, in my mind, by some of the alliances Brown the politician made with Quebec *rouge* figures in order to advance his own reform causes. These are not evidence of a pragmatic politician. The very last thing Brown could be labelled was a pragmatist.

In opportunistically clutching the anti-clerical ambiance of the anti-establishment francophones, he was hoping to put a quick end to the profound and far-reaching alliance between Tories in Canada West and the conservatives in Canada East. True enough, when his great moment in our history arose – the final struggle for Confederation – Brown proved himself a legitimate and even a fitfully imaginative visionary, although one does get the impression reading between the lines of his correspondence and editorials that he had at long last succumbed to some frustration at the lack of progress his professional and seemingly perpetual rancour had produced. And this is true too: towards the end of his life, when he was more openly exhausted from denominational warfare, he even tried a few bleak calls to end all the factionalism. For the most part, though, when he was in his prime and was caught consorting with Catholics (either the French-Canadian variety or, as he described them, the "squalid" new Irish immigrant sort), it is hard to see much other than an almighty hypocrite on the loose.

George Brown was a great editor and a definitive Father of Confederation, but he was a rotten politician. For the longest duration, he preferred to inflame anger than to placate it and tried to pass along his own resentments and frustrations to the electorate. Despite the historical picture of a man happy in engaged critical opposition, he lusted for office along with every other power-monger of his day. There's a wonderful description of Brown's posturing antics when he had a small taste of real power (it lasted for a mere forty-eight hours) during the 1850s in Christopher Moore's lively rendering of the Confederation era, *1867: How the Fathers Made a Deal*. Like J. M. S. Careless, Moore has a profound liking for Brown that I don't share and ascribes to him more generosity of spirit than I think he actually had. Nevertheless, there is no denying he rose to a statesman's stature, and Canadians – for however long we endure as a coherent nation – have cause to be grateful for that moment. But he was still a prig and bit of a jerk. When I was more involved in writing on contemporary politics in Canada during the 1970s and 1980s, it helped me whenever I needed to refresh myself on Canadian political history to transpose past political figures into contemporary roles. In this fanciful game, Brown always emerged as Paul Hellyer, the well-intentioned, arrogant, stubborn, and slightly ridiculous minister of national defence in the Lester B. Pearson administration.

Brown's Scottish wife, whom he found rather late in the day, certainly helped to ameliorate some of the rougher edges of his personality, but there's only so much a good woman can do! To me, it has always been hugely emblematic that it was an employee of *The Globe* who came gunning for him at the end, however drunk or mad the employee. He was only the first editor-in-chief of *The Globe* that disgruntled staff members have wanted to shoot. We live in more civilized times now, fortunately: the executioner no longer is a crazed printer skulking in a corridor. Now he takes the form of an inter-office memo and press release from Thomson Newspaper headquarters in the United States.

III

When it came time to eliminate William Thorsell as the editor-in-chief of *The Globe and Mail* after ten and half years, it was done quickly and relatively efficiently following consultations with Thomson Newspapers, the vast publishing organization that had owned the newspaper for more than two decades. In a nasty profession that makes a public spectacle of gobbling up its own and then mercilessly spitting them out, Thorsell was eradicated somewhat more gently than was his predecessor, Norman Webster, whose metaphorical claw marks on the editor-in-chief's desk at *The Globe* can still be felt. Thorsell, who was one of those who indirectly assisted Webster's bloody departure, was knocked off his own perch less than ten days after the publication of the Canada Day editorial quoted earlier. He was replaced by Richard Addis, a pleasant Englishman and Fleet Street editor who had once trained for the Anglican priesthood. When that singular fact was announced, you could almost hear John Strachan's ghost happily whistling through his teeth, while the spectre of George Brown gnashed its teeth. Within short order, Thorsell's name went from the top to the bottom of the masthead. What a tale was here, from start to finish.

It was inevitable the busy decade of Mr. Thorsell would end like this. The surprise was not that the end came after so many fascinating, bizarre, and often failed experiments in redefining the traditional newspaper, but that his reign lasted as long as it did. The sanguinary ducts of *The Globe and Mail* through which he slid out of high office had already been travelled not only by his own predecessor but also by three publishers he had seen off and at least five managing editors (one lost count of the subordinates Thorsell dispatched during his years of power). And this too: his ending was set against great turmoil – the fiercest newspaper war since George Brown's own day. But then so was his beginning at *The Globe* set against turmoil, yet then there had been no competition. As newspapers are being run these days by the scripts of revenge tragedies of the early seventeenth century, there was just the usual internal mayhem.

Like Aphrodite in her shell out of the sea, Thorsell seemed to arrive fully formed. In my mind, the inaugural moment came towards the end of 1988 at a dismal farewell party for the recently executed editor-in-chief, Norman Webster. It was held in Bronwyn Drainie's mother's home in deepest Rosedale, the *haut bourgeois* enclave in midtown Toronto. Drainie had been a columnist and book reviewer for *The Globe*, but her then husband, Patrick Martin, was a close friend of soon-to-be axed Geoffrey Stevens, who, in his turn, was Webster's closest colleague at *The Globe*. This was not so much a party as a blood reckoning, and you could sense the bad karma a block away, or at least I could as I approached the residence. It's fanciful, I know, but I believe I can remember thinking the very walls were seething with anger and the sense of betrayal. I always liked James Fleming's evocation of that party in his book, *Circles of Power.*

Machiavelli couldn't have envisioned a better scenario of high intrigue. Picture the members of the palace court (*The Globe*) gathering to pay their respects to a departing nobleman (Webster) at a party attended by leading members of the realm (former ambassador Stephen Lewis, publisher Peter Herrndorf, lawyer Clayton Ruby). Only the monarch (*Globe* publisher Roy Megarry) is not there. Held on a cold winter evening in January, the affair proceeds with decorum and civility. The host of the event (*Globe* journalist Patrick Martin) maintains the pleasant atmosphere with a heartfelt speech of appreciation, noting the guest of honour's achievements, presenting him with a cartoon portrait of himself and announcing that his supporters will create a university scholarship in his name.

Then Webster rises. In an emotional speech, he reveals that, contrary to first appearances, he was fired from his job and fears for the wellbeing of others in the room who, he says, are about to suffer the same fate at the hands of the monarch.

Reactions range from tears to acute unease because, watching from the corner of the room, is Webster's successor, William Thorsell, the man chosen to carry out these deeds. Thorsell remains the model of composure, even when the gathering is shocked later when Geoffrey Stevens (*The Globe's* managing editor) reveals that Thorsell has already fired him.

This tasty tale has one little denouement that I savour. The host of the evening, Webster's and Stevens' close chum Patrick Martin, was shortly afterwards caught out on a monstrous act of toadying to the new regime. Perhaps it was his impatience at getting a foreign posting in the Middle East that Webster and Stevens had apparently promised but never awarded before they got the heave-ho. In any event, it got back to the newsroom that Martin had somehow managed to leave a twenty-one-helium-balloon salute to Thorsell attached to his front door immediately following the official announcement of his elevation to editor-in-chief. On Thorsell's desk in *The Globe* newsroom, a disgusted colleague left a little note: "Next year, Jerusalem."

Boy, was I happy not to have any direct part in all of this. I had left *The Globe and Mail* only the year before, after seventeen happy and, for me, memorable and productive years. I had come to the famous newspaper in the early 1970s from the wreckage of the old *Toronto Telegram* and had, initially, an ill-defined but quite exciting job that reads today like an Irish stew: junior editor in the enter-tainment department; part-time feature writer on politics; dance and ballet reviewer; editor-in-chief-in-waiting. Well, the last assignment wasn't in the job description, but it was planted in my mind within a year or so, although it was never to be. I was one of a number of eager young men encouraged by the then editor, Richard "Dic" J. Doyle, constantly to aspire beyond where I found myself. I don't think there were ever any young women who fitted into this category, but I may be wrong. There is nothing more pathetic in journalism than contemplating yesterday's golden-haired boy still trying to bask in an extinguished sun, and I was determined not to be one of those. It is always best to get on with your life rather than to lust after what didn't come your way. I had a ball at *The Globe* and manipulated my "part-time" dance beat into something worthy of my own growing and fevered affection for the art.

From there, during the better part of the next two decades, I went on to become drama critic, Peking correspondent, acting Ottawa bureau chief, national columnist, and national editor. My final posting, in 1984, was as *The Globe*'s European correspondent based in London, which was a glorious lark. There was even a little garret apartment on Rue St. Jacques in Paris that went along with the gig, so I ended my days at *The Globe* on an almighty high. Well, perhaps it was down a notch or two from "an almighty high" as it turned out, because when I left the posting it was to become editor of *Saturday Night* magazine and that's when I discovered that it is hard to leave a newspaper on equitable terms.

The venerable magazine was in the midst of a dramatic change of ownership. The public-spirited Webster family, whose scion Norman was still the editor-in-chief of *The Globe*, had tired of the burden of enlightened ownership after nearly a decade of losses that were a continual drain on the family's charitable purse. The magazine was in the midst of its centennial celebrations and the nineteenth year of Robert Fulford's era-defining editorship when it was learned that the Websters were dealing with Conrad Black for the sale of the magazine. Or at least that was what we thought. After Fulford had resigned his post and after I had been asked to succeed him, it came time for the sale to be completed and that's when both sides, to their mutual chagrin, discovered they had been talking at cross-purposes. Webster was sure he had sold *Saturday Night* for a certain sum of money (not very much, I was told); Black was sure he had made a deal to take *Saturday Night* off the Websters' hands for a different undisclosed sum of money (ditto). This resulted in a standoff for a couple of days.

For me this was a two-fold embarrassment. In the first place, I was out there exposed as the editor-to-be with no magazine to edit, a bride at the altar with a no-show groom. I saw the humour in all this, but still it was hugely uncomfortable, especially when Joey Slinger of the *Toronto Star* wrote one of his trademark satirical columns trying to figure out which media mogul had screwed up the most. He took the trouble to indicate that whoever was doing the screwing, it wasn't being done to the new editor, whose relationship was still "unconsummated." In the second place, Webster was still my boss at *The Globe and Mail*, but it became immediately apparent when I went in to have my final interview with the publisher of *The Globe*, Roy Megarry, that Webster's days were numbered. Webster had told me that if things didn't work out at *Saturday Night* with Black, there was always a spot for me back at *The Globe*. That, apparently, was only the least of the errors he made, all from the goodness of his heart and with precious few thanks from anyone for shouldering the burden of *Saturday Night*'s losses.

"I'm really disappointed in the way Norman has handled this entire *Saturday Night* affair," Megarry told me solemnly when I went to see him in the midst of all this and before I even had a chance to sit down in the proffered seat. "He handled the business end of it ineptly and it has really made me question his judgement on a broader scale around here. More disturbingly, I know what he told you about coming back to *The Globe* and that was completely wrong. By all means, if you think you have a chance to improve *Saturday Night*'s position, go ahead. I suppose I can understand why you want to leave *The Globe* and become editor of a marginal publication, but being your own boss isn't all it's cut out to be, especially when you have an overseer like Conrad Black. So go, if you think that's right, but don't think you can just walk back in here if you don't like what you find. If you go, you go, and that's the end of it. There is no guaranteed return. Norman was wrong to say that to you and I've told Norman this. I also told him I was going to tell you."

Well, well, well, I thought to myself, *wasn't that pleasant after seventeen years at this wonderful dump!* I thought this too: if the publisher of *The Globe and Mail* is prepared to talk to a departing employee this way about his most important editorial colleague, Webster better start looking elsewhere for his future. I didn't hate Megarry, but I thought he was bringing a ruthlessness to *The Globe and Mail* that was altogether new and unwelcome. For all the perceived dangers of working for Black, the "Darth Vader" of Canadian publishing seemed to me a more direct, less insidious, and a more loyal employer than this steely and ambitious Irishman. Besides, I *was* anxious to run my own show and "marginal" *Saturday Night* was the best magazine in the country by light-years. I wanted the chance to prove I could be an editor-in-chief of a great publication.

I was thinking of all this as I approached the farewell party in Rosedale for Webster. He and Geoffrey Stevens, his managing editor and sidekick, had just returned from a world tour of *The Globe and Mail's* bureaus, which, in retrospect, seemed like a clever ploy of Megarry's to remove his twin irritations from the local scene when he was arranging a palace coup (he playing Tiberius and everyone else playing a minion, expendable or otherwise). By the time they returned and this party for Webster was about to begin, it was clear to most that Stevens would get the heave-ho too. William Thorsell, the "cool as a cucumber" editorial writer recruited from the *Edmonton Journal,* had by this time wormed his way into the publisher's confidence and it was known that he would be the next editor-in-chief.

There are any number of fascinating explanations and speculations on how William Thorsell became George Brown's editorial heir. My favourite, unverified, was that he simply parroted back to Megarry his own stated concerns about Webster's editorial rule and the publisher grabbed them and him gratefully because they supported his own views (naturally enough, since they *were* his own views). This amazed much of the rabble in the newsroom who *knew* Thorsell was gay and also knew about Megarry's strongly and often-stated homophobia. Despite knowledge of this open secret, it would be years before Thorsell publicly acknowledged his sexual orientation and it was done in a quiet and dignified way that befitted the man. It was also missed by most people. He made a speech in 1996 to the Toronto Gay Businessman's Association and, in effect, the news report of the speech was a "coming out" announcement, published discreetly on Page B-6 of *The Globe*'s "Report on Business." No closet was walked out of more gracefully and subtly than this!

And if there were to be a new editor, why not Thorsell? It was time for a shakeup at *The Globe,* or so many thought, and Thorsell was the first genuinely revolutionary figure to become editor-in-chief since its self-righteous founder gave up the ghost in the previous century. Not that what had preceded Thorsell was bad. It wasn't. It was glorious, so glorious and golden that it couldn't possibly have lasted. And don't you believe for a moment that old wives' tale that all journalists who have had a good time at a newspaper invariably refer to their own period as "the golden days." It was simply a coincidence that this unique golden era occurred exactly between 1970 and 1987, the precise years of my own time at *The Globe*. Michael Enright, the CBC Radio personality, claimed the golden era occurred a decade earlier when he was working at *The Globe*. Since this is my book, I can say with brisk authority that I'm right and he's wrong, although our old editor, Dic Doyle, would probably say we were both right because our dates together coincided with his own golden era.

Doyle was a dream of an editor and rereading his delightful, idiosyncratic memoirs, *Hurly-Burly*, reminded me forcefully of why he was so wonderful. Unlike either Brown or Thorsell, he was a largely anonymous figure outside the newsroom and executive offices of *The Globe and Mail*; indeed, he seemed to exult in his lack of public profile. That meant, however, that as an editor, and especially as an editor-in-chief, his ego was not a huge roadblock for the ambitious journalists all around him. By this I do not mean to imply that an ego-saturated editor such as Brown or Thorsell is bad for the paper. It just means it's a one-person newspaper, and to succeed in it you must form your journalistic career around that singular vision. In the case of Brown, it was exactly what should have been done: he was an originator and his vision carried everyone through. The verdict on Thorsell is still out, but in certain areas he was a revolutionary. What remains to be seen is how deeply his changes went inside *The Globe* and, therefore, how enduring they will be.

Doyle was neither an originator nor a revolutionary. He genuinely enjoyed the successes of his journalists, and it was their vision and energy that he embraced with such flattering enthusiasm. Only rarely did he give any evidence that he considered their success as a vindication of his judgment. I think this was because he knew in the very depths of his astute and sensitive heart that he sometimes made wrong judgments about young people. He seemed to think that all young people were a worthwhile risk, or at least young people who showed some gumption. What was so terrific about his style was that he encouraged each of us to be our own person, and if we performed well we were given excellent play for our stories and memorable subsequent assignments on which to nourish ourselves as journalists and human beings.

He was not hidebound by concerns of journalistic specialty or territory, which was lucky for me. I was plucked from the entertainment department and told I was going to be dispatched to China at a momentous point in contemporary Chinese history (1976, the year of Mao's death). In the ordinary way of luck in journalism, I had my life turned upside down from one foreign posting. Evidently he liked what I was able to do in the posting, as the result of which he made two mistakes, both from the goodness of his heart. He let me talk him into giving me a general affairs column that, at the time, I was not ready to pull off. That was the first mistake. The second was in trying to do the trick twice by sending another theatre critic to China. This was the egregious Bryan Johnson. Johnson, who could write extremely well, became something of a Conradian legend in short order: he so loathed China he lobbied hard to get out. But he had the Asia bug and lobbied just as hard to remain in the area. That earned him the chance to open the new *Globe* bureau in New Delhi, which he also loathed. Eventually, he got what he wanted, a freelance gig in the Philippines. It was there that he ended up as a part-owner of a girlie bar living off the earnings and favours of teenage hookers. In fairness to Doyle, this is not something that was easily discernible ahead of time. In fact, a few years earlier, Johnson had once written a brilliant front-page article about the tragedy of child prostitutes in Manila, so the adjective "Conradian" is apt.

From these mistakes, I learned a big lesson that Doyle already knew: failure can follow success in the newspaper game as easily as saying one-two-three, but there is no teacher greater than failure. That is why I think this man was such a great editor. He knew that even those assignments that looked as though they ended in failure could still bring a good return down the road. He had infinite patience, or so it appeared to me as I watched all the ambitious posturing that always seemed to be going on around the newsroom (I do not exclude myself here).

Dic Doyle's *Globe and Mail* was not a handsome paper to look at. It was cluttered and a bit of a hotchpotch. It would take an editor with a refined sense of design, William Thorsell, before the paper finally looked like the national newspaper it was always claiming to be. But the content of Doyle's paper retained right to his last days the capacity to startle and to deeply inform. If he had what he liked best and was always *trying* to put into place – an adventurous reporter, solid research, stylistic writing, an arresting picture, sensitive editing, and sound news judgment on the layout desk – then his *Globe* was the cat's meow. If he didn't get it, he would get restless and angry and dispatch his gauleiters, who could, under these circumstances, be absolute bitches.

The Globe and Mail's claim that it is a "national newspaper" has often been resented by those who felt it was simply a jumped-up Toronto rag, but the claim – which is only a few decades old – is largely hitched to its outstanding "Report on Business" and it has an absolute right to make it. Until the advent in 1998 of the *National Post* – the first Canadian daily newspaper specifically created as a national newspaper – there was no competition for the title. *The Globe* grabbed its illustrious central Canadian history, its comprehensive appeal to the business community, the dramatic postwar growth of Toronto, and built up a complicated, expensive national distribution system. All this conspired together under Doyle's regime to make *The Globe* one of the world's great newspapers.

Unfortunately, nothing stays static. Towards the end of Doyle's days, the editorial department was beginning to come apart at the seams. Maybe this always happens when it is perceived a long reign is about to end, but the heyday of Doyle's rule – when everything had seemed fixed in the firmament – had really ended when Roy Megarry turned up as publisher. Partly because Doyle was getting tired and partly because Megarry encouraged it, the gauleiters started to get restless and the sparking in the newsroom sometimes reached epic proportions. Megarry was an ambitious and busy publisher, but in effect, despite his own claims and those made for him, all that was left for him to do was figure out satellite publishing technology to facilitate the claim of being a national newspaper. That and, I suppose, pulling a clever little flim-flam on circulation propaganda that saw the newspaper withdraw from the Audit Bureau of Circulation (ABC). Most advertisers depended on the ABC to verify publishers' circulation claims. Megarry successfully argued that *The Globe* didn't need the traditional audit. Thus began the controversial policy of handing out free copies of newspapers at hotels and on airlines (and gas stations and hospitality centres and God knows where else) skewing the figures, and taking credit for the newspaper Doyle and his team created. It all worked beautifully until the day some real competition arrived.

In 1983, Doyle stepped down from his mighty perch and Norman Webster was made editor-in-chief. Megarry, to his credit, handled this transition well. The grand old editor was given a fine office in the executive suite, a colourful column to write in a prominent position, and all this was merely a prelude to his appointment to the Senate in spite of the degree to which he had railed against the upper chamber for most of his editorial-writing career. Still, he ended up in the same august parliamentary chamber as George Brown had a century earlier and he paid it the great tribute of taking its constitutional responsibilities seriously.

Doyle's successor at *The Globe* tried to take his responsibilities seriously too, and at the beginning this logical appointment looked as if it were going to be brilliant. There was a messy transference of power from the inherited managing editor, Cameron Smith, to his close colleague, Geoffrey Stevens. Many of us who didn't at all care for Smith's confusing management style nevertheless thought the way he was humiliated in demotion – he was offered a humble desk in the newsroom that was clearly an attempt to get him to resign – was a bad mistake. It set a precedent for the summary treatment that Webster and Stevens would themselves receive in relatively short order, as would every single one of their successors but the ones currently reigning (who also will be shown the door soon enough, although they will not believe it even when they see the doorknob turning).

A decade later, in the year leading up to William Thorsell's own editorial execution, one of the remarkable things he did before he was axed was to mark the end of the century and millennium by reproducing each day a different front page from *The Globe*'s 150-year past. I don't know if it is everyone's cup of tea and it may even have backfired a little as the brassy, young-at-heart *National Post* looked increasingly like the newspaper of the future and *The Globe* took the role of dialectical partner as the newspaper of the past. The verdict on this little footnote won't be clear until it is seen who won the newspaper war. In any event, the daily spectacle of the old *Globe and Mail* in all its many guises has been illuminating in the extreme. For the historically minded, it has been a wonderful way to see the changes wrought not only in the look of the newspaper but in its coverage of news. When he was allowed a few words in his own defence at his demise, Thorsell said his proudest achievement was that he had got his newspaper to redefine what was news, or, as cynics put it, that background stories belong on the front page. This very idiosyncratic definition of news was bound to depart with its progenitor. What the old front pages of *The Globe* tell us is two-fold: Thorsell had a genius for design and, secondly, he hadn't a sweet fucking clue about what made an exciting front page. His news judgment was whimsical and personal and he allowed stylistic design demands to crowd out variety and pace on the page. By the time the *National Post* came along, *The Globe* was one very fat sitting duck.

In *Hurly-Burly*, Doyle noted the phenomenon that all of George Brown's successors declined the political and social limelight that Brown thrived in. A possible exception might be Oakley Dalgleish in the 1950s, who is remembered as fondly in Doyle's book as I remember Doyle. But Dalgleish, like Doyle, was really a newsroom hero and not much of a public figure. When Robert Fulford came to write a profile of Doyle for *Saturday Night* in the early 1980s and, in the course of his research, interviewed me on my hero, I realized during a long and amiable lunch with the most knowledgeable journalist in Canada how little he,

Fulford, really knew about Doyle's personality, achievements, and complications. It amazed me that someone with the power wielded by the editor-in-chief of *The Globe and Mail* could be so little known and so underscrutinized, especially by the most curious journalist in Canada.

And so, it seems, the same can be said for all the successors of George Brown, as evidenced by the front-page reproductions throughout 1999. The newspaper fell into very distinctive periods. During Brown's days, it was reformist, anti-Catholic, pro-Confederation, moderately anti-establishment (and vociferously so during the Pacific Scandal that rocked the first Macdonald post-Confederation administration and led to its defeat). Under Brown's successors, the newspaper clearly embraced the Establishment, was pro-Empire, and by the time it merged with the Tory *Mail and Empire* in 1936 had pretty well abandoned its strong liberal ethos to the *Toronto Star*. Its war record was excellent, with vivid dispatches keeping people at home as well informed as possible under wartime censorship, and also helping to keep morale high. It's interesting to speculate, as one reads the war copy and the coverage of wartime debates in Parliament, what the post-Watergate journalists would have done to Mackenzie King and his administration (and what he would have done to them with the War Measures Act in place!). In any event, after the war *The Globe* solidified its reputation for being the newspaper for the Toronto intellectual, social, and business elite and its conservative credentials were almost the antithesis of what George Brown had created the newspaper for.

The other crucial and dramatic change from Brown's days, of course, was the question of ownership. Brown left a highly lucrative property behind. And soon enough after he died it was sold by his heirs and immediate successors and began the apparently cease-less journey of changing owners as "market forces" determined. The relatively benign ownership of the *Financial Post* chain, which controlled the newspaper when I first joined it, came to an end when Norman Webster's uncle, Howard Webster, the chairman of FP, decided he wanted out of newspapers and put the chain up for sale. The first to nibble was my old schoolmate, Conrad Black, and my first boss, John Bassett, owner of the CFTO television franchise and the former publisher of the *Toronto Telegram*. This was in 1980 and before a few weeks were played out, the vast Thomson organization rolled into the fray with all guns (i.e., tens of millions of dollars) blazing. I don't think Black and Bassett realized what hit them. Webster simply chuckled all the way to the bank as Thomson kept upping the offer. It's curious now to look back and realize that if Black had been successful, he might never have been lured to the British market and *The Globe* would probably still be ruling the national newspaper roost alone.

I remember those days vividly. Fear of Black caused hysteria in the newsroom. Almost any alternative was considered acceptable. That was a big lesson to me. I knew that Bassett and Black, though overbearing in many ways, were far better *newspaper*men than the heirs to the FP chain, and I also knew for sure they were more loyal to newspaper traditions than the Thomson chain. Yet *Globe* journalists worked themselves into such a froth that somehow Thomson – the dreaded chain that was reputed to have cost-reduced every newspaper it owned into editorial oblivion – seemed preferable.

The Thomson chain intrigued me because it damaged so many papers I admired and yet its founder and his son were both personable men who seemed to me to be admirable Canadian achievers on a grand scale. From afar, at least, I liked the way the company had started from so little and built up into the international monolith. I had met the first Lord Thomson (Roy) several times and had interviewed him when he was chancellor of my alma mater, Memorial University of Newfoundland, and I was the university correspondent for the St. John's *Evening Telegram* in the 1960s (later purchased by Thomson and degraded through cost-cutting and layoffs, and more recently purchased and nominally improved by the Black-owned Southam chain). Thomson was an original, and I respected his empire-building achievements in the United Kingdom even as I deplored what he did to the literate and feisty newspapers his machine gobbled up in Canada. When I was posted to London by *The Globe and Mail* many years later, it amused me to send Canadian friends and visitors to the crypt of St. Paul's Cathedral, not just to see Wellington's tomb but also to observe and inwardly digest the nearby wall plaque commemorating Thomson. I have it memorized and feel certain an Englishman wrote it:

ROY THOMSON
FIRST BARON THOMSON OF FLEET
An extraordinary man,
he came from nowhere and
accomplished great things

Occasionally a friend would remonstrate with me after seeing this and say that "nowhere" meant Timmins, Ontario, where Thomson made his first little fortune. "Nope," I replied, "you don't understand this place [Britain]. They mean the whole damn place, *a Mari usque ad Mare.*"

In any event, the second Lord Thomson of Fleet, Ken Thomson as he prefers to be known, is a very different fellow. I like him. He's a decent, mild-mannered, and considerate gentleman who, unfortunately, seems to stay out of the day-to-day business of running his newspapers. I wish he would bring his kindly personality to bear on some of the overpaid monsters who get control of the editorial agenda of *The Globe and Mail* until they too are dispatched to wherever failed Thomson executives are dispatched. But still, that's the way Thomson seems to like his company run, so he must live with the consequences. I say that laughingly knowing how considerable are the profits of his organization, but the turmoil *The Globe* creates is out of all proportion to its financial position within the Thomson chain.

There's a parallel here between the role The London *Times* played for Roy Thomson and that of *The Globe* for Ken Thomson, with the little proviso that *The Globe and Mail* makes money for the chain and *The Times* never did. Regardless. The parallel transcends profit or loss in both cases. Roy Thomson bore the losses at *The Times* manfully, as the old politically incorrect expression goes, because it was the price of his peerage and his self-perceived "duty" to his new position in the British establishment. When that position seemed secure and the losses beyond any sort of cure, he felt comfortable enough selling it. Ken Thomson bought *The Globe and Mail,* I suspect, so that he would have at least one newspaper in the Canadian chain to hang his pride on and to anchor his position in the Canadian establishment in whose midst he was most comfortable spending most of his time. I further suspect that if and when the public accountability for the ownership of *The Globe and Mail* becomes more rancorous and onerous than he cares to shoulder, it too will be sold.

It's not true that Ken Thomson doesn't care about the quality of his newspapers. He once explained in great detail and passion to me that his father felt so compelled to compete with the big international chains that he felt he had to squeeze his newspapers for as much profit as possible. It was an obsession, the son said. It hadn't been necessary for some time and any honest, dispassionate observer would see that the Thomson titles had improved. Despite our personal liking for each other, I'd taken a whack at the Thomson ownership in a column I used to write for the *Toronto Star*. His nibs was not pleased, and it is always distressing when you distress someone you like, but it is part of the price of being a public commentator. Anyway, by way of amends I felt I certainly owed Thomson enough of my time to scan his current array of Canadian newspapers properly and, I must confess I found them much improved. I was particularly impressed with what a nice paper the Victoria *Times-Colonist* had become and was about to write a column taking back – or at least amending somewhat – my snarky comments when, lo and behold! Thomson sold the little sucker.

And what a lot of newspapers he was selling in the 1990s and most of them were scooped up by Conrad Black's newly acquired Southam chain. "Hmmm," I said to the missus one day as another newspaper fell into Black's lap out of Lord T's ample bag, "something is up here and I'm damned if I can figure it out." At a certain point, Maude Barlow, the First Lady of Economic Nationalism, started to rant about the concentration of press ownership, and while I don't want to diminish anyone's sense of concern on this issue, I'm not sure concentration is the problem. For one thing, both the reading public and the journalists themselves would sound alarms very soon if there really was a concentrated effort to control our access to information and our thoughts. In the age of the Internet, though, it's just silly to speculate in this area very long. And even if concentration were a clear and present danger, all the government has to do to remedy it is to open the world of Canadian newspapers to outside buyers: concentration would get fractured in an instant.

What seemed then, and still seems, far more intriguing and far less discussed is what on earth was happening to the news business. On the one hand, one of the world's most successful newspaper chains – Thomson – was divesting itself of dozens of its newspapers all over the world and moving into niche publishing and electronic information retrieval and dissemination. On the other, Black and his various international newspaper holdings were expanding at an almost equivalent rate. Someone was surely making an epochal mistake here. Was Thomson, having sucked all the profits it wanted from its newspapers, moving too soon? Was Conrad coming in too late? Was this a case of a T. Rex fighting a raptor when both were ultimately doomed? Were they both correct, in fact, because they had different objectives?

You have to stay tuned to the future to find out the answers to these fascinating questions. All I know is that when I left that nasty party, held to say goodbye to Norman Webster and inaugurate the decade-long term of William Thorsell, the Canadian newspaper industry – with *The Globe* in the vanguard – was about to begin a roller-coaster ride that no one who was on it, or observed it closely, will ever forget. The landscape between then and now seems utterly changed and transformed, and the man who did much of the transforming became the principal victim of the change. I think this is called irony. Either that or hubris. In any event, it will be a long time before there is another editor-in-chief of any newspaper in Canada quite like William Thorsell.

IV

J told me this story about William Thorsell and I've always cherished it because it shows the seemingly austere editor's best human side and goes some way to compensate for the tales of dysfunctional management that were coming out of *The Globe and Mail* newsroom within weeks of his takeover. The story is set in Edmonton in Thorsell's native Alberta. It is some years before Patrick Martin's celebrated farewell party for Norman Webster. Thorsell is the editor of the *Edmonton Journal*'s editorial page. J was a summer intern at the same newspaper, grateful for his temporary job but in terrible turmoil over the disintegrating relationship between himself and his girlfriend.

The problem for J was fairly straightforward, although it may not have seemed so at the time. He was gay and struggling hard to come to terms with it. There were family and friends to deal with. There was his girlfriend. There was the rest of his life and all the attendant difficulties in being different, from being set apart from "normal" society. If he came out of the closet, what would this do to his vaunted ambition to become a television journalist? It is not for nothing that the highest suicide rate amongst men are young homosexuals trying to hide or to deal honestly with sexual instincts they never asked for in a society that, while definitely improving, still manages to register its general abhorrence of homosexuality in no uncertain terms.

J had heard that the editorial page editor was gay, although it didn't seem to be a big deal. He hardly knew the man, but nevertheless in his distress he sought him out and Thorsell agreed to listen. I heard this tale years later, in J's own telling, so I don't know all the details. The gist of the encounter, however, was that Thorsell told J that there definitely was a price to be paid for the inexplicable differences in his sexuality from the majority of men, but that society was changing its attitudes and he had a right to a decent life and a reasonable chance of success in his chosen field. "He told me," J reported, "that even though he accepted he could never be the editor-in-chief of *The Globe and Mail*, it didn't mean that he could not have a life of achievement. It was a matter of learning to make a reasonable assessment of the possible, protecting yourself, and – where necessary – sticking to your guns."

So far as I know throughout Thorsell's decade and a half at the helm of *The Globe and Mail*'s editorial department, his private life – much speculated upon within the newsroom – only became a public issue in one or two columns from competitor newspapers. Douglas Fisher, the veteran columnist in the *Toronto Sun*, let out a few homophobic farts in Thorsell's early days as editor-in-chief, and Trevor Lautens alluded to it in a *Vancouver Sun* column in the mid-1990s. But that's about it, if you exclude *Frank* magazine. On one level, that speaks very well of journalistic tolerance in Canada;

on another, it shows the usual hypocrisy the media adopts with its own. In any other important field of endeavour, a gay man's appointment to such a top establishment post in the 1980s would have been an instant *cause célèbre*. Look at how Svend Robinson was initially treated, and he was only a backbencher in the NDP federal caucus. Or imagine if a bishop, or the president of a bank, or a general of the Canadian Forces, or a member of royalty had been perceived as gay. Several times over the 1990s, *The Globe and Mail* itself allowed speculation about Prince Edward's sexuality to get into its columns based solely on the fact that he wasn't yet married. Yet only once did the editor-in-chief's homosexuality make it in – and even then the reference was indirect – after he addressed that meeting of gay businessmen in Toronto.

Yet Thorsell's greatest achievement at *The Globe* was probably not his redesign or his redefinition of the news or the repositioning of the editorial page. I suspect history, or at least "social history," will show that the true significance of his mandate over the national newspaper was that it was the first to report gay news as if it were ordinary news and, by the time his mandate was over, it was. I have no idea if this was by design – and, knowing Thorsell's propensity to let all points of view rage – I very much doubt it. Rather, the fact that he was gay probably let editors feel easier about carrying copy that was gay-related, some of it positive, some of it negative. Thanks to this, there really did seem to be a conscious effort over the Thorsell years to portray gays and gay-related news as part of everyday life. Certainly the volume of gay news, profiles of out-of-closet gays, and the gay sensibility in entertainment, travel, and the business world increased dramatically.

This undoubtedly enraged some, but I believe it has made a substantial difference to public attitudes and the tolerance of intelligent

Canadian society. There is irony here because Thorsell was generally thought of as a right-wing ideologue by many of his staff and by left-wing detractors. His gayness, only ever commented on in *Frank* magazine but widely known nevertheless in press and government circles, complicated the perceived ideological struggle for the soul of *The Globe*'s newsroom, but in fact the struggle was overstated. In the week Thorsell's demotion was announced, left-of-centre columnists such as Rick Salutin and Michael Valpy were still writing strongly worded articles and columns.

And this other strange thing happened too. Thorsell's own column, which was published on Saturdays and was regularly scrutinized by media addicts such as myself in much the same way as middle-ranking monsignors sniffed *L'Osservatore Romano* or Maoist cadres *The People's Daily*, seemed to go through a perceptual sea change. The column was always a clucking item while Thorsell held high office. One looked for gleanings into future purges, or political realignments, or the latest "disgusting" defence of Brian Mulroney, or – although it never came – the definitive outing column. Within two weeks of the demotion, however, the column was transformed into one of the most thoughtful, elegantly written, and idiosyncratic offerings from a Canadian journalist. Thorsell had been returned to *Globe* readers as he had arrived: a fascinating, off-centre, highly intellectual, and totally original presence in the most important newsroom in the nation. The only negative to mention here were all the corpses left behind in his wake, so much so that when it came to be his turn to take the cut, it seemed for all the world like Robespierre ascending his own scaffold.

Some people who have worked closely with Thorsell say that he seems rootless, unconnected to any particular part of the country or to any country in particular. That may make him a perfect editor for a national newspaper in a country such as Canada, but the sense of rootlessness has more to do with his intellectual detachment and the fact that he is very much a self-made man. Both his mother (Norwegian) and his father (Swedish) were immigrants to Canada. When he was born in Canmore, Alberta, according to James Fleming in *Circles of Power*, he spent the first year of his life in a garage with no running water. While true enough, it isn't quite as dire as it sounds, as his father, who had repaired aircraft during the war, was building a house for his family on land given to veterans on the outskirts of Edmonton.

Thorsell has written about his father in a moving column that was notable for its spare romanticism and eloquent respect. He has clearly been a quiet inspiration to the son throughout their lives together, and this inspiration may be part of the reason Thorsell himself was such a whiz at school, ending up in elected office at both his junior high and high schools. I'm sure I would have hated him, especially when he proceeded with excellent grades into the University of Alberta and spent his summers as an Alberta government promoter touring the North American fair circuit touting all that was fine east of the Rockies and west of Saskatchewan. I would have dismissed him as a "comer," to use that horrible American expression for an aggressively ambitious young man whose agenda is far too open to general scrutiny. That's to differentiate him from closet comers like me whose various agendas are compulsively hidden!

Another reason I would have hated him then was that this fieldwork for Alberta tourism stood him in such good stead, it led to his appointment as manager of the Western Canada exhibit at Expo 67 in Montreal. He was only twenty-one and got treated on a par with the other exhibit commissioners. I would have found that difficult to bear had I known him. His bent, then, was clearly emerging as primarily administrative, albeit with a strong academic thrust. After completing his BA in history, he went after two more degrees: an MA (also at the University of Alberta) in twentieth-century intellectual history; and a masters in public administration from Princeton's prestigious Woodrow Wilson School in Public and International Affairs. He then served successively both his alma maters in several administrative capacities, making the transition to journalism only in 1975. He ended up at the *Edmonton Journal*, but he started flirting with *The Globe* early on, taking his first job there in 1976 as an editorial writer. He quit shortly afterwards, however, missing the freedom he had had in Edmonton, where he soon returned, not coming back to *The Globe* until 1984. He took a 15 per cent drop in salary by this move east but ended up as editor-in-chief within five years.

Thorsell was a very different editor than what the old *Globe* was used to. All the others, without exception, had been traditional newshounds of one sort or another and had worked their way up the system, so that by the time they reached high office they had a practical sense of almost every aspect of newsroom operations. They also had deeply ingrained ideas – sometimes to the point of prejudice – about how news should be gathered, edited, and presented to the public. Thorsell had no practical sense of the newsroom, a huge impatience with the slow-witted or those set in their ways (or simply in his way), an intellectual confidence that was often indistinguishable from arrogance, and a lot of new ideas for newspapers – some of them brilliant, some of them either pretentious or silly.

Take "The Middle Kingdom." This "innovative" feature is as good an example as any of Thorsell transforming an initially stimulating intellectual concept into pretentious twaddle. It appeared before the readers' startled morning countenances during his initial revolutionary period and came with a lot of rhetoric on how the articles on this special page would transport us to another realm of journalistic thought and endeavour – deeper, presumably, more idiosyncratic, and definitely more meaningful than the old junk *The Globe and Mail* used to serve up. I believe a lot of innocent people in the newsroom had to listen to a barrage of stream-of-conscious reasoning from the editor-in-chief when this sucker tried to take off. But, stripped of its special logo and the fancy rhetoric, "The Middle Kingdom" was merely an update of the hoary features page, except that an editing edge had been lost and the pieces rambled on and on and on. It also left dark thoughts. If half the energy had been put into trying to produce better features rather than reconceptualizing what had been a given in contemporary newspapers, *The Globe* would not have had to go through so many absurd hoops. Being a cynical Old China Hand myself, I figured the editor had chosen the worst possible title and consequent imagery. He may have meant it to mean the kingdom of middle pages in the newspaper, but anyone who knew even a smidgen of history understood that "Middle Kingdom" referred exclusively to China. Symbolically it also meant a closed-off community where outsiders were unwelcome and which was sufficient unto itself for all needs: every other place was a mere tributary.

The single most dramatic change Thorsell made – and one that was successful, as few of these things are – was the redesign. Most newspapers and magazines change the way they look only when it is perceived there is something wrong in the design status quo. Occasionally, some foolish editors change the design just for the sake of change to announce their own suzerainty over the pages. Thorsell did it because the old design was provincial, clunky, and – thanks to years of minor tinkering – a mishmash of typefaces and layout styles. The look of the newspaper undermined all the hard work that went into the content.

Such changes do not usually exercise the public a great deal, but they are crucial internal events, upsetting years of deskmen's routines and affecting the very psychology of journalists whose writing stared back at them in different dress than they had ever seen before. Almost to prove that he was a bold revolutionary, Thorsell scrapped the century-and-half use of Gothic type for the masthead, chosen first by George Brown for *The Globe* and retained when *The Mail and Empire* was acquired and folded into the older newspaper. The new pages were, in a word, beautiful, but Thorsell's achievement was not so much aesthetic – important as that was – as in giving the newspaper the kind of look it had always needed to live up to its opinion of itself and that of many of its loyal readers. The design was elegant, sober, readable – and a hit with readers almost from the first day. There was a bizarre coincidence too, or perhaps it wasn't coincidence as Thorsell had a certain genius at times for catching the mood of the moment. Many of *The Globe*'s readers were learning the ins and outs of their computers and, among them, was the whole notion of personal choice in typeface and type size. It was a practical aesthetic moment that no one could have predicted a dozen years earlier. Many *Globe* readers were being *soi-disant* William Thorsells, tinkering with the way their own ideas could be presented in letters or memos. With that new insight, taken from a centuries-old craft at the heart of the newspaper business, this odd-sock editor invited his readership into a conspiracy of style and they could ride along with him as he discussed the merits of Times New Roman over Bookman Old Style or Garamond.

The only problem with the redesign was that it put a terrible burden on *The Globe*'s headline writers, who were getting hammered in two directions. From the editor-in-chief's office there were lectures about redefining what is and what is not news; from the layout department there was a clean and fresh look that was unforgiving to the second-rate. The writing of headlines, subheads, and cutlines is a real art. Believe me! They can tweak a reader's curiosity or mark solemnity or rattle you with their urgency and sense of crisis. Mishandled, they can give devastatingly wrong directions and misdirect, even misinform, thousands of people. They can also be banal. I have a vivid memory of an inside turn headline – across the top of an entire page – over one of those ghastly magazine-length essays Thorsell favoured in his early days. I believe the subject was pollution in the Northwest Territories, neither an unworthy nor necessarily a boring subject, depending on how it was written and presented. Anyway, the headline read: ARCTIC BEAUTY NOT AS PRISTINE AS ONCE THOUGHT. No indeed, I thought to myself. Nor is headline writing as demanding and effective an art as once thought.

The other casualty of the new redesign was the number of stories on the front page. On an average, the old front page in Dic Doyle's heyday had featured a minimum of seven and an average of eight or nine stories. Some of the front pages from the further past show that old *Globe*s and *Globe and Mail*s could manage more than twenty stories on the front. Once Thorsell's gargantuan Index and special feature and extended white space were accommodated, however, there was hardly room for four or five stories. This was a serious loss. It reinforced the notion that the newspaper had become a daily magazine, which may even have been the intention of the editor. This wasn't at all a bad concept, but it was wrong to signal the fact so concretely on the front page, which is still any newspaper's single most important selling page, where any impact or excitement has to be first registered.

Also, aping magazine culture at a time when readership of general-interest magazines and especially newsmagazines was in a free fall was not exactly swift thinking. On top of that, a lot of guff was heard throughout the 1970s and 1980s about television taking away the immediacy of news from newspapers, but all TV did was rob papers of the "first word." Newspapers remained the best means of conveying quick depth, and that's why the magazine concept was not without merit on an intellectual level, but it was paraded too ostentatiously on *The Globe*'s front page, exhausting readers before they had even perused the first paragraph.

But, all that said, what a lucky man was William Thorsell. For over ten years he had control of the finest newspaper in Canada, and with that control he did many interesting things, several of them important. He anchored arts coverage as it had never been before, and he brought to arts reporting a new *esprit*. There was irony galore when, eight years into his mandate, the brassy new *National Post* took his initial clever insight into expanding "leisure readership concepts" and with its larger and more dramatic "Arts" and "Life" sections made *The Globe*'s conscientious efforts look chintzy. There was a parallel here with the old *Toronto Telegram*, which pioneered the special Saturday arts section in the late 1950s only to see itself ultimately outpaced by both the *Toronto Star* and *The Globe*. Innovation of itself, then, can't save a newspaper. It has to be built upon with solid circulation and marketing values, something *The Tely* forgot to its peril.

Thorsell clearly loved the position of editor-in-chief and the power it wielded. He showed this early on with his most controversial relationship, the one with Brian Mulroney. The "most reviled prime minister in our history," as he was described once in the *Toronto Star*, was only the "most" reviled in the historically hampered journalists' mind. They had forgotten how reviled Pierre Trudeau was by the end of his mandate. And they didn't even know how reviled John Diefenbaker was, or William Lyon Mackenzie King, or R. B. Bennett, or – for that matter – Sir John A. Macdonald during the Pacific Scandal. To my eyes, however, Thorsell's hero worship of the reviled Mulroney says more that is interesting, valuable, intriguing, and even noble about *The Globe and Mail*'s now jettisoned editor-in-chief than any other action he took during his decade hold on power.

To the outsider, sympathetic or otherwise, it was clear from the start that the new editor admired strong authority figures. Every journalist who had followed Thorsell's career knew that he adored his first *Globe* publisher, Roy Megarry. It was more than the fact that he owed his big promotion to the man. He clearly liked Megarry's big-time style, his impatience with nay-sayers, and his global (well, Club-of-Rome-ish) viewpoint. Thorsell, obviously, was the biggest beneficiary of Megarry's favour, and he basked in it. There had been no such closeness between Webster and Megarry, or Doyle and Brig. Richard Malone, or indeed between any subeditors and George Brown. Editor and publisher, usually, are natural foes. It may not show at management meetings, but the sparring can go on behind the scenes with great fury.

Consequently, Thorsell's total identification with Megarry came as a considerable shock to the newsroom, which had been trained over the previous few years to loathe and beware anyone above the rank of editor. It was a flaw in the Webster-Stevens era that the rank and file of the newsroom were all too aware of their dislike for the publisher and all his works. I'm absolutely sure that Dic Doyle and his managing editor, Clark Davey, despised, or at the very least resented, Brigadier Malone when he was publisher in the 1970s, but I only came to believe this long after the brigadier had retired as Doyle or Davey never gave the newsroom a clue what the relationship was like. Not so with Webster and Stevens *vis à vis* Roy Megarry, and because everyone knew, the journalists became detached from crucial elements in the livelihood of a newspaper: from understanding the relatedness between good editorial and circulation; between confident, independent editorial and advertising; between knowing punditry and real power. They came to think that the publisher had no role whatsoever in the newsroom, and this in a newspaper where the publisher, right up until the 1980s, retained the full title of "publisher and editor-in-chief."

Set against this scene, Thorsell's love affair with Mulroney takes on a special flavour. There's some interesting background here too. Dic Doyle succumbed to the Mulroney blarney as well. I know this because I was his national editor at the time Mulroney was making his big move to eliminate the "feckless" Joe Clark and take over the leadership of the Tory party. Doyle was not an unsubtle man, and his support for the Mulroney thrust into higher politics took the form of nagging at the national desk about underplaying Mulroney's achievements and overplaying Clark's hold on the party. On this latter point, Doyle was right. Clark's hold on his party's loyalty was about as secure as a first-time filleter's hold on an eel. This is a Newfoundland image, appropriately enough, because Clark's subnemesis during his final days before leading up to his disastrous leadership review convention in Winnipeg was the former Newfoundland premier and Mulroney strategist Frank Moores. *The Globe's* editorial hierarchy had abandoned Trudeau's definition of Confederation years before, and Mulroney was clearly the white knight in attendance.

All of which is to point out that Thorsell wasn't the first national editor-in-chief to be bagged. Norman Webster wasn't part of this, however. Webster, whatever his views of Mulroney, came to see during his short mandate as editor-in-chief that almost anything horrible that could be said about Mulroney would resonate with the reading public. That he was too flashy and sleazy by half was taken for granted. Any suggestions of wrongdoing were happily believed and actual wrongdoing by anyone in his administration was gleefully reported. By the time Thorsell took over as editor-in-chief, Mulroney was the "most reviled" prime minister in Canadian history since the last "most reviled" title holder.

Mulroney and Thorsell talked a lot, it was soon apparent. That absolutely infuriated many of the political reporters at *The Globe*. In the post-Watergate era, that seemed tantamount to treason, although the tradition in Canadian politics and journalism is one of close relationships. Sir Wilfrid Laurier's door, for example, was always open to journalists in favour, and many Canadian political journalists of the pre-Watergate era prided themselves on their easy access to the top. My distant cousin, the late Blair Fraser, was a classic example of this cosy relationship with government leaders that would be so frowned upon now, but I'm not convinced the country or politics or journalism were worse off because of it. The only example of this now is *The Globe*'s Jeffrey Simpson, but his access is to the higher ranks of the civil service, where he could belong himself. Actually, I shouldn't use the phrase "pre-Watergate" in a discussion of Canadian political journalism, although the example of the Washington *Post* during the Nixon era certainly had deeply affected Canadian journalism. What I am talking about, the end of the comfortable and respectful relationship between pundit and pol, came with Peter Newman's influential and epoch-ending tome on John Diefenbaker, *Renegade in Power*. Newman's portrait of the demented Dief electrified much of the public, and Newman became the stylistic architect of political journalism for a generation or more.

Thorsell was the antithesis of Newman. It seemed, from the outside, that direct access to the top meant everything to Thorsell and he revelled in it, just as Newman revelled in indirect access to the top (via spies, snitches, trusted allies – the usual riff-raff) with a safe and swift exit. As someone who identified with power so much, who admired strong leaders, and who took an essentially conservative view of economics, Thorsell must have found access to the prime minister irresistible, and he resisted it not a jot. You can either deplore or admire this for the usual reasons, but what is truly amazing in retrospect was the editor's bold and dogged loyalty to the beleaguered Mulroney when it seemed everyone had abandoned him. Where were the merit and the rewards for the man in sticking by his guns and arguing that Mulroney's achievements were remarkable and outstanding? There were none. Not an Order of Canada, not a Senate appointment, not even a medal for courage or chutzpah. All Thorsell got was obloquy, venom, and distrust, both inside his newspaper and outside. It will be curious to see what the history books note in a half-century or so. Depending on how free trade and the constitutional wrangling evolve (and the memory of the gooey blarney subsides), the biggest shock in our collective futures may yet be the rehabilitation of Mulroney's reputation. And if that happens, Thorsell's prescience will be worth more than a footnote.

If free trade overwhelms us and the constitutional wrangling destroys the country, then we'll all be footnotes and it won't have mattered whose side who was on because the great game will have been lost. And what a game it was meant to be, with free trade, with a constant thrusting towards reform and egalitarianism somehow melded under the Crown, somehow different from the United States or the United Kingdom and yet incorporating the best of both. Somehow.

V

After George Brown helped make Canada during his version of six days and six nights, he did not rest. He continued to make trouble for Tories, Roman Catholics, and all the opposition newspapers in Toronto, especially the high Tory *Mail*. For its part, *The Mail* – not yet hooked up with *The Empire* but possibly sensing in *The Globe* not its own subsequent absorption but at least an

empire-builder and competitor of considerable tenacity – recipro-
cated by trying to make just as much trouble for him. In Brown's
curiously complex personality, the dwindling anti-Catholic
bigotry that nevertheless lay squat like a wart-ridden toad on his
soul tied in nicely, so far as *The Globe* was concerned, with his anti-
Tory politics and visionary genius as a newspaper editor. His audience – prosperous, Protestant, and, generally speaking, progressive
in a robust nineteenth-century way – was established and loyal in
both good and foul weather.

The business of being a statesman and nation-founder
was almost a by-product of his politics, and there's not much to
indicate that he was particularly happy as a pooh-bah of
Confederation. There are a few notable exceptions, but on the
whole newspaper people make crummy politicians and not very
good government administrators. There are several reasons for
this, but chief amongst them is the horror journalists feel at
espousing a particular cause, following through on issues, and
taking responsibility for the consequences. Journalists embrace
too much irony and scepticism to be comfortable in politicians'
garb. They are also too judgmental on one side, and too prone to
gullibility on the other: not a pleasant combination in politics. For
the most part, the exceptions – Nigel Lawson, the former editor
of *The Spectator* in Britain, is an obvious example, especially after
he became such an influential Chancellor of the Exchequer under
Margaret Thatcher – are usually zealots whose temporarily
leashed ideological passions curb their journalistic prowess and
independence. George Brown declined a knighthood, preferring
to remain "plain old George Brown" in J. M. S. Careless's felicitous phrase (if marginally inaccurate since he did accept an
appointment to the new Senate of Canada, thereby obtaining not

just the title Senator but also a Privy Council honorific, which ostensibly made his name The Honourable George Brown, on a par with the lesser children of a peer of the realm). From his friend Prime Minister Alexander Mackenzie he received an offer to become the lieutenant-governor of Ontario, but he declined that too. Instead, he expanded his newspaper and took to rearing prime shorthorn cattle at his new country estate, Bow Park, near present-day Brampton. The paper did fine, but the cattle became his financial nemesis.

Before the fancy cattle loomed so large in his life, though, Brown managed to do his bit to bring down the first post-Confederation administration of his hated political rival, John A. Macdonald, and he did it in the best way a newspaper editor knows how: by exposing corruption, bribery, and high-level hypocrisy. This was the Pacific Scandal and, like so many Canadian political scandals, close examination of the details and broad features shows both pettiness and venality on all sides. Considering the times, it was as bad a scandal as anything alleged against Brian Mulroney's Tory administration in the Airbus affair, but interestingly enough both scandals were caught up in huge sums connected to crucial transportation systems. During 1873, the man who had been granted vast land concessions and a federal charter to build the Canadian Pacific Railway was caught making equally vast election donations to most of the senior members of Macdonald's cabinet. Macdonald's Tories were not above taking advantage of their commanding governmental position, especially when it came to raising funds and pushing through their vaunted railway project both to woo and appease Western Canada and create new markets for Ontario and Quebec. And Brown and his Liberal colleagues weren't above making maximum political hay over the details of corruption, even while they almost certainly had a hand in stealing the tell-tale correspondence from a lawyer's office, and even while they gleefully tried to undermine what would eventually become one of the most binding forces — an east-west railway — of the early greater Canada.

A good newspaper out on a good cause is not required to have all the answers, nor any, really. Nor is it a prescriptive institution, though editors often have crackpot ideas for politicians to consider. Brown was unusual in that he came to believe deeply in the cause of Confederation and fought for it with all his wit and might, even putting aside for the moment and for the cause some of his most heartfelt prejudices. The business ameliorated and softened some of his hardest gripes, but it did not make him comfortable with the concept or the reality of actually governing. Even though he maintained the closest possible relationship with the first Liberal post-Confederation administration of Alexander Mackenzie — far closer than anything William Thorsell managed with Brian Mulroney — he was often uncomfortable with the compromises that this caused him, especially when he himself was often the issue. As an editor, I doubt if he ever looked finer than when he was chasing down Tories during the Pacific Scandal. He and his newspaper were wonders to behold, and the enthusiasm with which he beat Sir John A. over the head was spectacular. "The saddest spectacle the Canadian public has ever been called upon to witness," he called the whole mess, and he watched Macdonald's Tories go down in flames in the subsequent election with deep satisfaction.

By the time his own party and his friends assumed office, however, things had changed. The excitement of the chase, the happy electoral results – these stirring events worked in tandem to reignite in him what was essentially a depressive nature aggravated by painful, recurring stomach ailments that doctors couldn't really cure. Soon enough under the Liberals, internal party disputes had him spluttering in both his editorials and private discussions, even as his own political interests waned and his obsession with animal husbandry expanded.

By the mid-1870s, though, our man was an icon whose worst enemies still accorded him considerable stature. The later George Brown is so much more attractive than the earlier prig, it is sometimes difficult to reconcile the two. How much Canada owes his wife, Anne, for the kinder, gentler Brown cannot be fully known, but a lot can be inferred. They met in Scotland, shortly after 1860. Although it was only seven years before Confederation, he had gone there heartsick at the whole failure of colonial politics and the numerous setbacks for his great cause of reform. She was the daughter of Thomas Nelson, the progenitor of the famous publishing house. He had gone to school with her brothers, but a renewed acquaintanceship through a chance meeting in London brought him north. And thus he became, as happens often and happily enough, one of those lucky men who find a superb woman and, against all odds and common sense (on the woman's part), retains her affections. Anne was an attractive, lively, intelligent daughter of a proud and prosperous Edinburgh household. George snapped her and her considerable dowry up, and it was the single best thing he ever did for himself since making the decision to move with his Free Kirk-spouting papa from New York, New York, to York, Upper Canada. Anne plighted her troth, stood by her man for better and for worse, in sickness and in health, for richer and for poorer, till death did them part, as she vowed to do. When George brought his bride back to Toronto, five thousand of his supporters were there to cheer him on and sing "Annie Laurie" in her honour. She was enchanted with her new home and through her eyes he began to see the world around him and his fellow human beings in the light not of perpetual challenge and agitation, but of consummation, obtainable happiness, and measurable goals. From that moment on, Anne was there to rally his flagging spirits, assuage his neuroses and hurts, cheer his victories, and – when death came so unexpectedly – she was also there to rock him safely through his final journey.

There's a wonderful anecdote about Brown that happened towards the end of his life. It's in the vast and general category of "missed opportunities," and I loved it when Dic Doyle first told it to me many years ago because it humanizes the founder of *The Globe* in a way most journalists would smile at ruefully. The story came unsolicited during some amiable gossip about the Canadian investors in the board game Trivial Pursuit, which has had such a phenomenal international success. We were talking about a former *Globe* journalist we both liked and admired who had been offered a chance to be an initial investor for, I believe, $1,000. Either because he didn't have the loot or because he thought the game was a non-starter, he chose not to join with a group of ten or so colleagues. They, of course, went on to reap tens of thousands of dollars, perhaps hundreds of thousands, and our friend and colleague only got to contemplate the bile that must have risen in his gorge each time some obvious manifestation of the royalty cheques rolled into town. Trivial Pursuit was the merest blip in contrast to what Brown let slip through his fingers. I rather like J. M. S. Careless's sombre account of the matter in the *Dictionary of*

Canadian Biography because it leaves unsaid so many emotions and dark thoughts:

> From 1875 ... Brown was spending his time increasingly on affairs at his Bow Park estate. There his neighbour's son, Alexander Graham Bell, offered him ... a share in the rights to the "sound telegraphy" system Bell had invented if [Brown] would advance $600 and patent the device in England. He agreed to advance the money, and undertook to apply for a British patent for Bell in a forthcoming visit to Britain. But when the senator arrived in London in February 1876, the technical advice he received there discouraged him as to the value of Bell's invention, and Brown did not become part-owner of the future Bell empire. He was more concerned with his plan to launch a joint-stock company in Britain to build Bow Park into a major pedigreed cattle-raising venture. . . .

We know what happened to Bell and I'm afraid we also know what happened to Bow Park fancy cattle, even if we don't have the specifics. Generally speaking, as I have hinted at, journalists are better at reporting what people are doing than actually trying to do it themselves. We have trouble learning this, however.

George Brown died fussing over Bow Park and its costs. Ironically, it took some expertise from England to sort things out in the short term, and since he saw his entire life in the context of his final obsession – cattle – he seems to have died feeling he was a failure. How we downplay our achievements and play up our failures! In fact, he left a wonderful country and, not incidentally, a wonderful newspaper. He was always up-to-date with the latest technology, and although he doesn't seem to have given himself much credit for it, he retained a lively and inventive mind for editorial renewal. As late as 1876, when his passions were all caught up in four-legged creatures of "improving" provenance, he conceived and launched a weekly edition of his newspaper that was an instant hit and the precursor to the Saturday feature-laden editions that were more than half a century away. His *Weekly Globe* wasn't just a stuffy reprint of "the best" from the weekday offerings, either. There was real news from Europe by the most efficient cable service he could manage, lots of sports, and comprehensive coverage – features, news, illustrations, recipes, fashions – for "the ladies of the house" (and secretly scoured, as always, by the gentlemen who, then as now, were trying to figure out where they stood with the "fairer" sex).

Before we meet his assassin, it is worthwhile to take a short look at Brown's mellowing anti-Catholicism. There are two ways to go about this business. The first way is rather pleasant. In 1871, a few years after Confederation, after all the church-state battles of the anti-Anglican coalition had been won and Bishop Strachan's side lost, Ontario's English-speaking Catholics approached Brown in a delegation and asked why reform-minded Catholics should not join common cause with the Liberals as they once had many years before – before, that is, Brown had whipped the whole of Protestant and Orange Canada (well, Canada West actually, but then as now Ontario had always felt itself to be "all of Canada") into a fever pitch of anti-Catholicism. Why not, said Brown, and he penned his famous open letter in which, as Careless carefully points out, he retracted nothing but allowed that perhaps Roman Catholics might have something of value to contribute to the Canadian experiment.

If he didn't say sorry for all the hatred and the generation of animosity he had caused, he had learned how to deal with his colic-ridden past with a sense of whimsy. I give the credit for this to Anne Brown. I hear her warm and welcoming laughter coming out of Brown's mansion (which still stands on Beverley Street, about four or five blocks from my own house) every time I cycle past it. Here is how he ended his open letter. The "they" he is addressing are those very Roman Catholics he had attacked with such venom a decade earlier:

> All I ask is that they shall forget for a few minutes whose name is attached to this paper and read calmly what is written. Let them blaze away at George Brown afterwards as vigorously as they please, but let not their old feuds with him close their eyes to the interests of their country, and their own interests as a powerful section of the body politic.

That's the nice version. The obverse, or nasty, version is that he had discovered that English-speaking Catholics in Ontario were about as enamoured with the French-speaking Catholics of Quebec as he was and there was, at long last, a possible common cause amongst reform elements to keep those damn papist frogs from controlling the country. It's an old Canadian story. I suppose the truth, as usual, lies somewhere in between.

So now "Enter the Assassin," as the stage direction might say. This *mise en scène* is direct from Careless's last chapter of *Brown of The Globe: Statesman of Confederation 1860-1880*:

> March 25, 1880; four-thirty on a dull afternoon. Brown was working quietly at *The Globe* office in his room that opened off the landing of the staircase up from King Street, which went on to the editorial room above. There was a tap at

the door. He looked up from his desk to see a sallow little man, not much more than five feet tall, thin-faced, with a straggling moustache and goatee, standing uncertainly in his doorway. George Bennett was his name, the intruder mumbled, employed in *The Globe* engine room for the past five years. He had the paper with him – fumbling for it – and if Mr. Brown would sign –.

Brown was impatient. He did not know the man. He did not know Bennett's record of drunkenness, neglect of duties, and wife-beating, or that he was now out on bail after being arrested for non-support. Least of all he did not know that Bennett, drinking heavily and brooding heavily on his wrongs, had bought a revolver before coming to *The Globe* that day, and written down wild vows to kill his enemies at the newspaper office. The one thing Brown did know was that he had been needlessly disturbed by the unprepossessing little creature, who had no doubt got what he deserved.

Gruffly he told Bennett to take his paper for signature to the head of the department where he had been employed. The foreman there had already refused to sign it, said Bennett, moving into the room and half closing the door behind him. Then take it to Mr. Henning, *The Globe* treasurer, who would have the record on the books – Brown grew uneasy. What did this man want? Bennett came forward to the desk. "Sign it – sign it," he demanded harshly. Brown rose. Angry refusal brought fierce insistence; the sound of rising voices could be heard in the editorial rooms. Now Brown's temper was soaring – when Bennett, white-faced and staring, suddenly snatched out his revolver and cocked it. *The little wretch might be meaning to shoot me,* flashed through Brown's mind. Impulsively he leaned forward, grabbing Bennett's wrist. There was a moment of mad struggle. The gun fired as Brown managed to deflect it downward. "Help, help – murder!" he shouted wildly. But his far greater strength quickly overcame the assailant. Forcing Bennett back out of the room and onto the landing, he held him there against the wall as he wrenched the still loaded weapon away.

The shot, the cry, and the noise of the struggle brought three editorial staff members, Thomson, Ewan, and Blue, pounding down the stairs from above. Aghast, they rushed to seize hold of Bennett, while Brown, grey and trembling, leaned against the wall. "Are you hurt, Mr. Brown?' Blue asked anxiously. "I don't know," Brown answered in a daze. Blue pointed sharply at the other's leg. "There," he said urgently. On the outside of the left thigh there was a clean hole in the broadcloth trousers. Brown slowly ran his hand down, and behind his leg a little lower. It came up stained with blood.

They called the police and the doctor, while Brown went back into his room to lie down. Dr. Thorburn arrived and quickly dressed the injury. It seemed to be only a flesh wound, and quite superficial; *The Globe* director had already appeared to be recovering, as he joked and talked about his "assassination" with excited members of his staff. Undoubtedly it would make a good news story for a rather dull day. He even walked down out of the building to take his usual hired carriage from the West End Cab Company home to Lambton Lodge. He expected merely to have a short stay in bed while the wound healed. But he would never return to *The Globe* office.

Shortly afterwards, the acid-tongued Goldwin Smith wrote to John A. Macdonald: "The czar of King Street has had a narrow escape. If [Bennett] had used a horsewhip, perhaps the wave of public indignation would have been less universal." Oh dear! Brown did have his enemies. Well, to be a good (or bad) editor is to wake each morning and prepare yourself for making ten new enemies, at least. For George Brown, all enemy-making was coming to an end. Despite the doctors' and Anne Brown's best efforts, the wound refused to heal and gangrene set in. A little over a month later, he died, writhing in pain. In due course, George Bennett would hang. Both deaths were handsomely covered in *The Globe*.

VI

For only a few months, William Thorsell, formerly of Edmonton, Alberta, and Kenneth Whyte, also formerly of Edmonton, Alberta, were editors-in-chief of Canada's two national newspapers. There were two national newspapers in Canada for only a few months when an Englishman replaced Thorsell, but still the spectacle of two Westerners at the helm of the flagship newspapers of both the Thomson and Southam chains was arresting. The advent of the *National Post*, though much ballyhooed and anticipated, nevertheless caught *The Globe and Mail* by surprise. With the new newspaper starting from ground zero, clearly the battle – in editorial, in circulation, and most crucially in advertising – was *The Globe*'s to lose. As it turned out, between the announcement that the *National Post* would be a reality and Thorsell's demotion, *The Globe* offered Canada and the newspaper world a textbook case of how not to meet such a challenge. And there was this little item too: in the ten and half years Thorsell was editor-in-chief of *The Globe*, he worked through four publishers (Roy Megarry, David Campbell, Roger Parkinson, and Philip Crawley) and six managing editors (Geoffrey Stevens, Tim Pritchard, John Cruikshank, Colin Mackenzie, Margaret Wente, and Edward Greenspon). Each of these people represents a different facet of the Thorsell leadership style, but their numbers speak loudly of the dysfunction at the helm of *The Globe* as it slid all unprepared into battle with the new *National Post*.

But first, how on earth did it happen that two Alberta journalists took over the national press of Canada? Sheer fluke? Maybe. No one can really say for sure, but I have a theory that was forged in the wake of the messy business of Conrad Black's mucked-up peerage over in London at the House of Lords. The proprietor of the *National Post* and the fine old Southam chain is the third Canadian press baron to loom over the British newspaper world this century. He follows Max Aitken (Lord Beaverbrook) and Roy Thomson (Lord Thomson of Fleet). How did that happen? Well, I think the same way the Albertans took over the national press in Toronto. Never underestimate ambition tied to a strong sense of being on the outside looking in, especially when there is rot at the centre.

Both Thorsell and Whyte, from very different perspectives, entered national journalism in Toronto with considerable Western chips on their editorial shoulders. Thorsell has subsequently embraced Torontoism with passion and is busy tending to his own version of Bow Park, minus the fancy cattle. But the former chief editorial writer of the *Edmonton Journal* was very capable of admonishing central Canada on its sins of neglect towards the West, and indeed these strictures were a large part of his effective pungency as *The Globe*'s great pontificator on the right. Whyte, who succeeded me for a few years as editor of *Saturday Night*, was a product of Ted Byfield's feisty *Alberta Report* empire and he still hasn't fallen into Toronto ways, perhaps because his view out of his office window is of a parking lot somewhere around Highway 401 and the Don Valley Parkway. It is not a view to inspire local identity. In any event, both men clearly had something under their skins that seems to me strikingly similar to what lay under the skins of Beaverbrook, Thomson, and Black in London. A desire to preside, certainly, and to make a mark in what is not exactly enemy territory, but nevertheless a part of the world regarded with mixed feelings from whence they came. Whyte and Thorsell were highly successful outsiders who found the core of what they once considered an impregnable fortress to be soft, pliable, and easily adapted to their own purposes. So did the three Canadian press lords in London.

But, of course, you have to be a press lord to stay in power. What happened to Thorsell in mid-1999 will probably happen to Whyte some time before the first decade of the third millennium is over. It seems impossible to conceive, but it will happen and probably at the very moment of most relaxed success. That's the way it goes in the nasty newspaper business, which eats its own with a voracious appetite. It cannot be said that Thorsell served himself up as a tastier treat in this process than anyone else, since less crafty souls than he have also been given the proverbial boot. I think especially of Kevin Doyle of *Maclean's* magazine who, like most editors good or bad, have a hard time seeing the writing on the wall. The only thing that can be said about the situation at *The Globe and Mail* is that the editor was mostly inept in handling newsroom psychology and his bedside manner was the pits – the deep-down, dark, and forbidding pits. On a one-to-one personal level he could be charming, but he did not have the first clue how to engender enthusiasm and loyalty. *If the helots working for him did not understand how lucky they were to have such an original mind saving their newspaper for the twenty-first century, then they should clear out.* Thorsell never said that and may never have thought it, but he gave the effect of it and that was the same as saying or believing, at least in the newspaper business.

Watching his decade unfold, I found it dizzying to behold the extremes of what he could achieve, both for good and ill. The redesign and some clever rethinking of newspaper geography, like back pages of sections, always had to be balanced against his inability to understand the importance of sports coverage and his dismal front pages. Both his successes and failures, I think, sprang from his dislike of listening to other people. If he had listened, especially to the old hands at *The Globe*, he would never have pulled off such a bold and successful redesign. If he had taken more advice on "The Middle Kingdom" and not simply heard what the house syco-phants told him, he would have been saved the daily embarrass-ment it became until, like the Cheshire cat in *Alice in Wonderland*, only the sardonic smile was left and then it went too.

The Globe has lived with and triumphed over intense direct competition before, but not in most people's memory. Right now it is facing the most intense challenge of its venerable life. It is still loaded with prestige and has many loyal subscribers, but in its fervour and passion the *National Post* more clearly resembles George Brown's original newspaper than *The Globe* does today, and it is not at all clear whether both will survive in a reduced market or if one of them will have to lie down and die. That so many Englishmen were brought over to help start up the *National Post* and that *The Globe*'s publisher and new editor-in-chief should also be recently acquired Englishmen is an irony almost too spicy to savour. It is not just what would George Brown have thought – he would have fumed and stormed – but that the mother country, which had to suffer brash colonials taking over its print media throughout the twentieth century (Beaverbrook, Thomson and Black), has returned to the old colony to take over its print media. The old Queen who ushered in the departing century might have had a small smile on her face had she known. Her great-great-grand-daughter presumably is far too politic to say anything. At least in public. That's part of the reason why she's still the Queen of Canada, despite the fact that *The Globe and Mail* has called for the monarchy's demise. Since 1952, when she ascended the throne, she has chalked up eight *Globe* publishers, seven editors, and an uncertain number of managing editors but certainly no less than a baker's dozen. *Honi soit qui mal y pense!*

1867: How the Fathers Made A Deal, by Christopher Moore. Published in
1997 by McClelland & Stewart.

Brown of The Globe (Volume 1: "The Voice of Upper Canada 1818-
1859"; Volume 2: Statesman of Confederation 1860-1880), by
J. M. S. Careless. Published in 1959 by Macmillan of Canada.

Circles of Power: The Most Influential People in Canada, by James Fleming.
Published in 1991 by Doubleday Canada.

Dictionary of Canadian Biography, Volume X 1871 to 1880. Published in
1972 by the University of Toronto Press.

Hurly-Burly: A Time at the Globe, by Richard J. Doyle. Published in 1990
by Macmillan of Canada.

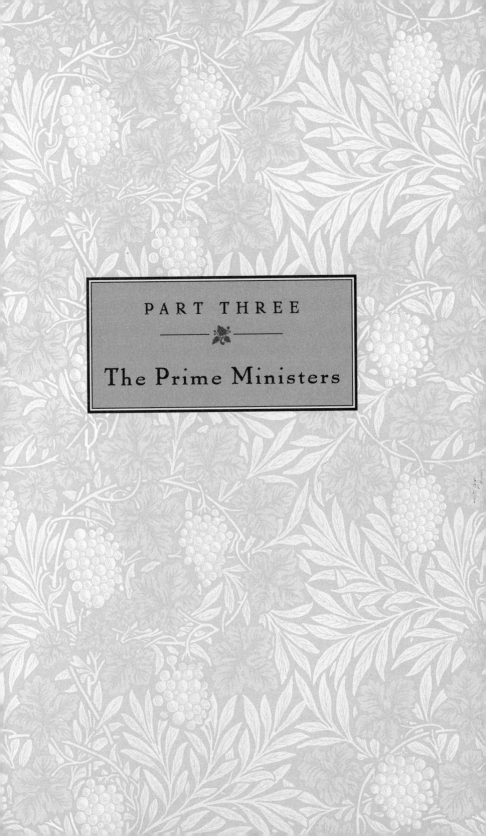

PART THREE

The Prime Ministers

I

The concise definition of "betray," according to the *Canadian Oxford Dictionary*, is fairly straightforward and suits most discussions on Quebec, in history or during our own time:

betray, *v.tr* 1. place (a person, one's country, etc.) in the hands or power of an enemy. 2, be disloyal to (another person, a person's trust, etc.) 3. reveal involuntarily or treacherously; be evidence of this (*his shaking hand betrayed his fear*). 4. lead astray or into error.

The notion of betrayal, in one form or another, is so deeply imbedded in the psyche of Canadian anglophones and francophones that we are often totally unaware we are operating under notions more appropriate to the War of the Spanish Succession than to the pursuit of democratic happiness, state medicare, and a decent pension. Who, of a certain age, cannot be aware that Alberta felt betrayed by the federal government's National Energy

Program during the Trudeau administration; that Quebec felt betrayed by the other provinces in various federal-provincial constitutional undertakings, particularly by their rejection of the Meech Lake Accord; that Newfoundland felt betrayed both in the fight for Confederation in 1948 and later in onerous forced deals over Churchill Falls hydroelectric power with Quebec; that English Canada felt betrayed by francophone Ottawa in patriating the Constitution; that separatists in Quebec felt betrayed by the anglophone and allophone Quebecers in the 1995 referendum; that British Columbians regularly feel their economic expansion is betrayed by Ontario; and so on and so forth?

When you peel away the rhetoric, the altruism, the pragmatism, and even the selfishness, it sometimes seems that at the heart of all Canadian political action – regional or national – is betrayal. The end of the twentieth century, the one Sir Wilfrid Laurier said belonged to Canada, finds the lucky 30-million in a generally cynical mood, which is a useful filter to observe this particular phenomenon. Betrayal may not seem to fit easily into the notion of the "kinder and gentler" country to the north of the forever-enemy, but then Prime Minister Jean Chrétien's administration has apparently betrayed us hook (free trade), line (magazine policy), and sinker (G.S.T.) to the same forces it accused the Mulroney administration of betraying us to. It was not only in *Hamlet* that the "funeral baked meats did coldly serve the marriage tables." When the Newfoundland and Nova Scotia delegates stormed out of the Confederation talks in the 1860s, they were looking to avoid charges of betrayal. When they returned – in the case of Newfoundland, not until the middle of the twentieth century – they were still charged with betrayal. In Canada, the process of demonization has developed into a high art and can begin, in some cases (as with Brian Mulroney or Joe Clark in English Canada or Chrétien in Quebec), the moment we cast our ballots. This seems to be directly related to our disgust at actually having to elect someone or some group to govern over us. The wonder, then, is not at the plethora of suspicion and distrust that afflicts our national life, but that we ever got over it long enough to create a country and that we have staggered more or less intact through nearly a century and half of multifarious betrayals.

A few years ago, when I was browsing through my own miscellany of a library in search of some Canada Day inspiration for my editor's column in *Saturday Night* magazine, I stumbled across a book entitled *The Tragedy of Quebec: The Expulsion of Its Protestant Farmers* by Robert Sellar. At the time I pulled the maroon-coloured tome off the shelf, I was still reeling from a powerful excursion into the late-nineteenth-century anglophone views of Quebec as presented by my own magazine. It's important to appreciate that Sellar is not an aberration for his time and place and that he wrote with a more measured and thoughtful pace than the heated prose of my own dear organ in its earlier guise. Here's a typical snippet from Edmund E. Sheppard, the redoubtable founding editor of *Saturday Night*, writing in a July 1891 issue following a recess of Parliament to honour St-Jean-Baptiste Day:

> I do not know how the rest of Canada feels but I do not care how many saints the French-Canadians have had or have. They have not had saints enough to make them either clean politicians or patriotic citizens. . . . [English-Canadian politicians] are not there [Ottawa] to loaf around on saints' days; they

are down there to attend to our business, and I imagine that if they quit this queer work and told some of the greasy-haired Jean Baptistes to go and take a bath, there would be a lot less public money spent, both directly and indirectly, than now is being squandered on keeping some very unimportant people quiet. . . . I for one am not prepared to subscribe my very unimportant name to the list of politicians and writers who desire at every cost to conciliate French-Canada, but as I watch the development of everlasting evidence that clericalism and politics united produce a state of corruption which cannot be tolerated, I am more and more prepared to shoulder a shot gun rather than lie down before a lot of one-horse corruptionists who are all wind and no courage. We have had too much of it. If we cannot govern these self-seeking disturbers we can coerce them. As I have said a dozen times in these columns, the Ottawa River is our Mason-Dixon Line.

Regular readers of *Saturday Night* at that *fin de siècle* – the bulk of whom comprised the Protestant Toronto financial establishment – were familiar with Sheppard's line. If it is wrong to brush the whole lot (my grandparents included) with this intolerance, it is still worth pointing out what a phenomenal success *Saturday Night* was almost from its first issue in 1887. Sheppard certainly felt comfortable writing about the difficult issue of separate schools in Ontario less than two years after his first edition (March 1889):

But why beat about the bush? What are we [the English-Canadians] here for? Why did Wolfe take the trouble to fight Montcalm? Was it not to conquer Canada? Was it not to make the Anglo-Saxon supreme? The British troops fought in vain, Wolfe died in vain if we are to yield today and abandon the fruits of that victory. . . . Why the hocus-pocus about separate schools? There should be none. What is good enough for one child is good enough for another. If sectarianism cannot be maintained without isolating children, let sectarianism and every other "ism" which suffers by contact with free institutions, go, and good riddance to it. If it is God's will that the Roman Catholic Church be as great in the future as in the past, it will be so; if otherwise, who shall say the ends of providence have been defeated by one law for all, one school for all, equality for all, privileges for none . . . If there is any body of men in this country, particularly in this province who have a right to say, "Go, and he goeth, come, and he cometh," it is those who said it on the Plains of Abraham, and there will have to be another fight before the verdict is changed.

By the time I started reading *The Tragedy of Quebec*, then, I had been softened up. The author seemed strangely familiar and I believe, in one form or another, I have known him all my life – as a relative or a teacher, as a pundit of the moment or a doomsday merchant. The specifics, obviously, have changed (but not all that much, as you will read), but the aura of anger and sense of betrayal are as Canadian as maple syrup. Sellar's particular theme is fairly straightforward:

Supposing a number of men, ambitious of obtaining power over their fellows, organized themselves into an oath-bound society, and, further supposing, in carrying out their plans, they found it required the driving away of people who were hostile to them, would not their first move be to get control of the land? Possession of the soil means sovereignty. Villages and towns may decay and become effete, but the soil remains, and to whomever the men who plow and reap pay allegiance, will be the actual, though they may not be the nominal, rulers. The priests having got a legislature that was their creature, were absolute in every part of Quebec except in those sections where the land had been grants of the British Crown. To exercise the same domination over that land as they did in the old seigniories was their purpose. The assault was first upon the Eastern Townships, and the priests thrust into them two wedges to effect their purpose, the parish system and separate schools. Bring these free townships under parish law and the English-speaking farmers will not want to stay; deprive them of their public schools and reduce them to the alternative of sending their children to confessional schools, and they will be compelled to go. . . .

The obstacles [the priests] had to overcome were such as to any other class of men would have been insuperable. Here was a body of English-speaking farmers spread over eleven counties, who had held the land for sixty years and more, who had completed their social and municipal organizations, and developed a characteristic individuality. The Protestants were largely massed in six counties. Stanstead, Sherbrooke, Waterloo, Missisquoi, Brome, Huntingdon, and in these counties in 1867, the year that Quebec passed under the rule of a Catholic legislature, the Protestants numbered 56,600, the Catholics 25,583, mostly employees of the English. With a clear majority of some 31,000 the Protestants felt secure. They were passing rich as riches go in rural Canada, prosperous and aggressive, wielding a political influence not in proportion to their numbers but of their wealth and intelligence.

The design of the priests was that this self-confident, self-reliant and enterprising people should be brought under pressure that would constrain them to leave their fields and homes to be occupied by French-Canadians. That a farm population could be so supplanted seemed incredible, and those who suggested such a design being entertained were laughed at.

Out of a population of eighty-two thousand in 1867, thirty-one thousand was a sweeping majority, and appearances pointed to an increase, for each summer saw the number enlarged by immigrants from Britain. Left alone, these counties in another generation would have counted a hundred thousand Protestants. *But they were not left alone.* The Legislature, sitting at Quebec, was working hand-in-glove with the priests to work their downfall, and how far that has been accomplished let the census of 1911 tell: –

Catholics 174,004
Protestants 57,926
Majority of Catholics 116,078

Thus in forty-six years a majority of thirty-one thousand Protestants had been changed into a Catholic majority of one hundred and sixteen thousand! Since the days of the Dragonnades has there ever been such an extraordinary displacement of Protestants from their homes and native land? How, in the face of these official figures, can any man have the conscience to assert Home Rule has been a grand success in Quebec, and, having wrought no injury to Protestants, Ulster need not dread a Dublin parliament? When Quebec was separated from Ontario all six counties had a Protestant majority. Only one, Brome, is in that position today, and its majority of 9,652 forty-six years ago has fallen to 3,318, and grows smaller each year. . . . There are instances of not a single Protestant family being left in a township. The clerical newspapers boast openly of the "peaceable conquest" by the priests of the Eastern Townships, the Protestant stronghold of Quebec, and with reason, for it is a conquest without parallel.

I'm not quite sure why I had purchased this old book in the first place and for a while I couldn't even remember where I had got it. Then it came to me. It was among a number of curiosity items I'd found at the annual Trinity College book sale in Toronto. It's a personal quirk: I like interspersing my library with surprises and I'll buy bizarre old books on a whim. I like books and art and objects that transport me back in time without any intermediaries, no matter how dark or mistaken the viewpoint.

In the case of Sellars and his popular book (already in its fourth edition), a very concrete understanding of historic post-Conquest settlements and familiar bicultural grievances can be gleaned in all the passion. It's important to remember it in any consideration of a French-Canadian prime minister of Canada who is prepared to embrace a nation that features periodic – but regular – outbreaks of both anglophone and francophone tribalism. Here is Sellars, lumbering towards his book's ending, on the subject of dual languages in Quebec, circa 1911. This was the year Sir Wilfrid Laurier's long term as prime minister came to an end and after he had struggled so hard to bring about reconciliation between the two "founding" races:

> The assertion that the system of two languages works well in Quebec is so frequently and positively asserted that many believe the assertion. Such is not the case; the existence of two official languages in Quebec works badly, and is a hindrance to its prosperity. Look at a few instances in proof.
>
> The commerce of Quebec lies in the hands of the [English] minority – blot them out, banks would close, steamships cease running, railways shops disappear, factories shut their doors. The great employers of labour, the directors of gigantic enterprises, the suppliers of capital, are English-speaking. It is from them the Provincial Government draws most of its revenue, Montreal constituting the milch cow from which Quebec politicians replenish the provincial treasury, yet no consideration of gratitude prevents wanton interference by the Legislature with the English minority in its modes of doing business that pays their salaries and supplies the funds they spend. Twice has the Legislative Assembly adopted a bill to compel commercial companies to use French. That these companies, in their own interest, will use French wherever called for is plain, but the proposal is to coerce them, by fines, into using French where they consider there is no need, and an opening is given to lawyers to harass and prey upon them by recovery of prescribed fines. Is there another British dependency where companies, which have received no state aid, are punished for not using another language than English? How would the manufacturers of Toronto like to be dictated to in this manner, yet that is what

the recognition in Ontario of French, as co-equal of English would bring them. Take the issue of two languages in court. Here is an illustration. An action is taken out against an English-speaking farmer. The document notifying him of what he is ordered to do is served upon him in French. He is unable to read it, and asks for an English copy. The reply is that French is an official language in Quebec, and he has no right to ask for a translation: the document served upon is according to the law of the province. He attends court, all that is said is in French, for, unless the charge against him is criminal, he cannot claim to have evidence of witnesses repeated in English. All he knows of what is going on is what his lawyer whispers to him. The judge takes the case en *delibere*, and when he comes to a finding the farmer gets his decision in a long French document. To learn what the judgement is that has been passed on his case, he has to search out someone who can read it to him, perhaps paying for a translation. . . .

There is more of Sellar, much more, but I think this is more than enough not to dismiss him out of hand but to recognize in him many of the blind-sided frustrations of English-speaking Canadians in dealing with the federal government's efforts to keep this country together. As long as there is a Canada, there will be a Mr. Sellar. His francophone counterpart exists as well, obviously. In terms of political mentors, think of Preston Manning and Jacques Parizeau. Then think of trying to govern a democratic country where both can live in peace. So far in our history there is only one way to do it and that is to betray them both.

II

It has been customary in Canadian journalism when analysing the life and style of a current prime minister to look for historical antecedents. Or at least it has been since John George Diefenbaker's day. He had no precedents, as Peter Newman made clear in the very title of his famous and influential political page-turner *Renegade in Power*. Both Pierre Trudeau and Jean Chrétien have been compared numerous times with Wilfrid Laurier. Physically Trudeau and Laurier share a patrician elegance, which, in their respective epochs, pleased their countrymen to behold, whether or not they agreed with their political philosophy or legislation. But Laurier was a progenitor who wrote all the archetypal definitions on what constituted appropriate compromise in the Canadian situation, while Trudeau didn't know how to compromise himself out of a wet paper bag. Any evidence of compromise during the Trudeau administration – and Chrétien has always been generous in attributing great compromising skills to Trudeau – can invariably be traced back to pressure from cabinet colleagues or officials, not to any inherent respect for the normal Canadian political process by the great immovable Buddha. Either that or it was a cynical and disgusted retreat from a position he knew to be proper and which the fools and charlatans he was required to surround himself with were incapable of pulling off or sustaining. Think of anything from the initial deal he made at his own leadership convention in 1968 with Newfoundland's Joey Smallwood to almost every political and patronage decision he made with his ubiquitous fixer, Jim Coutts. Trudeau never suffered fools gladly, whereas Laurier saw them as part and parcel of the Canadian condition and useful if properly deployed. No doubt that was why he liked many journalists while Trudeau loathed most of them. Towards the end of the twentieth century, Trudeau despised John Diefenbaker and his Prairie mysticism; at the beginning of the century, Laurier patted Diefenbaker on the head and told him – a paperboy on the hustle – that great things were expected of him.

Jean Chrétien, as prime minister, has identified more strongly with Wilfrid Laurier than with any other Canadian prime minister, but they are a mismatch too, despite the remarkable parallels in their lives and careers. Yes, they are both French Canadians who became prime ministers. That's significant. Yes, they were both beloved by many English Canadians and dismissed as traitors or *vendus* by nationalistic Quebecers. Yes, they both rode the Liberal party to power in the wake of disgraced Tory administrations that were more a coalition of non-Liberals than they were recognizable political parties. All that's true enough and interesting on a certain level, but the non-parallels are just as interesting. No, Laurier was definitely not from a working-class background as Chrétien was. No, Laurier never had to backtrack on his views on free trade. No, Chrétien doesn't particularly enjoy the company of women, but he has never swerved his loyalty and affections from his wife, Aline, as Laurier did to his wife, Zoë. No, Laurier had almost no experience of governing before he came to great power save a minor cabinet post in the final days of Alexander Mackenzie's

Liberal administration of the 1870s. Chrétien held a total of a dozen cabinet posts — including Finance, External Affairs, and Justice — in the administrations of both Lester Pearson and Pierre Trudeau. And no, that is not Chrétien's face on the five-dollar bill.

So where does that leave us? We look to the past for guidance and perhaps for moral justification and armour, so it is not surprising that Trudeau and Chrétien both sought to identify their causes with that of Laurier. In his time, he was the most admired man in Canada, and he was the first Canadian leader to leave his mark in the Empire and the world beyond. He cut a much bigger figure in his day than Sir John A. Macdonald, who was notorious to his enemies as a boozer, an architect of sleazy backroom deals, and a merchant of corruption. Laurier's enemies, even in the heat of battle, were in awe of his stature, his passion for Canada, and his great natural dignity. The man who ultimately defeated him and became Canada's first wartime prime minister, Sir Robert Borden, admired Laurier so much he felt daunted in victory and found it difficult to conceive of himself cutting such a noble figure. A classic liberal, much influenced by Gladstonian liberalism, Laurier was a superb orator, the greatest prime ministerial speaker the country has ever produced. Considering the competition, I realize, this statement is not difficult to defend, nevertheless Laurier was hugely esteemed for the passion of his oratory in his own lifetime. Subsequently, the only near equal on the podium was John Diefenbaker, but the Chief's passion was tinged with paranoia, and in his final days you were never quite sure if the white-coats were going to have to come and cart him off. He was no Sir Wilfrid.

In fact, no other Canadian leader has ever been able to match the sense of perfect unity between the office and the man, except

Georges Vanier as Governor General. That parallel is telling because both men brought a spiritual quality to their calling, even if those who discount the spiritual in public life cannot quite recognize it. Here is what the drama critic and political commentator Augustus Bridle wrote of Laurier shortly after his death:

> He swung in a great romantic orbit of political sentiment. We never had a statesman who could smile so potently. Never one with such mellifluous music in his voice, such easy grace in his style, such a cardinal's hauteur when he wanted to be alone and such a fascinating urbanity when he wanted to impress a company, a caucus or a crowd. The Romanist whom Orangemen admired, the Frenchman who made an intellectual hobby of British democracy was the kaleidoscopic enigma of Canada.
>
> Laurier was nearly all things to all men, the kind of man to whom other people naturally happened. He was a human solar system, in which many people wanted to gravitate, even to the ragged little girl on the prairies who picked him the wildflowers he wore in his coat as far as she could see him on the grain platform. He was sometimes many things to himself. One moment he could be as debonair as Beau Brummell, the next as forbidding and repellent as a modern Caesar. He was consistently the best-dressed public man in Canada. A misfitting coat was to him as grievous as a misplaced verb in a peroration.
>
> Laurier could perform obvious tricks with consummate grace. And he performed many. There was never a moment of his waking life when he could not have been lifted into a play. His movements, his words, his accent, his clothes, his

facial lineaments were never commonplace, even when his motives often may have been. He was Debussy's *Afternoon of a Faun*. . . .

Not much of this pertains to Chrétien, who has operated all his life at a level much lower than Laurier or Vanier or Trudeau, and different again from the faintly Rotarian aura of Louis St. Laurent. Here's a famous tale, which I've heard or read in at least a half-dozen versions, including from Chrétien himself. I love it because it is both self-deprecating and at the same time skewers unconscious arrogance. When Trudeau and Chrétien were both novice ministers in the Pearson administration and once found themselves sitting beside each other on an airplane as they awaited takeoff, Chrétien tried to make polite small-talk with his intellectually lofty seatmate. "Look, Pierre, it's raining outside," he said. Trudeau looked up from the papers in which he had been immersed. "Jean," he said, "if it's raining, it's inevitably going to be outside." Ditto for the tale of Chrétien and the mega-pompous Jacques Parizeau in which Chrétien deployed his undeserved reputation as a "pea-souper" to stinging effect. At the time, Parizeau was the outsized minister of finance in the first Parti Québécois administration and Chrétien had only recently been appointed to the federal cabinet. This is journalist Peter Stockland's account of the confrontation from *The Toronto Sun*:

> Chrétien was attending a gathering of federal and provincial ministers. The meeting opened with the pontifical Parizeau giving a long-winded, professorial speech on everything that was wrong with the Canadian economy.

The main federalist error, he insisted, was continued reliance on the theories of John Maynard Keynes, the British economist who advocated increased government spending during downturns in the business cycle.

"Canada must," Parizeau concluded with a flourish, "throw Keynes right out the window."

Seizing the microphone, Chrétien rasped:

"'Dats okay wit me – I never knew dis Keynes guy anyway. Let's throw him out and get on with the meeting."

Parizeau sagged like an empty parachute. . . .

No, there are few parallels here between Chrétien's style and that of either Laurier or Trudeau, although it should be noted that Chrétien served Trudeau loyally for all the years he was prime minister. They were never soulmates, yet their professional relationship was probably the biggest single personal factor in keeping Quebec a part of Canada during very turbulent times. The Canada they were keeping together was, to a great extent, Laurier's Canada, which – rough-hewn though it was – had been inherited directly from the better visions of Sir John A. Macdonald and Sir George-Étienne Cartier.

One of the most important things to know about Laurier was that during much of his active political life in Ottawa he was considered a betrayer of Quebec by his compatriots, a *vendu*, as was Vanier, as was Trudeau, as was Chrétien. Chrétien more than any of them. And another important thing to remember is that for much of Laurier's youth and young manhood, he thought he was going to die of tubercular "consumption," as his mother and his sister had died. He had only been seven when his mother passed away, but he had a strong memory of her heaving, dry coughs, just like the ones wracking his own body. So strong was the sense of imminent demise that for a long time he eschewed marriage for fear of leaving a widow who might not even be thirty by the time of his expected death. Sometime during the twentieth century we lost sight of the general imminence of death. Unique in the history of civilization, we made such leaps and bounds in medicine that the very notion of medically unpreventable death seems risible. Even with the setback of AIDS, most of us remain convinced a "cure" is just around the corner. AIDS seems so sinister and evil to us precisely because it has not yet been eliminated, but the nineteenth century – and every century before it – knew dozens of diseases with the same definitive consequences as AIDS. Laurier's "consumption" – the most familiar "wasting" disease of his time – was one of them. On July 1, 1867, when the Dominion of Canada was proclaimed, and Queen Victoria was in residence at Balmoral, and George Brown lay exhausted in Toronto after making his newspaper miss two deadlines with his seemingly unending salute to the new nation, and Bishop Strachan was just weeks away from his death, Wilfrid Laurier was gripping the edge of his desk to brace himself against another coughing jag. The slight improvement in his health the month before had clearly been a lull, and the consumption that ruled his life was seemingly back with a vengeance.

Except that it wasn't consumption. It was chronic bronchitis, which was bad enough at the time but not life-threatening. He was not to know that until nearly a year later, when he thought he had lost the love of his life to another and after he had abandoned any sort of long-term ambition. He was a young lawyer who eked out a sort of professional existence, but the high hopes his father, Carolus Laurier, had pinned on him seemed forlorn. The father was a land surveyor, and the son of a land surveyor, in the pretty village of St-Lin. This was a profession that marked the family out for respect rather than affluence. And yet this adventurous father, something of an anti-clerical philosopher, gave his son a most unusual education for a French Canadian of that time. Wilfrid was shipped off at the age of ten, three years after his mother died, to the neighbouring English-speaking town of New Glasgow to attend a Presbyterian school and study English. He was given permission to absent himself from the religious readings and observances of these flinty Protestants, but his natural curiosity and his father's open mind prevailed and he found great satisfaction in comparing and contrasting Presbyterianism with Catholicism.

Later, when he went to a classical Catholic and French-speaking college for which his cash-strapped father and step-mother sacrificed much, there was no one quite like him, with his bilingual proficiency and denominational sophistication, either amongst the student body or on the faculty. So he was marked off as different, both intellectually and through the recurring rigours of his ill health. In due course, he studied law at McGill, as well as working in the Montreal law offices of a noted Liberal named Rodolphe Laflamme, and it was during this period that his skills as an orator started to be appreciated by a growing audience. He had a particular success with anglophones, who were reportedly awed by this handsome, articulate French Canadian who could speak their own language more beautifully than they could. At McGill, he was voted "speaker of the year" and was the elected valedictorian for the graduation class of 1864. It was a mystical speech, much of it in French, this valedictory address, redolent of high hopes expressed as realities even if they were not yet so. But in this rapture of trying to will Canada into his own concept of the peaceable and decent kingdom, it is possible to see the greatest romantic of Canadian political life at his public onset. This is clearly the same man who later and famously said the twentieth century would belong to Canada:

It is to our glory that race hatreds have ended on Canadian soil. There is no longer any family here but the human family. It matters not what language the people speak, or at which altars they kneel. You have heard French and English names here, graven on the tables of honour. You have heard some address you in English and I am now speaking to you in my mother tongue. There is glory in this fraternity of which Canada can never be proud enough. Mighty nations, indeed, may well come to us to seek a lesson in justice and humanity.

With all his evident promise, it is not surprising that Zoë Lafontaine fell in love with the most romantic lawyer in Montreal. She could hardly have avoided him. They first met when his law studies began in 1861 and they both boarded at the Montreal home of friends of the Laurier family, Phoebé and Séraphin Gauthier. It developed into a proper nineteenth-century relationship, one part flirtation and nine parts chaperoned etiquette. That one part can be very strong, though. Through all the agony of Laurier's attempts to figure out what was the best or most appropriate course of action, finally determining to move to the Eastern Townships both to free Zoë (and himself) from the inevitable obligations of courtship and to bring purer air to his beleaguered lungs, Zoë never really faltered in her ambition, even when she accepted the proposal of another man. Of course it is impossible to figure out all the delightful and melodramatic machinations going on at the time, but even so, a century and half later, the denouement of this tale still tugs at the heart.

He was in the middle of preparing for a murder trial when the telegram arrived on May 12, 1868. *"Viens à Montréal tout de suite, j'ai quelque chose a très grave à te dire. Séraphin Gauthier."* [Come to Montreal at once. I have an urgent matter to tell you.]

And so he came and learned from his medical friend that he was not tubercular but bronchial, that he could marry, that Zoë would break off her engagement to another – was desperate, in fact, to break off the engagement – if he would propose to her. So he did. Then and there. And she told him she wanted to be married that very same day. And so they were, and he was on the train back to the murder trial in the Eastern Townships that very night, married and with a future that would take him he knew not where, but not to the grave, at least not immediately.

The Chrétiens of Shawinigan have a different tale to tell of their crown prince than the Lauriers of St-Lin, but it is no less worthy given the later era with its own definition of poisoned politics. And although Canadian demographers and historians would certainly class Laurier's parents as middle class and Chrétien's as working class, there are nuances to be tricked out that tell a much more interesting story than such bland classifications indicate.

Most Canadians who follow the details of national life seem to know that Chrétien was born of a mother who had nineteen children, nine of whom survived, and that he was number sixteen. This sets him apart from most Canadians today, but it is not a strange phenomenon in Canadian history, at least not in Quebec or Newfoundland. When I went as a university student to Newfoundland in 1965, I encountered many families – Protestant as well as Catholic – where a dozen and a half pregnancies was the sign of healthy libidos and bad luck in the days before birth control ruled almost supreme. (It wasn't until the formal papal ban on birth-control devices was read out in parish churches that many Newfoundland Catholics in the more remote outports even knew the pill existed. Inquiries into where to get it began the moment the mass was over; the same may have occurred in Quebec). What was remarkable about the Chrétiens was how they handled their huge brood. Perhaps it is enough to know that their children became eminent doctors, nurses, business entrepreneurs, lawyers, and so forth. And, of course, one became prime minister.

The frailty of the francophone reality in North America has always stood at odds with the paranoid view in English-speaking Canada that Quebec – and Quebec's francophones – always get what they want. Even most anglophone Canadians who have a visceral affection for Quebec and understand that without it there is no Canada do not really understand the internal dynamics of minority psychology. The only exception are those anglophones who remained in Quebec after all the separatist scares and came to identify their own minority status and future within the French fact of Quebec. These anglo stay-behinds can be divided into two interesting camps: the *enragés*, such as the columnist and English-language-rights advocate William Johnson, who are broadly sympathetic with the French reality but outraged at the hypocrisy and racial myopia of the *"pure laine"* zealots and separatists; and the *wusses*, such as philosopher Charles Taylor, who have a profound understanding of Quebec culture and a broad sympathy for its survival but who, like Lenin's "useful idiots," tend to look foolish in their efforts to accommodate ancient grievances, almost to the point of condoning double standards. It is forgotten that the two categories exist, and have always existed, for francophones as well. Wellie Chrétien for example. Jean Chrétien's father, a humble machinist for all his working life, had a keen sense of the fragility of the French language and also great strength of character. In *Straight From the Heart*, the wonderful book of memoirs Jean Chrétien published in 1985 after he lost the Liberal party leadership campaign to succeed Pierre Trudeau and was facing a political void when no one whose opinion counted ever expected him to become prime minister, he wrote about the insight into North American language realities Wellie Chrétien had garnered during his younger days when he worked in the United States:

> My father taught me that survival of the French fact in North America was due to Quebec's association with Canada. He had learned from experience. My father spent his early years in New Hampshire, because his family was part of the wave of Quebeckers who moved to the United States in search of work. They returned to the Mauricie when the economic situation improved; but my father never lost his interest in the fate of francophones outside Canada. He was a director of the *Association Canado-Américaine*, an organization dedicated to the survival of the French in New England, for forty-five years; he subscribed to French-language news weeklies from Massachusetts and even from Michigan, and

knew about the history of the French in Louisiana and the American West.

The assimilation and loss of influence of the French in the United States contrasted dramatically with what happened in Canada, so my father always looked on Canada as a good protector. He was aware, of course, of the difficulties French Canadians had outside Quebec, and he used to worry about how francophone minorities would survive and flourish from coast to coast, but he never blamed the English for that. His attitude was always positive, concerned with the future rather than obsessed with the past. My father had become a strong Canadian under Laurier, a *rouge* Liberal whom he greatly admired.

Like all our prime ministers, Chrétien has been so demonized since his electoral victories that it is difficult sometimes to remember the strong motivations that propelled him to Ottawa, not all of which were vainglorious. The conservative media in English Canada, and even a Liberal newspaper such as the *Toronto Star*, bemoan his "lack of vision" and a "business-as-usual" legislative agenda. Trying to hold on to the middle ground in Canada is a complex matter, not all ideological, especially when the vilification in Quebec of a pan-Canadian nationalist such as Chrétien brings with it a degree of abuse unmatched in living memory (perhaps the only parallel is the contemptuous hatred felt for Brian Mulroney in English Canada, which is not shared in Quebec). The animosity for Chrétien in Quebec has its roots in the role he played in the "betrayal" during the constitutional process Trudeau initiated and left ominously unconcluded. In a very real sense, Chrétien has had to pay the price of Trudeau's

"Forget Quebec, let's sign the damn thing" arrogance. To appreciate how unfair this all is and also how battle-hardy Chrétien was when the moment of testing came, it is worthwhile remembering that no prime minister ever began in office so well prepared in cabinet government. Certainly far better than Laurier.

III

Old Quebec by Gilbert Parker and Claude G. Bryan (with illustrations) was published by the Copp, Clark Company in Toronto in 1903. It is a very fancy book, with numerous uncut pages of heavy stock, a beautiful dark-red binding with gold lettering plus a bold bas-relief, also picked out in gold leaf, of the Citadel in Quebec City. My grandfather bought it for $1.25 in 1938, and his bookplate is pasted in front, below where the second-hand bookstore pencilled in the price. The bookplate is delightfully arch. An Elizabethan gentleman, in a ruff collar and pantaloons, is seated at a table reading a book by the light of an oil lamp. Inscribed above my grandfather's name is this fine and worthy sentiment: "Far more seemly were it for thee to have thy study full of Bookes than thy purses full of money. – Lilly." Indeed! As my grandfather was a founding partner of Dominion Securities with Sir Edward Peacock, I take the sentiment as proof of his own romanticism. He had a fine library, including all the splendid volumes of the historical Champlain Society. He voted for Laurier in 1911, the year he married my grandmother and the year before my own father was born. He cast his ballot for free trade and lost the vote. It must have been during a brief radical period, for it was the only time he voted Liberal in his life. Still, according to my father, he admired Laurier enormously.

Old Quebec is a rambling, gaseous, and often wildly inaccurate history of Quebec City, but it is infused with such love of the old fortress and of French Canadians, I know why my grandfather loved it. He was one of very few Toronto businessmen of his era who worked directly with French-Canadian business colleagues, and while I suppose some of the florid, almost paternalistic condescension in the following conclusion to *Old Quebec* probably coincided with his own sense of anglo business superiority, there is nevertheless a measure of gracious affection and defensiveness on behalf of French Canada that is worthy of its time and place. Here are the last two paragraphs of the book – old-fashioned paragraphs – after nearly five hundred pages in more or less the same vein. I appreciate that they would make a contemporary Quebecer throw up, but then much that was written a century ago about Canada's "pivotal" role in the British Empire would make most English Canadians throw up today too. Ditto for the Roman Catholic Church's late-nineteenth-century views on Quebec piety. We have, it seems, very delicate digestive systems for our past:

Valiant as she was in asserting her predominance for so long, there was however a siege against which the fortress and bastions of Quebec were of no avail. Left behind in the march of progress, commercial and political, her prestige as a centre of national influence slowly declined, and Montreal and Toronto took over that pre-eminence which had been hers for centuries. Yet nothing could rob the city of her maternal grandeur. She saw no longer in the west the wild prospects and the fertile wastes, but a sturdy nation settling down to its destiny, and spreading out over half a continent; so realizing her ancient prophecy, so fulfilling her laborious hopes, the reward of zealous toil and martyrdom. The great Colbert's dream was now come true, save for the flag, which floated over the happy homesteads in the peaceful land. These homesteads of the west, in the region of the great lakes, were indeed to be the centres of growth and progress and vast wealth; yet the venerable fortress on the tidal water was, and still remains, the noblest city of the American continent. There still works the antique spirit which cherishes culture and piety and domestic virtue as the crown of the nation's deeds and worth. There still the influence of the ancient priesthood, and a university in some respects more distinguished than any on the American continent, keep burning those fires of high tradition and a noble history which light the way to national grace of life, if not to a sensational prosperity. Apart from the hot winds of politics – civic, provincial and national – which grow across the temperate plains of their daily existence, the people of the city and the province live as simply, and with as little greedy ambition as they did a hundred years ago.

The rumble of the calèches and the jingling of the carrioles in the old streets are now pierced by the strident clang of the street-car; and the electric light sharpens garishly the hard out-lines on the stone mansions which sheltered Laval, Montcalm, and Murray; but modern industry and municipal emulation sink away into the larger picture of fortress life, of religious zeal, of Gallic mode, of changeless natural beauty. No ruined castles now crown the heights, but the grim walls still tell of

"Old, far-off unhappy things,
And battles long ago."

The temper of the people is true. Song and sentiment are much with them, and in the woods and in the streams – down by St. Roch and up by Ville Marie – *chansons* of two hundred years ago mark the strokes of labour as of the evening hour when the professional village story-teller cries "*cric-crac*" and begins his tale of the *loup-garcou*, or rouses the spirit of pure patriotism by a crude epic of some valiant avatar; when the parish fiddler brings them to their feet with shining eyes by the strains of *O Carillon*. They are not less respectful to the British flag, nor less faithful in allegiance because they love that language and that land of their memories which they know full well is not Republican France of to-day when the Church suffers at the hands of the State. If ever the genius of the Dominion of Canada is to take a high place in the fane of Art, the soul and impulse of the best achievement will come from Old Quebec, which has produced a sculptor of merit, Hébert; a renowned singer, Albani; a poet crowned by the French Academy, Louis Fréchette; and has given to the public life of the country a distinction, an intellectual power, and an illuminating statesmanship in the persons of Étienne Taché, Sir George Cartier, and Sir Wilfrid Laurier. Enlarged understanding between the two peoples of the country will produce a national life marked by courage, energy, integrity, and imagination. Though Quebec has ceased to be an administrative centre of the whole nation, the influence of the people of her province grows no less, but is woven more and more into the web of general progress. The Empire will do well to set an enduring value on that New France so hardly won from a great people, and English Canada will reap rich reward for every compromise of racial pride made in the interests of peace, equality, and justice.

Laurier's journey to Ottawa was leisurely and came after a sojourn in the Quebec legislature, which began in 1871 but lasted only three years. It was possible in those days to be elected to both the federal and a provincial parliament at the same time, and so Laurier – the new *rouge* in town – began his political life at the age of thirty in close proximity to some of the great Worthies of Quebec in the struggle for Confederation, not the least being Cartier himself. The Quebec legislature, like the national parliament, was dominated by the Confederation Tories, and Laurier, who had a more radical past than he currently espoused (he had actually opposed Confederation at one point), was content for the most part to bide his time in the provincial legislature, interspersing legal work with political speeches that continued to build his reputation as one of the best orators in the land.

In 1874, he resigned his seat and ran for the House of Commons in Ottawa in the federal riding of Drummond and Arthabaska. Sir John A. Macdonald was defeated in the wake of the Pacific Scandal and Laurier's party – the Liberal party of

George Brown headed by the new prime minister, Alexander Mackenzie – came into office. Before the Liberals, in turn, were turfed out, Laurier had a brief fling as a cabinet minister (Inland Revenue – to keep his romanticism in check, perhaps!). This brief chronology is necessary to make a seemly entrance to the year 1877 and Laurier's famous speech in defence of liberalism.

If I were Dictator of Canada, I would make every schoolchild study and memorize huge hunks of this speech, just as education authorities in the People's Republic of China made millions of children study and memorize Chairman Mao's famous funeral essay on "Comrade" Norman Bethune, the Canadian doctor who died tending to the wounds of Mao's revolutionary army. I first heard part of it from my father, who read it aloud to me when I was thirteen or fourteen. He had recently inherited much of my grandfather's library and was reading O. D. Skelton's *Life and Letters of Sir Wilfrid Laurier*. I confess it meant nothing whatsoever to me and I was irritated at being required to listen to my father pretend he was Sir Wilfrid. Later I studied the speech at university, where I was somewhat more impressed, but it wasn't until a close friend got me whipped up about Laurier that I read it seriously and it has been a kind of beacon in my life ever since. I think I have returned to it a dozen times. It seems to me that only in a country as confused and forgetful about its history as Canada could such a wonderful public display of political wisdom, sectarian generosity, and progressive aspiration be allowed to lapse into obscurity.

The occasion of its presentation was memorable, and so too was its location in the heart of Old Quebec. It was at a meeting of the Canadian Club on June 26, 1877. Laurier was on the threshold of becoming the leader of the Liberals in Quebec, and he was just a few months away from assuming his first cabinet post in the

Mackenzie administration. The issue was, at the time, huge and potentially lethal to Laurier's future political ambitions. Powerful ultramontane elements within the Roman Catholic Church had been sounding alarms against "godless liberalism" for a generation in Quebec. The advent of Confederation, which returned to Quebec a provincial structure and responsibility for education unfettered by the concerns of the old English-French union of Canada West and Canada East, had brought some of the passion to a white heat. If it is hard to summon up today a sense of how bitter these disputes could be, perhaps those who had strong views on the free-trade debate – on either side – might recall the feelings of bitterness or triumph at the battle and the results. It was similar in the Quebec of 1877. Here are two study documents, researched, summarized, and translated by Skelton in his Laurier book, that will serve to give something of the flavour of the growing rancour:

From the "Catholic Programme" for voting guidance in elections published first in the *Journal des Trois-Rivières* on April 20, 1871 and which was supported by numerous bishops and other higher clergy as well as leading laymen: *1. If the contest is between two Conservatives, it goes without saying that we shall support the one who accepts the platform we have just outlined; 2. If on the contrary, it is between a Conservative of any shade whatever and an adept of the Liberal school, our sympathies will be given actively to the former; 3. If the only candidates who come forward in a constituency are both Liberals or oppositionists, we must choose whichever will agree to our terms; 4. Finally, in the event that the contest lies between a Conservative who rejects our programme and an opportunist of any brand who accepts it, the position would be more delicate. To vote for the former would be to contradict the doctrine we have just expounded; to vote for the latter would be to imperil the Conservative party, which we wish to see strong. What position should we make as between these two dangers? In this case we should advise Catholic electors to abstain from voting.*

Four years later, in September 1875, a joint pastoral letter was issued by most of the bishops of Quebec, headed by Archbishop (later Cardinal) Elzéar-Alexandre Taschereau, the most powerful ecclesiastical voice for French Canadians in Canada. It is true that Archbishop Taschereau, with guidance from Rome, later repented somewhat that he had signed this letter, but that happened only after an official Vatican inquiry into all the turmoil in Quebec and after Laurier made his classic and courageous defence of liberalism and the Liberal party. The letter was meant to administer institutional poison into all the works of liberalism and *rougiste* machinations. More specifically, it was designed "to shut the mouths of those who, to sanction their false doctrines, find pretexts for escaping the teachings of their own bishop by invoking the authority of other bishops which unfortunately they abuse, deceiving good people."

Distrust above all [the pastoral letter ran] that liberalism which wishes to cover itself with the fine name of "catholic" in order to accomplish more surely its criminal mission. You will recognize it easily from the description which the Sovereign Pontiff has given of it: 1. The endeavour to subordinate the Church to the State; 2. Incessant attempts to break the bonds which unite the children of the Church with one another and with their clergy; 3. The monstrous alliance of truth with error, under the pretext of reconciling all things and avoiding conflicts;

4 Finally, the illusion, or at times the hypocrisy, which conceals a boundless pride under the mask of religion and of fine assurances of submission to the Church. No one, therefore, may in future with good conscience be permitted to remain a "Catholic Liberal."

This was more than "serious." This was a political life-and-death issue that Laurier, for all his growing spirit of compromise and reconciliation, could not avoid. He was on the verge of accepting high office, and he knew if he did and made his true views on the church's interference in the electoral process clear, it could scuttle his future electoral chances. Writing in 1875 to a friend who had asked him if he would take on the issue, he frankly admitted his reluctance and pointed out how "quiet and happy" he was in his life with Zoë. "The moment I accept office, I will go into it actively and earnestly, and from that moment my quietness and happiness will be gone. It will be a war with the clergy, a war of every day, of every moment. Political strifes are bitter enough in your province [Ontario], but you have no idea what it is like with us and I will be denounced as Anti-Christ. You may laugh at that, but it is no laughing matter to us."

Two years later, this reluctant anti-Christ stood up before the standing-room-only crowd at the Club Canadien in Quebec City. From the onset, he made clear that he was out to disabuse people who were convinced liberalism meant heresy in faith and revolution in politics. Citing the attacks on his party and philosophy, he made a compelling argument that Catholics were given only one choice: vote Conservative or abstain from voting altogether and indeed abstain from political life altogether. He then spoke forcefully on how it was possible to be a Liberal as well as a good Catholic. Laurier's inherent instinct to draw together all people of goodwill was a constant throughout his life. To his mind the differences in conservatism and liberalism were "matters of temperament." As Skelton reports it, there was no moral superiority in either tendency. The conservative might do good in defending old and tried institutions, or much evil in maintaining intolerable abuses; the liberal might be a benefactor in overthrowing these abuses or a scourge in laying rash hands on hallowed institutions that still had much to offer the nation. Then he reached the heart of his endeavour that night and to do this he reached into his own heart:

For my part, I am a liberal. I am one of those who think that everywhere, in human things, there are abuses to be reformed, new horizons to be opened up, and new forces to be developed. The principle of liberalism is inherent in the very essence of our nature, in that desire for happiness with which we are all born into the world, which pursues us throughout life, and which is never completely gratified on this side of the grave. Our souls are immortal, but our means are limited. We constantly strive towards an ideal, which we never attain. We dream of good, but we never realize the best. We only reach the goal we have set for ourselves, to discover new horizons opening up, which we had not before even suspected. We rush on towards them and those horizons, explored in their turn, reveal to us others, which lead us on ever further and further. And thus it will be as long as man is what he is, as long as the immortal soul inhabits a mortal body; his desires will always be vaster than his means and his actions will never rise to the height of his conceptions. He is the real Sisyphus of the fable; his work, always finished, must always be begun again. This condition of our nature is precisely what which makes the greatness of man, for it condemns him irrevocably to movement, to progress; our means are limited, but our nature is perfectible and we have the infinite for our arena. . . .

In our adversaries' party, it is the custom to accuse us of irreligion. I am not here to parade my religious sentiments, but I can declare that I have too much respect for the faith in which I was born ever to use it as the basis of a political organization. You wish to organize a Catholic party, to organize all the Catholics into one party, without other bond, without other basis, than a common religion. Have you not reflected that by that very fact you will be organizing the Protestant population as a single party, and then, instead of the peace and harmony now prevailing between the different elements of the Canadian people, you throw open the door to war, a war of religion, the most terrible of all wars?

Our adversaries further reproach us with denying to the church the freedom to which it is entitled. They reproach us with seeking to silence the administrative body of the church and to prevent it from teaching the people their duties as citizens and electors. They reproach us from wanting to hinder the clergy from sharing in politics and to relegate them to the sacristy.

In the name of the Liberal Party and liberal principles, I repel this assertion.

I maintain that there is not one Canadian liberal who wants to prevent the clergy from taking part in political affairs if they wish to do so.

In the name of what principle should the friends of liberty seek to deny to the priest the right to take part in political affairs?

In the name of what principle should the friends of liberty seek to deny the priest the right to have and to express political opinions, the right to approve or disapprove public men and their acts, and to instruct the people in what he believes to be their duty?

In the name of what principle should he not have the right to say that if I am elected religion will be endangered, when I have the right to say that if my adversary is elected, the state will be endangered?

No, let the priest speak and preach as he thinks best; such is his right and no Canadian liberal will ever dispute that right because everyone has the right not only to express his opinion, but to influence, if he can, by the expression of his opinion, the opinion of his fellow-citizens. The right exists for all, and there can be no reason why the priest should be deprived of it.

I am here to speak my whole mind, and I may add that I am far from finding opportune the intervention of the clergy in the domain of politics, as it has been exercised for some years. I believe, on the contrary, that from the standpoint of the respect due his character, the priest has everything to lose by meddling in the ordinary questions of politics. Still, his right to do so is indisputable, and if he thinks proper to use it, our duty, as liberals, is to guarantee it to him against all denial.

This right, however, is not unlimited. We have no absolute rights amongst us. The rights of each man, in our state of society, end precisely where they encroach upon the rights of others. The right to interference in politics, therefore, ends where it would encroach upon the elector's independence because the constitution of the country rests on the freely expressed will of the elector. It is perfectly legitimate to alter the elector's opinion by argument and all other means of persuasion, but never by intimidation. As a matter of fact, persuasion changes the elector's convictions, intimidation never does. That is why if the opinion expressed by the majority of the electors is not their real opinion, but an opinion snatched from them by fraud, by threats or by corruption, the constitution is violated, and you have not government by the majority, but government by the minority.

I am not one of those who parade themselves as friends and champions of the clergy. However I say this: like the most of my fellow-countrymen, I have been educated by priests and among young men who have become priests. I flatter myself that I have among them some sincere friends, and to them at least I can and do say: *Consider whether there is under the sun a country happier than our own; consider under the sun if there is a country where the Catholic Church is freer or more privileged that it is here.* Why then should you, by claiming rights incompatible with our state of society, expose this country to agitation of which the consequences are impossible to foresee?

I address myself also to all my fellow countrymen without distinction, and to them I say: *We are a free and happy people, and we are so owing to the liberal institutions by which we are governed, institutions which we owe to the exertions of our forefathers and the wisdom of the mother country.*

The policy of the Liberal Party is to protect these institutions, to defend and extend them, and, under their sway, to develop the latent resources of our country.

This is the policy of the Liberal Party: *It has no other.*

Just copying this speech on my laptop has given me goosebumps again, and I'm a Tory! And we have let this good man slip from our practical consciousness even though he inherited from Macdonald, and further established, the only means by which Canada can be effectively held together and governed: through an accommodation between French and English. Macdonald called his administration "conservative" and Laurier called his "liberal," but in effect they were similar in that they both had a clear vision of what the beasts of race and language would be like if released unfettered into the politics of the "happy" land. It is, perhaps, why the most successful leaders in Canada have been the ones most irritating to zealots and those who have absolutely clear definitions – economically or ideologically – of where we should go. Macdonald, Laurier, King, St. Laurent, Pearson, Mulroney, Chrétien: some were eloquent and others were drones, some condoned more corruption than they should have and others led impeccable administrations. None of them though – and this is what separates them from Borden, Bennett, Diefenbaker, and Trudeau – tried to push a personal agenda through, however well intentioned, that forgot about Canada's special beasts. Accommodation to the central reality of Canadian life remains the only key to successful governance of this country after nearly 150 years and dramatically changing demographics. As Quebec's population has dwindled in proportion to the whole of Canada's, and significant parts of the population – particularly in the West – have agitated for different arrangements, there has never been a more important time to remember Laurier.

IV

"The Prime Minister is calling you."

The message came fourth-hand, via the prime minister's secretary, via my assistant, via the registrar of Massey College, who picked up the telephone in her office at the back of the quadrangle around which we all work. I raced back to my own office, and halfway there realized how short of breath at fifty-five I had become, despite an attitude of mind that was not much above the age of consent. During the last ten seconds I ceased sprinting and tried to catch my breath, the better to consider quickly how best to open the conversation.

"Oh, I say there, Prime Minister? How nice to hear from you. . . ."

No. That wouldn't do. We'd only met three times. Breezy insouciance has its place, but perhaps not here.

"Prime Minister, is that really you? Wow!"

Ditto. Enthusiasm has its proper place, but perhaps not here. Certainly not from someone who is fifty-five, out of breath, and carries the title "Master."

"Jean, be a pal and hold for a sec till I deal with this other call."

Familiarity with a dash of one-upmanship is almost always okay if you are actually familiar with a person. A prime minister, however, is a prime minister.

"Hello . . ." is what I said.

"Mr. Fraser?" said a strong, assertive female voice.

"Yes," I answered, wondering where his accent had gone.

"The Prime Minister would like to speak with you. Would you hold for a few seconds?"

I had invited Himself to a college event a couple of weeks earlier, using a high-placed intermediary to make sure the invitation actually got to him and not to a phalanx of flunkies all such folk are surrounded by. As a result, I already knew he would not be able to attend because of the G8 Summit in Ireland. So the phone call was a courtesy and I took it as a high honour.

"Hello, Mr. Fraser?"

"Yes, Mr. Chrétien," I said. "How are you?"

"I'm fine, but I can't accept your nice invitation unless you can tell me how to be in Ireland and Canada at the same time."

"D'Arcy McGee used to do it all the time till the Fenians came gunning for him," I joked. A Confederation joke too! How often do you get a chance to make a joke with a prime minister? But would he get it?

"Yeah, well dat guy lived in the age of miracles, and I'm stuck here in the age of the *National Post*. I'm getting a little angry with your newspaper calling me corrupt . . ."

And we were off. I don't have a recording of the conversation, nor did I make notes, so these scraps are something of an anecdotal or imaginative recreation. "My newspaper" had only recently become the *National Post*, where I was writing a new weekly column of media criticism, but it was a freelance position and I was at least two knight's moves removed from editorial policy. The prime minister vented very politely. He was incensed at what he described as the half-baked innuendos and unsubstantiated "evidence" of his personal corruption in the form of a government business grant to help a constituent in his riding. The *Post* had made much of the business of local friendships, former associations, and quiet understandings (the sort of stuff Stevie Cameron did with Brian Mulroney), and while it was already fairly well established that the prime minister knows how to make the federal government work for his riding, the absence of anything truly horrendous or even mildly outrageous was – at the time of our phone call – increasingly more obvious. In our conversation, which was amiable and clearly intended to be passed on, he summoned up his entire political career – wholly unblemished by any taint of corruption – to argue that at the very least he had earned enough credit for the benefit of a modest doubt until all the facts were exposed and examined. The *Post*, he argued, wasn't even operating under a scintilla of doubt, but was charging off in all directions and insinuating he was responsible for the darkest deeds. I pointed out, gently, that his administration had already got through an entire majority term without any real corruption problems or media heat, and that with truth on your side, patience was the best course of action. He argued that he would like the *Post* to employ "some of dat patience" before they published their "dirty" insinuations.

The conversation touched on other matters, so I don't want to paint the prime minister as obsessed with one subject. We talked about the recent visit of the new King of Jordan, the *National Post*, the upcoming G8 economic summit, the *National Post*, the initial reason for the phone call (to attend a gala performance to honour the Russian ballet superstar Mikhail Baryshnikov, on the twenty-fifth anniversary of his defection in Toronto), the *National Post*, the time I accompanied him across the Atlantic on his last briefing to the Queen on the country's new constitutional arrangements, the *National Post*, mutual friends, and the *National Post*.

I was struck by two things after I hung up. Well, more than two really, because it is both moving and disconcerting to be talking so directly to the centre of governance, especially for a part-time journalist who likes to observe politics closely but from a safe distance. Chrétien's English is a lot better than journalists make out, at least in private conversation. Personally, I like his accent a lot. If it has a negative effect on people, it surely compensates for all the fractured French poor French Canadians have had to put up with for a century and half from English-speaking politicians and Governors-General (but *not* the Queen, ironically, who speaks beautiful schoolgirl French). When we spoke briefly in French and the full panoply of my fractured syntax emerged (*"Malheursement, je parle français comme une vache Ontarienne,"* I said), he backed off from a full deluge on the subject of *"votre journal."* It was a kindness, under the circumstances, which I appreciated.

And this too. As with all creative people – and politicians are creative, ego-driven people just like writers and artists and the more dramatic kind of lawyers – there is a longing for approbation and appreciation. Jean Chrétien is a much more serious person than his fifteen-second nightly news clips, or the satires on "The Royal

Canadian Air Farce," would indicate. He has a colourful public persona that is not unrelated to the everyday man, but it is – or it was once – a consciously adopted performance. He even admits as much in his memoirs when he talks about his early image in Ottawa as a "peasant pea-souper." His parents clearly expected much of him, and from a very early age he was a driven soul. He is also a great survivor, and that is his most warming characteristic, along with his generous and loyal heart. He is not a small man, and I believe, like Laurier, his generosity of spirit is what has helped him to govern such a difficult country as Canada in the same way all the successful prime ministers of Canada have: from the eternal centre, whether it tilted to the left or the right; constantly trying to douse language or cultural discord; never letting the left hand know what the right hand is up to; never using oratorical passion to inflame one side at the expense of another; honouring the land; keeping the constituents happy; watching out for the media; and looking after your friends and allies and forgiving all enemies who can possibly be of use to you in the future. This is not governance to everyone's satisfaction. Here, for example, is Christina McCall's assessment from *Grits* on Chrétien's two most successful francophone predecessors:

But both Sir Wilfrid Laurier and Louis St. Laurent had turned themselves into the kind of readily understandable stereotypes that soothes the Anglo's racial unease. Laurier was the silver-tongued orator, the lawyer from the country town who loved the Empire and, until the racial conflicts that erupted in Canada during the 1914-18 war, praised all things British as beautiful whenever he had the chance. St. Laurent was Uncle

Louis, the half-Irish Quebec City lawyer with the cooly precise private manner that made him the ideal token French Canadian in the corporate boardrooms, coupled with the comfortingly folksy public façade that made him acceptable in legion halls and church basements in the rest of the country.

McCall's seminal book was published in 1982 when Canadian liberalism, with its Trudeau-esque colouring, was going through serious internal re-evaluation. While McCall was writing, there had been Trudeau's brief defeat and Joe Clark's even briefer administration followed by a return to Trudeau. Then John Turner's own brief fling and Brian Mulroney's historic takeover of the Liberal party's centreground, complete with a crucial francophone phalanx. Then Kim Campbell's briefest of flings, and finally the Liberal party's reclamation of Parliament Hill. The contempt for Chrétien himself, however, lingers. Here's an academic update on Chrétien liberalism from Professor Michael Bliss, the influential and assertive Canadian business and political historian. This is from an op-ed piece in the *National Post* in 1999:

> What vision does the government of Canada have of our future as we face the next millennium? Where is Liberalism taking us?
>
> The answer is unclear, though clearly unexciting. Jean Chrétien's government stands for pragmatic, managerial Liberalism. The politicians are content to keep the country more or less on its present course. Liberals squat happily on the middle ground of Canadian politics. If the centre shifts, they

can be expected to waddle along with it, as they often have in the past. Whether or not the right unites, the governing party will not surrender the centre easily.

No one, including the man himself, would accuse Mr. Chrétien of being a visionary prime minister. He is not cut from the cloth of a John A. Macdonald, a Pierre Elliott Trudeau, even a Mackenzie King or a Brian Mulroney. Rather, he seems to be a socially conservative, politically adept, benign "chairman of the board" of Canada Inc., presiding over the affairs of a firm that's doing fairly well, thank you. Routine business. No serious problems. When is tee-off time?

Sir Wilfrid Laurier was much like that during Canada's first great economic boom, almost exactly a century ago, and Louis St. Laurent filled the role during the great post-war boom of the early 1950s. History is uncannily close to repeating itself in 50-year cycles as Jean Chrétien rides the amazing expansion of the late 1990s.

Bliss continued in this vein for some considerable length, excoriating Chrétien and his Liberals for doing so little to prepare the country for the future and for being such dullards in the general business of inspiring the nation. After invoking the improbable spectres of Sir Robert Borden and John George Diefenbaker, he concluded his passionate jeremiad with a question: "Who will be the next politician with really new ideas, with something like a new vision for this country?" Those of us who feel we are still paying through the nose – both fiscally and in terms of a ruptured national governing polity – for the "visions" of John George and Pierre Elliott may perhaps be forgiven if we take a little distance from

Bliss's passionate search for a new Galahad. I prefer the identifiable ambitions of the Baie Comeau salesman or the *p'tit gars* from Shawinigan because I like my metaphysics restricted to religion and visions to be of saints or dearly remembered mothers.

V

In case I have inadvertently left the impression I was attempting a dispassionate examination of Jean Chrétien, I should admit I bonded with him on two notable occasions in my life. The first was when I travelled to London with him. He was taking the final constitutional package for passage through the British parliament (for the last time) as well as to brief and advise the Queen. We had a long talk on the airplane. He was the minister of justice then and cock of the walk and I was left with a strong sense of the sheer pleasure he got out of government and being such a key player.

The second occasion, a gala party to celebrate the Quebec elitist newspaper *Le Devoir*, was a much more sombre affair. We were both wallflowers: I, because I was an outsider, and he, because he was a notorious *vendu* and traitor to Quebec, thanks to that little trip when he took that Constitution to London without Quebec's agreement. By this time, Chrétien was Opposition leader and at his lowest-ever political ebb – "Yesterday's Man" the media called him – and a politician seemingly going nowhere at a snail's pace.

The exuberant Chrétien is a wonder to behold. As we sat in the airplane in the early hours of a mid-Atlantic morning, he traced all the travails and hopes that were pinned to the new constitutional process. When I asked him about Quebec, he frowned and admitted it was a big problem, but that the process had to proceed or nothing would get done. I could see he believed that strongly; he had bought Trudeau's cold logic and the two of them were confident that they could speak for Quebec's eventual acceptance. No anglophone prime minister or justice minister would have dared to be so presumptuous. It was something of a defining moment for me as I realized that in Chrétien's bubbling enthusiasm, all the hopes of liberal nirvana for Canada were contained, whereas I *knew* in my bones this was a false hope. I *knew* – in a sort of defining moment of my own latent conservatism – that the rusty old inadequate constitutional package we already had (the British-North America Act and various pieces of itinerant constitutional legislation) had one shining asset the Trudeau constitution lacked, and that was Quebec's consent. Even as I was sitting beside this decent and hugely optimistic man and started liking him more and more, flattered by his attentions and impressed at his own personal achievement in the world, I knew I could never share his outlook exactly. As Laurier said, it is a matter of temperament. I was pretty sure the known chaos would be better than the unknown. I ventured on this point a little, but it sparked no interest in him and when he detected in me slightly less enthusiasm than he felt, he changed subjects and we talked a little of London and royalty. He had once come knocking on the Queen's door with yet more constitutional rejigging arrangements. When she caught sight of him, she smiled good naturedly and said, "Not you again!"

I loved that story and the way he told it because it illustrated his carefree humility in high office and the fact that he doesn't take himself too seriously. Somehow, in the course of our conversation, I mentioned that my mother was a big fan of his, and that she was ill with a bad heart but was excited that we were both off on this "great adventure." Before the flight was over, he handed me a handwritten note to her, which she subsequently framed with a Canadian flag decal at the bottom. It stayed close to her bedside almost to her death, and I'm sure it was only because she donated her earthly remains to the anatomy department of the University of Toronto that it wasn't buried with her in a coffin. Chrétien's genius as a "people politician" can be sensed in the fact that he never forgot he wrote that note and whenever we met, even on the briefest of official occasions, he would ask after her health; after she died, he did not fail to commiserate. The late Tory politician George Hees was also like that. People laughed and even scoffed a bit at some of his political cartwheels in his various ministries, but they liked them too. They thought well of him thereafter, even if they disagreed – sometimes strongly so – with his policies.

I cannot begin to tell you the rage the Chrétien administration's policy on China and on refugee status brings out in me: how unimaginative and craven is the former, and unnecessarily cruel and cowardly the latter. And the Liberals' song and dance over Canadian magazine policy in the face of really repugnant bullying from south of the border was merely embarrassing. Yet knowing the man, I do not think him unimaginative, cruel, craven, embarrassing, or cowardly. Just the opposite. I think he will probably go down as one of our best prime ministers because he brought the country back from the brink (where, it is true, some argue he took it) and set it on as steady a course as was possible. And while this infuriates passionate folk such as Michael Bliss, I do not believe Canada can actually be successfully governed in any other way. That is why Laurier's administration looked so much like Macdonald's, and why Mulroney's looked like Mackenzie King's, and why Chrétien's crowd stole all of Mulroney's much criticized achievements – from free trade to the almighty GST – and made them Liberal policy.

It was not the genial conversation on that airplane that really cemented my affection for Jean Chrétien, though. Journalists who believe that flattery from politicians extends farther than the newspapers they write for are fools. While there are real friendships that evolve from professional relationships in politics and the media, they are rare: the politician discovers this when he or she loses office; the journalist learns of it just as abruptly when she is fired or moves into public relations. No, it was our conversation on the more sombre occasion of Le Devoir's anniversary gala that convinced me we had, in Chrétien, a leader for all seasons. I had been invited to the event because at Saturday Night I had supported Le Devoir and its editor, Lise Bissonnette, during a financial crisis. A fair bit of Toronto loot had been sent Quebecward, and so I was invited to the big event to thank all those who had helped out. I went with my best friend, the eloquent historian of French Canada and its most loyal anglophone advocate, Dr. Ralph Heintzman, who knew many of the distinguished guests drawn from Quebec intellectual society. I kept my mirth to myself, but in this crowd heavily weighted towards separatism, I was amused that the event was staged at the Hôtel Reine Elisabeth.

I knew hardly anyone and was terrified to deploy my crummy French, so I dispatched my date to make the rounds before we sat down to dinner, while I tried to find a potted palm to hide behind, not a usual quest for my loquacious self. I cannot remember if there was a palm, but I found a sequestered spot. It turned out to be where Jean Chrétien had already staked out his territory. We were near the bar and he looked as happy to see me as I was to see him. He didn't immediately remember me from the airplane trip, but once I reminded him we were off and soon discussing our pariah status at this event. On at least two occasions in this crowded room, eager conversationalists moving around the room would hover near, catch sight of him, and their jaws would drop as they quickly put some distance between them. That was how demonized he had become, thanks to the intellectual and media onslaught against him after the "betrayal" of Quebec in the constitutional process. It seemed to me that he had to take not only flack for his own role, but most of the shit that should have been sent Trudeau's way but wasn't since Quebecers rather liked his patrician style and arrogance and were happy to dish it out to Chrétien.

Whatever. He was in Opposition now. Brian Mulroney's Tories seemed to be doing just fine by Quebec's yardstick, but Chrétien, one of the great sons to come out of Quebec and a man whose career is a lesson to every young person anywhere in Canada that this remains a country of enormous opportunity, was seen as a traitor and a loser and utterly risible.

"You can imagine," he said, "this is not an easy place for me. I just try to keep a smile on my face and don't talk to anyone for very long. I am not popular here!"

"Does it bother you? I mean really bother you."

He didn't give me an immediate answer, but looked out around the large crowd. I thought I had asked a question out of turn and that he was angry, but no, I think he was searching for the right response.

"Yes," he said finally. No embroidery or supplementary. Just "yes."

He took a gulp of his drink and smiled again. "But dat's politics, you know. You always take the good with the bad."

I can't remember specifically what else we talked about that night, although we chatted for most of the reception prior to the dinner. I believe Mme. Bissonnette came up to us at one point and said a polite hello. She is a brilliant but humourless woman, and since I had made my appeal on behalf of her organ I had also published Mordecai Richler's views on her and on anti-Semitism in Quebec, so in a sense both Chrétien and I were united in the doghouse. She was, of course, a gracious hostess and moved speedily along to more agreeable company.

When Chrétien and his Liberals were finally elected to office, I wrote an editorial in *Saturday Night* – one of the last before I moved on to Massey College – paying tribute to Chrétien's endurance and faithfulness to the political process. My record as an astute public commentator on politics was not bright, as half a year earlier I had chosen one of Brian Mulroney's lower moments to tout in my magazine his administration's extraordinary achievements, despite the failure of the Meech Lake Accord and his own lugubrious style. I got only one bit of support for that piece and it was from the dearest old man I ever knew: Professor Emeritus Douglas LePan, whom I would later come to know intimately as he was the doyen of my college and held court there almost to the day he died. A former civil servant, twice winner of the Governor General's Award for poetry, war hero, educator, and intimate of some of the great figures of his day (Lester Pearson, Vincent Massey, Charles Ritchie, Pauline Vanier, T. S. Eliot, and on and on), LePan had come to the conclusion that Mulroney had inherited what he called "the Canadian mandate of heaven." By this he meant that Mulroney had grabbed the ideological centre along with a sturdy faith in Quebec's importance to the very idea of Canada, and had run with it. To LePan, free trade – originally a Liberal plank of Laurier's – was the inevitable consequence of geography and pragmatic economics. As for Mulroney's treacly, self-puffing personality, LePan looked at me with benign condescension and said, "You were spared Mackenzie King's opinion of himself, and thanks to the primitiveness of media and the politeness of journalists then, so was the country. Mulroney actually reminds me of King a little. They both needed a lot of coddling. You know Pierre [Trudeau] and I were once colleagues and friends, but I'd have to say he really did do a lot of damage to the country."

I asked him, just for the fun of it, if he thought Chrétien could win a majority government (this was before Mulroney stepped down, but when his popularity polls were low) and how he would do as prime minister.

"I don't see it, as bad as Mulroney is doing today," said LePan, as good a political prophet as myself, "but if he does win he would be an improvement on Pierre. At least Chrétien talks to you, not at you. It's a useful trait, especially if you want to have a dialogue! Now that you put it to me, I think I'd like to live long enough to see Jean Chrétien become prime minister. I think his mind is open to wonder. I only met him once, a long time ago when he was minister of Indian affairs. He came to University College [at the University of Toronto, where LePan was principal at the time] for a conference. All his predecessors had been disasters, but he was wonderful. It's also nice to see conventional political wisdom tossed out the window. 'Yesterday's man' wins today! I like that thought a lot."

And he did live long enough.

This is taken from *Straight From the Heart*:

During the 1968 election I was campaigning in British Columbia when someone asked, "Mr. Chrétien, what will the policies of the Trudeau government be for the Indians of Canada?"

As I was Minister of National Revenue at the time, I was somewhat taken aback. "Do you want a frank answer? I don't know a damn thing about it!" Everyone laughed. Three weeks later Trudeau invited me to become Minister of Indian Affairs and Northern Development.

I didn't think I could accept after what I had said in Vancouver, but Trudeau looked at it another way. "Nobody will be able to say that you have any preconceived views of the problems," he argued. "In fact you represent a similar background. You're from a minority group, you don't speak much English, you've known poverty. You might actually become a minister who understands Indians." I was also being pressured by my young assistants, John Rae and Jean Fournier, both of whom had worked in the North as students and were in love with it.

So I agreed. Before me the Indians had had seven ministers in seven years. I stayed six years, one month, three days, and two hours, and I loved every minute of it. My fondest memories are of travelling in the north those years, the kind people, the remote villages, the scenes of unusual beauty and isolation. After fifteen years, for example, I vividly recall many wonderful moments such as the visit to Coppermine, NWT, with my wife, two of my children, and a sister in early 1970, the North's centennial year. The day was extremely cold but sunny, and there was a ceremony for us in the assembly hall of the Anglican church. The men were laughing and the women were feeding their babies, and there was a really nice exchange of gifts and good wishes. The town had never seen a cabinet minister before.

At the end of the formalities, the Inuit wanted to do something special, so they sang "God Save the Queen" in their own language, with all the verses that are sung in church, finishing with a recognizable "Amen." They sang it like a hymn. You know French Canadians have often felt uncomfortable with the monarchy, because it has represented the Conquest for many of them, but that day I understood a dimension that had eluded me; these people were singing a hymn to the head of their church and they sang with such beauty and respect that my sister had tears in her eyes.

VI

When Sir Wilfrid Laurier died in 1919, he was fairly convinced his life's work had been a failure, that all his optimism in an English-inspired liberalism had been misplaced, that his patient efforts to bring about reconciliation between French

and English had blown up in his face thanks to the 1917 conscription crisis which had divided the country, and that the world
itself was being torn apart in a horrible war that would, in the
end, tear Canada apart as well. Defeat at the polls in 1911 no
doubt contributed to his sense of failure, and it is difficult for
anyone in the midst of rejection to remember, let alone enter into
the balance, the years of acceptance and great success. He was
attacked physically too, by jeering, nationalist youths in Montreal,
who had been inflamed by a speech from Henri Bourassa, Laurier's
compatriot and nemesis, who played a role in his life not unlike
the one René Lévesque played for Pierre Trudeau and Lucien
Bouchard played for Brian Mulroney. The young people were
roving the streets in gangs after a political meeting and lucked into
the prime minister's car on its way to the train station. They
stopped and surrounded it, pounding on the windows and shout-
ing crude and cruel epithets. Their spiritual descendants would
harass Georges Vanier and Pierre Trudeau and Jean Chrétien in
their turn: "Sellouts," "Traitors," "Scab."

Laurier was the first to prove that the politicians most adept at
keeping Canada together were the ones who came from Quebec,
or who knew how to make Quebecers and francophones feel connected to the federal government, and to make anglophones feel
connected to Quebec, yet they were also the very ones to suffer the
crudest attacks. St. Laurent got off easy, but still he was subject to a
certain measure of contempt from the Quebec intelligentsia, not
the least from Trudeau in his Young Turk period. Curiously, the
only Quebec-sensitive prime ministers to escape such attacks were
anglos – Sir John A. Macdonald and Brian Mulroney. Since they
were anglos, they presumably were selling out English Canada and,
indeed, from Orange Lodges for Macdonald and angry westerners

for Mulroney, they did get their fair share of venom. Lester Pearson deserved to be let off the hook in Quebec for similar hypocritical reasons, but it was his bad luck to be prime minister during the Quiet Revolution, and despite all his best efforts, he was made initially to seem as a menace and finally as irrelevant in Quebec.

Hateful and hurtful as all the mud-slinging was, Laurier knew how to deal with it because he had "religion" and an invincible faith in the country he had nurtured so well for so long. "I am branded in Quebec as a traitor to the French and in Ontario as a traitor to the English. In Quebec, I am branded a Jingoist, and in Ontario as a separatist. In Quebec I am attacked as an Imperialist, and in Ontario as an anti-Imperialist. I am neither. I am a Canadian. Canada has been the inspiration of my life. I have had before me as a pillar of fire by night and a pillar of cloud by day a policy of true Canadianism, of moderation, of conciliation."

Achievements in politics – enduring achievements, that is – tend not to be acknowledged for decades and are savoured mostly by historians. As for Sir Wilfrid Laurier's achievements, by the end of his life he had ceased enumerating them even to himself for they had become dull and distant, offering little if any release from the sense of failure. The close relationships he had valued with strong and feisty female friends, to supplement his warm but one-dimensional marriage, no longer cheered him, while male friends or colleagues who had once been especially dear and close to him were distant or even studiously unfriendly. Spiritually, he was sufficiently ambivalent about the balm offered by the Holy Mother Church that he only rarely found solace in the metaphysical.

Yet, as even his more acid-tongued detractors might admit on a fair day, his achievements had "not been inconsiderable" (the double-negative phrase is Sir Robert Borden's). From 1896 to 1911 – fifteen continuous years in office, three successful general elections in a row — he steered Canada into the new century and through endless shoals of regional discord and founding-race conflict. He began his first mandate in the midst of the Manitoba School Crisis and only by being French Canadian and struggling to be fair to all sides, thereby alienating the nationalistic francophone population, did he reached some sort of workable accord. But still, he did it and with great courage and, for better or worse, a new province could get on with its life. He created two other new provinces as well, and for as long as Saskatchewan and Alberta exist as political entities, their people can give thanks to the patrician French Canadian who shepherded their birth from conception through to the first cries of Western alienation (which — surprise, surprise — had an anti-Catholic, anti-French flavour). The day before I started writing the first draft of this section *The Globe and Mail* reprinted its September 2, 1905, front page celebrating the creation of Alberta:

GREAT INAUGURATION OF ALBERTA PROVINCE

Edmonton Gay With Bunting and Crowded with People

YOUNG GIANT OF THE WEST

A Most memorable Day Of Merrymaking and Ceremony

LAURIER TO THE ALBERTANS

In the course of his speech at Edmonton yesterday at the inauguration of the Province of Alberta, Sir Wilfrid Laurier said in part:

"When I look about me on this sea of upturned faces, I see everywhere the fine determination of the new Province. I see everywhere hope. I see everywhere calm resolution, courage, enthusiasm to face all difficulties, to settle all problems. If it be true everywhere, it must be especially true here today: 'Hope springs eternal in the human breast.' (Cheers)

"In order to bring this new province to the standard we have set for it, it is necessary that we have the hearty co-operation of all the people, of all the citizens of Alberta. We must have the co-operation of the old settlers and pioneers, the men of the old provinces, chiefly of the Province of Ontario, who came here when the land was a desert, and made the desert smile. We must have the co-operation also of the new citizens who have come here from all parts of the world to give Canada, to give Alberta, the benefit of their individuality, of their energy, of their enterprise.

"And since it just happens that I have the great honour of occupying the post of the first servant of the Crown in this country, let me say on behalf of the Crown, with the concurrence of His Excellency the Governor General, that to these new fellow countrymen, to these new subjects of the King, I offer the most cordial of all welcomes, cordial to one, cordial to all.

"Let me say also to our new fellow countrymen that the Dominion of Canada is in one respect like the Kingdom of heaven. Those who come at the eleventh hour will receive as fair treatment as those who have been in the fold for a long time. (Laughter and cheers). *What we have, we want to share: our land, our laws, our civilization. Let our new fellow citizens take their share in the life of this country, whether it be municipal, provincial or national. Let them be electors as well as citizens. We do not anticipate and we do not want that any individuals should forget the land of their origin or their ancestors. Let them look to the past, but let them also look to the future: to the land of the ancestors, but also to the land of their children. Let them become Canadians, and give their heart and soul, their energy and their vows to Canada, to its institutions, to its King, who like his illustrious mother, is a model constitutional sovereign."* (Loud cheers.)

What a good year 1905 was for Laurier! In addition to creating new provinces, he was presiding over a healthy economy and one of those extended periods in which Canadians could take the best possible measure of themselves, dreaming whatever dreams we do during economically beneficial times. He was constructing new railways to stitch the country together through east-west trade, creating new federal ministries of enduring worth and might (Labour and External Affairs), and building up the notion of an independent (of Britain) Armed Forces. His special worth to English Canadians was the good side of the coin Christina McCall turned over in *Grits* when she noted cynically that Laurier soothed anglo racial anxiety. He was also the first French-Canadian leader to make English-speaking Canadians take pride in their country's unique and still emerging bicultural complexity, although it would never have been thought as that at the time.

But for me, Laurier's greatest contribution can be found in the remarkable subtext of that genial speech to the Albertans in 1905. The special emphasis he placed on addressing what we now call "New Canadians" sounds a trumpet that will forever resound in our dear land as long as it remains identifiable as Canada. I am, perhaps foolishly, trying to deploy the language of the times because, however florid it may sound to today's ears, it is hard to escape the extraordinary optimism and grandeur of those days when Canada was "feeling its oats." I think it must have been a good time to be alive and embrace hope. Under Wilfrid Laurier, the notion of Canada as a great immigrant country – a land dependent upon constant infusions of new energy from "beyond the seas" – came to a glorious initial resolution.

His remarkable minister of the Interior, the thirty-six-year-old Clifford Sifton, going deaf even at that age, bloomed under Laurier's total approbation until their extraordinary collaboration collapsed in the acrimony over free trade with the United States. In the glory days, though, Sifton cleared away all the cobwebs of obfuscation and red tape that had encumbered the old Department of the Interior, and therefore all immigration to Canada, prior to his arrival. With Laurier's insistent urging and approval, he set about populating the country with people looking for a new chance from almost anywhere (then acceptable) on the known globe. In Laurier's great decade, the first of the new century, more than a half-million new immigrants came, most of them heading west. It had the single most dramatic effect on Canada as anything since Confederation itself, and stayed a unique phenomenon in our history until two later Liberal administrations, those of Pearson and Trudeau, removed the unwritten but real racial quotas, and within a period similar to Laurier's era of great change, the face of Canada dramatically altered again.

All this seems to be clear, and mostly wonderful, at the end of the century. I doubt, though, whether it brought the old man any solace at the end of his days. He had gone down in flames pushing reciprocity with the United States. This had been overwhelmingly rejected by the electorate as the Tories wrapped the Union Jack around themselves and accused the Liberals of selling out the country to the United States. Laurier, the great lover of all constitutional gifts from England, was deeply wounded at the charges. As usual, his vision was a noble one. He rejected the argument that reciprocity would mean annexation to the United States, just as he rejected the argument that weakening Imperial ties through North American free trade would undermine the traditions and constitutional form of government that had evolved from the English system. Instead, as his great biographer, Joseph Schull, points out, he offered both sides "something better" than either had dreamed of. "There may be a spectacle, perhaps, nobler yet than the spectacle of a united continent," he said in a speech on March 7, 1911, "a spectacle which would astonish the world by its novelty and grandeur, the spectacle of two peoples living side by side along a frontier nearly four thousand miles long, with not a cannon, with not a gun frowning across it on either side, with no armaments one against the other, but living in harmony, in mutual confidence and with no other rivalry than a generous emulation in commerce and the arts of peace."

It didn't go down well at all. Canadians were not ready for "a generous emulation in commerce and the arts of peace" and who knows, maybe it was too soon in the evolution of the country's economy. Nevertheless, reciprocity had been part of the Canadian concept of continental partnership from day one in the country's constitutional history. It is amusing to watch the issue played like a tennis game between the Liberals and the Tories throughout all of our history. Our necks almost got twisted as we looked to the left and then the right to see who was hitting the ball hardest in the great free-trade debate that Brian Mulroney led. There was a studied irony that this historic wrangle ended up back in the Tory ranks, where it began in Sir John A. Macdonald's day, with Alexander Mackenzie's Liberals dead set against the notion. Perhaps knowing how the issue had already bounced back and forth across the ideological divide, and knowing how it would continue to do so in the years ahead, Laurier was comfortable with prophecy in this sphere. And prescient! When Sir Robert Borden's administration called its first session of Parliament, the usual ragging of the defeated by the victors took place in various venues, including, of course, the House of Commons. Laurier's response was plucky: "O men of little faith," he flung back on the Tory benches when he was told free trade with the United States was as dead as any issue ever could be. "O men of little faith, that seed will still germinate." In the election, he had likened Sir John A. Macdonald to "the Moses of reciprocity" who had not been able to get his country to the Promised Land. He then offered himself as the "Joshua" who would take everyone there, which was not to be. Those who are not offended by an irreverent Judeo-Christian allusion will perhaps forgive me for noting that at the end of Laurier's century, it was Brian Mulroney who got to play Jesus Christ in proclaiming the Good News of free trade only to be crucified by the rabble baying for his blood, including a stone-throwing Jean Chrétien, who got to play St. Paul by converting and turning himself into the great apostle of reciprocity. But perhaps this is a little over the top.

The gloom that descended upon Laurier's life after his administration fell did not mean he was an ineffective leader of the Opposition. He had had the job before when he was on the rise and watched all the successors of Sir John perish one way or another (including one, Sir John Thompson, who died practically on Queen Victoria's hearth at Windsor Castle, where he had gone only weeks after being asked by the Governor General to form a new Tory administration in 1894). Laurier was a good leader of the Opposition: tenacious, loyal to the institutions of Crown and Parliament, and gloriously stubborn when he felt the need. He was successful enough in fighting Sir Robert Borden's naval defence bill, which enraged him. The issues seem clear enough to us today, but that is because all our attics are cleared of any lingering sympathy for the British Empire. "Empire" is a bad word for starters. Amongst other nasty things, "the Empire" can strike back, as we all know from *Star Wars*. The notion that Canada was a comfortable part of the British Empire and that even many French Canadians, primarily via the Roman Catholic Church, admired the status quo of Empire and loyal Dominion, seems today almost impossible to believe. That's because, as I wrote in the introduction to these essays, we seem to feel we have the world's most inconvenient history and Canadians seem to prefer not knowing any of it. It's easier that way.

Still, when Sir Robert Borden, early on in his new administration, proposed that Canada simply send loot to the Mother Country to help build up "the Empire's navy," many Canadians felt this was entirely appropriate and looked upon Laurier's opposition to it as treason. Now no one in Canada loved England and its traditions of liberal democracy more intelligently than Laurier. No one in Canada, not even in English Canada, loved the monarchy more intelligently than Laurier, even though he had resisted accepting a knighthood in 1896 and had fought back all of Sir Joseph Chamberlain's efforts to centralize the running of the Empire in London by herding all the dominions and colonies into willful subservience. Laurier was, to my mind at any rate, the perfect Canadian because he could encompass the optimism of basic liberalism, the respect for tried and true institutions of conservatism, the generosity of the well-intentioned rich, the cautious scepticism of those living next to someone even wealthier, and the pride of the essentially self-sufficient. These traits, which were his personally and which, through some spiritual osmosis, he managed to bequeath his fellow Canadians, meant that he had a clear conception of how to deal with Canada's evolving and increasingly complex political situation. He may have been the first to understand deeply how to detach the sovereign – and his own Dominion – from domestic British policy.

In any event, when Borden pushed through his naval bill and suddenly found himself facing a full filibuster from the Liberals with the old leader in full fury, he did the only sensible thing an uptight WASP could possibly do (I speak from the heart of the tribe): he broke out in boils and imposed closure. No doubt ringing in the poor man's ears were Sir Wilfrid's stinging phrases:

"O ye Tory jingoes, you give England two or three dreadnoughts to be paid for by Canada but to be equipped, maintained, and manned by England. You are ready to furnish admirals, rear-admirals, commodores, captains, officers of all grades, plumes, feathers and gold lace, but you leave it to England to supply the bone and sinews. You say that these ships shall bear Canadian names. That will be the only thing Canadian about them. You hire somebody to do your work; in other words you are ready to do anything except the fighting." The long years of Liberal ascendancy had packed the Senate with a pliant group of the faithful and, in the end, the Tory bill was defeated in the Upper House, occasioning neither the first nor the last calls for its reform.

All of this counted for nothing to Laurier at his end. When war was declared, he pronounced quickly that Canada stood side by side with Britain and the Empire, but when Borden asked him to join an administration of national consensus and coalition, he declined. For Laurier, the trap was wide and vivid. By resisting the coalition, he would be accused of being anti-British and hurting the war effort. By succumbing, Quebec would be isolated in the inevitable conscription battle and all the painstaking work of a lifetime would go up in flames. It seemed an impossible choice, but it wasn't, of course. Although it must have wounded him deep down, he knew he had to resist the coalition. For a country struggling to be at peace with itself, the closing off of a national party that was the only home of the moment for Quebec federalists would be an unmitigated disaster with consequences for the future far beyond the war aims of the Empire. And so, with taunts of traitor ringing in his ears, he went his lonely way. And he was very much alone in the Conscription Election of 1917, for although he kept Quebec within the Liberal fold, it was still isolated within a party that had lost all outwardly perceptible grip on any other part of the country. That was how it seemed at the time. William Lyon Mackenzie King was already a busy beaver in the wings of Canadian liberalism and his first stage entrance was only months away, and a starring role only a few years away. But that is all from the benefit of hindsight and we can see, also from the benefit of hindsight, that Mackenzie King rode to electoral success on Sir Wilfrid's considerable coattails. The old man saw none of this. What he saw were all the friends who had deserted him. He seems to have minded that the most. Pasted onto the fly-leaf of his well-thumbed Bible, the psalm that resonated for him (Psalm 55) in his final days was bleak and desolate:

> For it was not an enemy that reproached me; then I could have borne it: neither was it he that hated me that did magnify himself against me; then I would have hid myself from him. But it was thou, a man mine equal, my guide, and my acquaintance.

But he did keep Quebec within the federal fold, he did get to see war's end and, at the age of seventy-eight, after suffering two paralytic strokes in February 1919, he died. His last words, whispered to his wife, were: "*C'est fini.*"

Mais, ce n'est pas vrai. Grâce à Wilfrid Laurier, ce n'est pas encore fini l'histoire du Canada.

Canada: The War of the Conquest, by Guy Frégault. Published in 1969 by the Oxford University Press.

Grits: An Intimate Portrait of the Liberal Party, by Christina McCall-Newman. Published in 1982 by Macmillan of Canada.

Laurier: The First Canadian, by Joseph Schull. Published in 1966 by Macmillan of Canada.

Life and Letters of Sir Wilfrid Laurier: Vols. 1 & 2, by Oscar Douglas Skelton. Published in 1965 by McClelland & Stewart.

Old Quebec: The Fortress of New France, by Gilbert Parker and Claude G. Bryan. Published in 1903 by Copp, Clark Ltd.

The Prime Ministers of Canada: Macdonald to Mulroney 1867-1985, by Christopher Ondaatje. Published in 1985 by The Pagurian Press.

The Private Capital: Ambition and Love in the Age of Macdonald and Laurier, by Sandra Gwyn. Published in 1984 by McClelland & Stewart.

Sir Wilfrid Laurier and the Romance of Canada, by Laurier L. Lapierre. Published in 1996 by Stoddart Publishing Company.

A Social History of Canada, by George Woodcock. Published in 1988 by Viking Books.

Straight From the Heart, by Jean Chrétien. Published in 1985 by Key Porter Books.

The Tragedy of Quebec: The Expulsion of Its Protestant Farmers, by Robert Sellar. Published in 1907 by Ontario Press Ltd.

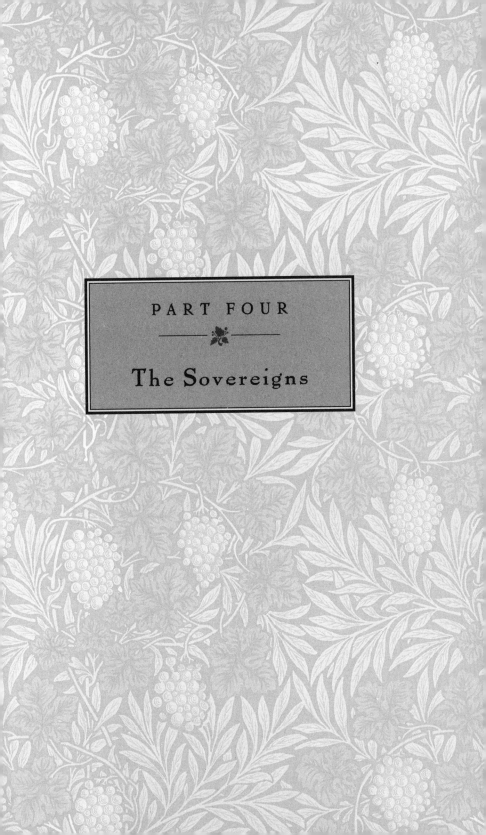

PART FOUR

The Sovereigns

I

I remember the moment it was first switched on. It was 1953 and I was not quite nine. Barrie, my bossy older sister, had just had her eleventh birthday. My mother was seated in one of the two armchairs of the upstairs study. This was "the twice-around-the-clock room," as described in *Canadian House and Home*: a master bedroom by night, a family study by day – a clever 1950s variant to all the subterranean "wreck" rooms being carved out of dank old basements. My grandmother, Granny Dickinson, my mother's mother, was seated in the other armchair. We waited for what seemed an hour while my father was on his knees diddling with the dials.

The cacophonous volume came first and a little pinprick of light on the screen. We could make no sense of the sounds – just occasional, seemingly unconnected words – but my friend, Johnny Harbinson, and I kept our eyes glued to that tiny pinprick of light. It disappeared for a moment and then flashed on again even larger. As it slowly started expanding, the disconnected voices went lunar and whined. Granny D clutched the breast pocket of her silk shirt to turn down the volume on her hearing aid, to no avail.

The whining became louder and then quite suddenly there was an explosion of shapes filling out the entire screen, all seventeen inches of it. The shapes were zigzaggy and volatile. Father fiddled even more with the dials – I later came to know those dials as intimate friends, the Vertical Hold and the Horizontal Hold – but in truth he hadn't a clue what he was doing. I had watched him trying to make sense of the operating booklet and after a minute or so he put it down in some annoyance. "Cath," he said to my mother, "I'm just going to plug the damn thing in and see what happens."

I had gone running out to let my sister know . . . *what*? That the television revolution was about to begin, I guess. And it was beginning at my own house, the only house in the neighbourhood, so far as I could find out, to have a set. The survey, I admit, was selectively conducted among the only people in the world who counted: Johnny Harbinson, Bryce Hunter, Patty Robertson, Jamie McGeough, the Kingsmills, Aunt Laura and Uncle Seymour. There was a rumour that some people on Lascelles Boulevard had one before us, but since they didn't have kids they didn't count.

"He's going to turn it on," I shouted down the stairs. My sister and a couple of her friends came running up the stairs and bounced into the room, giggling and whispering at the same time in that annoying way girls do. They were eating popsicles and my mother told them to go back outside until they were finished. "Aw, Mum, just this once," whined my sister. My mother was remorseless. "Out," she said.

That's how I remember it, anyway. It happened in Toronto in the house with the brass lion's head knocker, the grandmother from Glasgow on the second floor, and the most loyal nine-year-old royalist on the third. The television set had been purchased so that we could watch the coronation of Queen Elizabeth II on June 2, 1953, a date that was emblazoned into my cerebellum months earlier when it was first announced.

In my class at Oriole Park Public School, we had just been given a large copper coronation coin each, with the Queen on one side and the royal cipher – E II R – on the other. I don't think I had ever received anything as precious as this before, or since for that matter. I saw it somehow coming mysteriously from Buckingham Palace itself and I kept it with my treasures in a tin box carefully tucked away inside the big drawer of my locked desk. *Locked desk?* My God, I had a tight chain around the entire thing and through its drawer handles. These were secured by two padlocks – a combination lock and a key lock – to keep my sister's prying eyes and snooping fingers O...U...T.

Just before my father died in June 1998, I reminded him about the television set – the first of so many in our lives – and said that in my boyhood fantasy I thought it would be the Queen herself who I would see first when the television set was turned on. There was a bit of disappointment when it turned out simply to be a humble weather reporter. I think the confusion came because we had talked so much about getting a television set to see the coronation. It would be a while before I realized my life would not be worth living unless I saw each week's episode of Roy Rogers and his faithful horse, Trigger.

My father snorted at my royalist memories. Perhaps the coronation was one of many factors he said, with the kind of accountant's harumph he used to put down what he considered my more flamboyant memories of a shared family past. The only real reason he bought it, he added, was because "your mother was flat on her back and bored to death." It's true my mother had had severe disc problems and had been put to bed rest for several weeks, and it may well have been my father's intention to divert her with the new contraption. If so, the diversion didn't appeal for long. Before the end of May, when I and my sister stormed into "the twice-around-the-clock room" (which my mother was now calling the "I'm-never-getting-out-of-here room") to see the latest of Roy Rogers's exploits, I definitely heard the F-word come from my mother's mouth. And not just once, but twice in almost the same breath. She was reading a magazine and my father was reading some business papers when Barrie and I came in and turned on the set. As the program started, my mother turned to my father and said, "Fuck Roy Rogers. Fuck Trigger." Later she insisted she had said "Phooey," but my father agreed with me that she had said the F-word. I was shocked, but he smiled. Nevertheless, the blunt explosion marked the end of total infatuation with the miracle of television in our house.

As for the coronation – the real reason for the television set so far as my grandmother and I were concerned – we knew all the details. The British Broadcasting Corporation was going to film it and two or three special jets of the Royal Canadian Air Force, outfitted with dark rooms for film development, would take off, each with a precious reel on board, and speed their way to Canada. We would be watching the coronation in instalments literally on the same day it happened. To watch something this extensive in North America that had happened in Europe the same day was an historic first, and John Anderson Fraser and his grandmother, Barbara Forrester Dickinson, were on top of the story from beginning to end.

Granny D had even bought me a special coronation coach and regimental lead soldier set for Christmas, and I was constantly trotting out the poor Queen and Prince Philip and all the Queen's horses to march down The Mall yet again to Westminster Abbey. As I could lift the lid on the golden state coach, I could always check to make sure the Queen was still sitting correctly, with her right hand up in a permanent wave to her people, which included me and my granny and all those handsome Zulu warriors and their barechested wives from the *National Geographic*, not to mention the colourful Sikhs of India, the busy Chinese in Hong Kong, the dour Boers in South Africa, the beautiful Maori from New Zealand, the well-wrapped-up Eskimos from the Northwest Territories of Canada, and Harry Belafonte from Jamaica. We were all hers and she was ours. There wasn't a jewel in the Imperial State Crown whose dimensions I didn't know. My granny and I knew the weight of the big orb and the little orb, the length of the jewelled sceptre, and the engraving pattern on both sides of the Sword of State. We knew how many little ermine it took to form the border on her coronation robe and how far below the knee the buttons on the silk breeches of the pageboys were fastened.

We also knew that during two very holy moments in the service – when the Archbishop of Canterbury anointed her head and *naked breast* with holy oil, and later when she took communion (the wine for which came from vines near Bethlehem while the sacred water, following purification, was from the River Jordan) – the television cameras would look away. I was relieved to hear this. Ever since I had read an account of the forthcoming service in the *Illustrated London News* and learned that the Archbishop of Canterbury, Dr. Geoffrey Fisher, was going to make the sign of the cross on *her naked breast* with holy oil, I became concerned about her right to privacy. I don't think I minded if I saw her naked breast. I would respect the privacy and be proud of the viewing privilege. But I didn't think the world should see it. In fact, I was pretty sure the world shouldn't see it. I mean all women's breasts were a private matter and whose could be more private than the Queen's?

Years later I read Roald Dahl's wonderful memoir of his childhood, *Boy*, and discovered that he went to a boy's school in England where the headmaster, the self-same Dr. Fisher, before he became such a mighty prelate of the church, got his jollies by savagely caning little boys. When I read that, it twigged my old concern out of its storage cells. "Well," I thought, "so I needn't have worried after all. The Queen was perfectly safe."

It was a black-and-white coronation on television, of course. It would be two days before the movie houses had the colour version. We all went to that too, standing up for "God Save the Queen" at the beginning of the show, as we did before every matinee movie we went to in those days. Only on this occasion we were still trying to get used to singing the word "queen," which sounded funny after all those years of singing "God Save the King." The change was nice, though. She was nice. Everything was nice. It would be years before we actually met and I cannot claim we lingered long on each other's conversation (about eight seconds, I believe). But like many Canadian kids of the same age in 1953, I bonded with her tightly that June day she processed down the Abbey aisle and mounted the throne of King Edward the Confessor, which contained the Stone of Scone and had the carved initials of centuries of errant boys who had managed to get their pocket knives out when no one was looking.

The Stone of Scone is gone from the throne: packed up and shipped off to independence-minded Scotland. Hong Kong is gone. Australia was on the brink of going. The whole family's been dismissed as dysfunctional. In Canada, after nearly a half-century on the throne and serving as a constitutional safety net during some of the most fractious and turbulent crises in the history of our confederation, Elizabeth II is seen as an embarrassment, a temporarily unavoidable relic of our colonial past. We don't want her, but we can't do without her.

II

Elizabeth's detractors in Canada and the enemies of the Crown have had lots to say about her and the institution of monarchy over the past few decades. She is now so disregarded or disdained in some circles that she may almost be the definition of the perfect Canadian. This is a somewhat metaphysical point that, to be fully appreciated, requires us to go back to the world of her great-great grandmother, Queen Victoria, who rarely meddled in Canadian affairs.

That's misleading, actually. To say Victoria "rarely meddled" suggests that she was actually keeping track of Canadian affairs, that she was interested in them but nevertheless stayed out of them. This wasn't the case at all, as she wasn't in any but the most peripheral way interested in the vast territory. We were a large, and largely uninhabited, part of the growing global red of the British Empire. Much more to her taste, at least during her long and lonely vigil as the widow empress, were her Sikh servants from India or her Scottish gillie, John Brown. There is no record of her warming up to a colourful Mohawk chief, or chuckling at the patois of her faithful French-Canadian Lady-of-the-Bedpan. They didn't exist for Victoria, and even if they did exist they would have been irrelevant to the adoration she was held in across Canada, including Quebec. Affection for her and loyalty to the Crown were hinged on a system that simply required her to be seen presiding over the greater part of the globe and to which English Canadians used to feel a total sense of identity and French Canadians, following the lead of their church, supported with a smile or a shrug.

That the annual Victoria Day holiday is still maintained in many parts of Canada seems to some perverse, but it is redolent of that past. In its specifics today, I must admit, it's a little sad and tawdry, but that's because officialdom can hardly even pay token attention to it. In 1998, by accident, my wife and I took her ninety-year-old father out for a stroll in his wheelchair while he was recovering from a bad bout of something that had required a short stay at the Women's College Hospital in downtown Toronto. Following the sound of bagpipes, we walked two blocks to Queen's Park just in time to catch the tail end of the Victoria Day parade, which concluded in front of the portals of the provincial legislature.

Oh dear, oh dear, what sights were these? The usual collection of marching cadets displayed the splendid hodgepodge of races that are such a feature of the Armed Forces cadet program today.

Marching expertise and élan, however, continues to elude them, which to my mind speaks well of their program and of Canada. There was a high-school pipe band, and the sound of the pipes still goes down well almost anywhere in Canada. And then there were the marching Loyalists and representatives of Canadian monarchical societies, either in blazers or in period costumes.

As these clowns went by, my venerable father-in-law turned around and looked up at us. His eyes were wide and his wonderful smile as broad as it could be. "Is this what's left of the Queen's guard?" he asked. We said nothing. Nothing needed to be said.

Pulling up the rear was a large van hauling the final ghastly float. God only knows what had preceded it. The theme here was "Canada's kings and queens," and there was token tribute made to Louis XIV and XV of French-ruled Canada before the gouty Georges of the House of Hanover spread their triple chins up against the trim beards or clean-cut jaw lines of the House of Windsor Georges. Cardboard cutout images of all these monarchs were affixed to the float: Louis XIV, Louis XV, George II, George III, George IV, William IV, Victoria the Only, Edward VII, George V, Edward VIII, George VI, and Elizabeth II. The only trouble was that all but five had been flattened by the wind, and a pretty perverse republican breeze at that because four of those that remained upright were the worst of the lot: Louis XV, George IV, William IV, and Edward VIII.

Queen Victoria alone withstood the May wind to represent the monarchs who gave more than they got. In truth, there might have been no monarchy at all had not she ascended to the throne in 1837 after so many years of the ancient institution being regarded as something of a pestilence. And she was no Tudor

Elizabeth, as serene in the confidence of her own ability to master the art of governance as she was in her God-given right to rule. Victoria and the monarchy survived largely because an outsider – Albert, the loving consort – was an underrated genius who understood not only that traditional monarchy was a spent force but that the mystical monarchy could be revived and hitched to the notion of a constitutional head of state.

Albert didn't give two figs for Canada either, but his good work assisted this country in concocting a constitutional framework that, for all the fractiousness it embraces, has held the country together for nearly a century and a half. Or maybe you thought Sir John A. Macdonald and all the Fathers of Confederation did it by themselves.

III

The first trip Elizabeth took to Canada was in 1951. As a beautiful princess of the "blood royal" and the heiress-presumptive to the throne, she was bound to have an ecstatic welcome in those days. Her parents, King George VI and Queen Elizabeth (now the Queen Mother), had made the first visit to Canada by reigning monarchs in 1939 and it was one of the most memorable moments in Canadian history. People still alive today who saw the royal couple in their own cities and towns have indelible memories tied to all sorts of bizarre places because that is where they caught a glimpse of the stuttering, unconfident man who never expected to be king and his wife, the Queen Consort, who rewrote the textbook on royal spouses until Diana came to transform the role into an upmarket soap opera.

I had a dear old friend in Toronto who told me she never went into the Ontario Liquor Control Board premises at Summerhill Avenue – once a midtown train station whose now-faceless clock tower still stands – without a skip in her heart because that was where she first saw the shy but smiling face of King George VI. And he looked straight into her eyes, of that she was convinced until the day she died. It was a nice mixture of heightened nostalgia and reality since once her memory passed, presumably, she would continue with the business at hand, which was usually the purchase of rye, but occasionally gin.

The children of the King and Queen, the princesses Elizabeth and Margaret Rose, were in their day the most famous sisters in the world. George and Elizabeth inculcated in their solemn eldest daughter notions of service and duty that she still personifies today, whether the world still gives such notions any regard. The rigorous seriousness of her commitment to reign honourably but not to rule arbitrarily was not so evident in 1951. She had married the handsome and arrogant Philip only a couple of years earlier, and the conventions of the court were much more hidebound than they are today. The trip to Canada – a classic grand tour that foreshadowed many subsequent trips to her diminishing realms across the seas – was a wild success after a slow start (the first demands that she smile more often in public occurred on this journey and came not from the deferential Canadians – but – typically and ominously – from the capricious British press).

A picture from the tour of a square dance in Calgary in which Elizabeth is looking adoringly into Philip's eyes as they do-si-do each other is usually trotted out in any collection of images from her life. As much as you can tell from a photograph, she looked very happy. If so, I'm sure it was the last time she was "happy" here. How on earth could anyone be "happy" touring such an uncertain and often spiteful place that took increasingly less interest in its history and institutions? Certainly, very few commentators gave her any credit for her quiet, dutiful efforts to retain the grace notes of civility in our exhausting struggle with an imperfect constitution.

Although it is hard to believe that she would harbour any real affection for Canada, the Queen does appear to have some bemused fondness for our fractured selves. This is gauged from the usual questionable journalistic sources – the inevitable assumptions that are made in royal coverage, a bit of direct conversation at official functions, and small clues here and there (a wry smile at the absurdity of some of the things she is made to do, such as touring the Purity Biscuit factory in St. John's, Newfoundland; her matter-of-fact tolerance of Margaret Trudeau's flakiness right up to the last second Pierre Trudeau was in high office; an undeniable exuberance in the high Arctic).

When Jean Chrétien turned up at Buckingham Palace that time and the Queen said, "Not you again!" Chrétien reported that she was smiling. I've seen that smile, a fetching, ironic smile that seems to be both wearied and forgiving. I was on that trip with Chrétien, reporting for *The Globe and Mail*, and I believe the "you" then was not so much directed at *le p'tit gars* from Shawinigan, of whom she is apparently more fond than any of her previous Canadian prime ministers. No, it was directed through him to all of us. "Not you again!" *Yes, us again and again, and this time we've really fucked it up, Ma'am, because we couldn't get Quebec to agree, but we want you to sign it anyway and make it legal.*

And she signed it, although I expect she put the gears to the government for failing to include the most important of the original partners of Confederation in the new arrangements. She would not, however, have been so graceless as to point out that what was already in place was infinitely preferable to this new and aberrant creation, since what already existed included Quebec by Quebec's own signature. Nor would she have bothered to point out that, if permitted, she was prepared to stick around and help clean up the mess the new constitution created long after Trudeau had quit the scene.

None of this, I realize, is the stuff of high emotion and never could or will be. The closest Elizabeth ever came to expressing precisely her regard for the country was in the late 1980s in the midst of one more of our publicly embarrassing constitutional contretemps: the political rhetoric was unusually charged at the time, the federal government seemed impotent in the face of regional intransigence, and the breakup of the country looked imminent. It was on this occasion that she announced that she was not just "a fair-weather friend" and through the means of this little-understood cliché she implied that she, and the neglected institution she personified, was at Canada's disposal.

Also implicit was the quaint notion that a sovereign of Canada – which has existed in one form or another since the French explorers first laid claim to the land of the aboriginals – was a concept that still worked, still marked us off as different sort of North Americans from the citizens of Mexico and the United States, and still might not be an insignificant means to deflect the vicissitudes of our unending conflicts. Our incoherence as a nation, it seems to me, has miraculously preserved the monarchy because we cannot agree how to eliminate it or what to replace it with. If we were wise enough to see past colonial hangups and other banalities and into a postmodern Canada, we might start embracing the usefulness of this remarkable institution. If we were subtle enough to understand how lucky we are to have it, that is. And if we were clever enough to know that you can use the phrase "postmodern" just as conveniently as "reconstituted monarchy" provided that it is useful and works!

It is not at all clear if we are wise or subtle or even a bit clever, alas. When have we ever properly thanked her for her steadfastness? We don't know how. It's not that it would be embarrassing. We don't even think about it. I'm not so sure more than a handful of people under fifty were even listening to that speech. Yet here is this curiosity: because it functions blamelessly as a symbol above the fray, the Crown in Canada has been largely non-controversial over the past quarter-century. To a considerable extent it has been domesticated through the offices of the Governor General and the lieutenant-governors and since most of these appointments are now political rather than from the ranks of exemplary Canadians, they are not even thought of as "the Crown" (one only has to contrast the transparent nobility of George Vanier against the pleasant but inconsequential Ed Schreyer or Romeo LeBlanc to see the distance we have travelled in vice regality).

Yet many Canadians are only discovering in 1999 and 2000 just how potent the governor generalship can be with the appointment of Adrienne Clarkson to Rideau Hall, the first sign in decades that a Canadian prime minister had an inkling of how to rejuvenate this historic post. Prior to that, the only contrasting concept of monarchy available was when Diana surfaced on the international consciousness – surfaced, glowed, glowered, and then exploded. The hagiography of Diana is crucial to an understanding of the nature and the future of the monarchy, because the degree of admiration and identification felt for the "people's princess" in Canada – which so far as we know she didn't give two figs about – was remarkable. It has only two precedents: Edward VIII during the period he was an adult Prince of Wales (roughly from the First World War to his abdication in 1936), and – surprisingly enough from the vantage point of our contemporary ignorance – Queen Victoria, who I daresay cared even less for our more delicate sensitivities.

IV

In Professor Donald Creighton's seminal study of our early years of nationhood, *Canada's First Century*, there is not one single indexed reference to Queen Victoria. Creighton doesn't even bother to trot out the only vaguely known act of direct intervention – pointing, mid-century, her pudgy finger on a map to Bytown, Ottawa-to-be, on the border of old Canada West and Canada East to try to locate a compromise capital for the proposed new experiment in federation in 1867. She's to blame for Ottawa! An anti-monarchist could conceivably rest his case right here, but, one suspects, Professor Creighton wasn't much of a jokester.

When, in 1994, the *Dictionary of Canadian Biography* published Volume XIII, which dealt with eminent Canadians who died between the years of 1901 and 1910, there was no biography of the old Queen. The rule, apparently, to make it into the dictionary is that you have to have actually stepped foot on the land. In other words, even if you are the head of state of Canada, you don't make it into the game unless you actually came here. And why should she be there, many will ask in agreement. I'll tell you why. Because if you look in the index for this and many of the previous volumes, the most cited name is "Victoria, Queen of Great Britain and Ireland," and it is a scandal that a special Canadian biography was not commissioned for Volume XIII. Even a brief article would have painted a different picture of the monarch than prevails in any other country over which her name held sway. Her relations with the first seven Canadian prime ministers alone would surely justify a separate biography, but there was also all the richness of her views on vice-regal appointments, especially when one was her difficult son-in-law, the Marquess of Lorne.

So, it came to pass that in the otherwise excellent *Dictionary of Canadian Biography* a decision was made not to include biographies of this crucial sovereign of Canada. We can read about Sir Joseph-Philippe-René-Adolphe Caron, who was knighted by Victoria. We can see numerous references to the first Baron Shaughnessy, whose path to ennoblement began in Victoria's reign. There is Louis Riel, who was hanged in her name, and also Sir John Thompson, who practically died in Victoria's arms at Windsor Castle, where he had gone to "kiss hands" upon succeeding Sir John A. Macdonald to become Canada's third (and very short-lived) prime minister. You can read about people who settled in Victoria or Regina or Jubilee or Prince Albert and not have a clue where these strange names came from, or why. You can also read about three winners of the Victoria Cross, the highest award for bravery for most of Canada's history, but you cannot read a specific biography of the woman who was responsible for all of this, or in whose name decisions and awards were taken and given.

My favourite entry in Volume XIII is that of Richard Rowland Thompson, who was born in Ireland and died in Buffalo, New York. Immigrating – briefly – as a kind of remittance man to Canada after a desultory schooling at the end of the nineteenth century, he twiddled his thumbs for a few months until the Boer War mercifully beckoned and where he proved himself to be a man of uncommon bravery. He was recommended for the Victoria Cross, which he didn't in the end receive, but he liked what he saw of South Africa so much that he even went back there after the war to work for the local constabulary and after that in security work for De Beers Consolidated Mines (where, if we were to learn anything of his responsibilities, I expect we would be appalled). There is only one reason this otherwise forgettable little man has made it into the dictionary. His singular acts of courage in the Boer War (amongst other deeds, he crossed "200 yards of bullet-swept ground to reach a wounded soldier") brought him to the attention of his sovereign, who gave him one of four scarves she designed and knitted for the four bravest soldiers in her overseas dominions and colonies. Thompson was the only soldier from Canada to receive one. Although officially it didn't rank as high as the Victoria Cross, sentiment and the fact that there were only four placed it much higher. So, thanks to this scarf, Thompson makes it into our most important history books, but the royal knitter remains excluded.

In the Creighton book, there are numerous references in Canada's first century to the "Victorian era" and "Victorian decorum" and even "Victorian imperial politics," but She who gave her name to the era makes nary an appearance. Since the book covers our first century after Confederation, it goes up to 1967, but the only sovereigns actually mentioned are the two Georges, V and VI, and then only to note that such-and-such a prime minister trotted off to London to attend their coronations. In the inevitable telescoping such a popular history entails, Creighton decided, wittingly or unwittingly, that the Crown was largely irrelevant. I suppose that it is also remotely conceivable that he thought the monarchy was so obviously indispensable that he didn't even think of referencing it. Somehow, I doubt it.

Now contrast this familiar neglect – Creighton joins a mighty throng of national historians in largely dismissing the pertinence of the sovereign to Canadian affairs – with Wilfrid Laurier's comments in Parliament on the passing of the old Queen in 1901, five years after he assumed the premiership of the Dominion of Canada and she had been well launched into the seventh decade of her reign:

> She is now no more. *No more?* Nay, I boldly say she lives in the hearts of her subjects; lives in the pages of history. And as the ages revolve, as her pure profile stands more marked against the horizon of time, the verdict of posterity will ratify the judgment of those who were her subjects. She ennobled mankind; she exalted royalty. The world is better for her life.

Even if you dismiss some of the language here as part of the extravagance of the era and of Laurier's own romanticism, you can still detect the same sort of identification that so many of us made with Diana when she was killed in Paris. Unless we accept that identification amongst so many English Canadians and a fair number of French Canadians, I don't think the Victorian era in Canada can be comprehended.

It didn't matter that Victoria rarely bothered herself with Canadian affairs. She was the symbolic ideal, and the farther away her subjects were from the reality of the nineteenth-century monarchy and the specifics of the lonely old widow in Balmoral, the more fervent was the identification. This is not so surprising. Didn't we learn endless sordid little details of the wretched Dodi Fayed's life only to have it embellish our sense of Diana's loneliness in reaching out to someone so unworthy of her love? Diana may have gone in and out of favour with the tastemakers and other cognoscenti, but as we now know after her death that fickle approbation simply skimmed along the surface of the deeply felt and strongly held affection she aroused worldwide.

So it also was with Victoria. Her subjects knew that she had become something of a grumpy recluse, that she'd gone to fat, that she was a stern mother, and so on. At several junctures in her reign, her advisers warned her about arousing republican sentiments through avoidance of "public responsibilities." But out on the streets, with merely a few flicks of the wrist in her ridiculously tiny carriage, she put paid to all the sententious theorizing and other drivel of her day. People, it turns out, really do connect to symbolic leadership that balances pomp with practicality, liturgy with action, formality with controlled familiarity. Even polar opposites in personality such as Victoria and Diana both came to understand that the longing of ordinary people to identify with them was the strongest single source of their power and mystique.

The only contemporary Canadian history I have read that has any real sense of how central the figure of Victoria was to

Canadian affairs and Canadian lives is Sandra Gwyn's *The Private Capital: Ambition and Love in the Age of Macdonald and Laurier.* That's because Gwyn puts such useful and intelligent reliance on the practical documents of the age: newspaper and magazine articles, diaries, records of parliamentary debates, and correspondence. In all of these sources, Victoria – either personally or as sovereign – looms larger than life because her personal qualities were always mixed up with her symbolic roles ("Mother of the Empire," "Protectress of the Red Indians," "Defender of the Faith," and so on.) If contemporary historians write Victoria out of the Canadian story by minimizing her role, they undermine their own profession. They also have to take some responsibility for the sense of dislocation and lack of connection Canadians "feel" about their past. Victoria's role as a remote, supreme figure in the Empire has a direct parallel in Elizabeth's restrained and distanced role of today. This is repugnant to some people who want to feel emotionally closer to their heads of state. To such folk, I recommend bonding with President Clinton, either standing upright or on their knees.

V

The parallels between the lives of Diana and Edward VIII, who, shorn of his crown in the 1936 abdication crisis, ruled a few ranch acres in Western Canada and a suburban hidey-hole in Paris as the lacklustre Duke of Windsor, are instructive. In his young manhood, he was thought to be the definition of hand-someness. People could not get enough of his pictures: profile, full face, from a distance, closeup, in and out of uniform, in evening dress and in swimsuits. He was what men wanted to be and whom women wanted to be with. He did not have to purchase this fevered esteem. His good looks were luck, but the rest came with his position and was fuelled by people's own fevered imaginations.

So it was with Diana. Given the different eras and the wildly different access to personal information, they still seem to share remarkably similar stars except that Edward was unlucky enough to live on. Their choice of unworthy mates is almost melodramatically obvious, but so was the contrast people felt existed between their free and honest expression and the uptight, protocol-bound court they were both fighting to escape. We know now that Edward didn't have the heart to be a king, and I suspect that Diana – her husband's sexual betrayal overwhelming her thoughts – eventually didn't want to be a queen. They both understood the power of gesture, and the media caught on to both their fairly obvious games quickly. The big difference, as I said, was that she had the wit to die young and extravagantly, while he simply went on and on and on. Diana never actually married silly Dodi, while Edward obliged himself after the abdication to marry bitchy Wallis. He allowed his idolaters to see all the tarnish while all Diana's surfaces remained highly buffed. Had she lived, I'm sure she would have dwindled into a sad, superfluous figure such as the Duke of Windsor or Margaret Trudeau. Instead, there is talk of *beatification*! She has a nasty brother to attend to all that, and in the meantime we are left to deal with the ex-husband who cheated on her: the would-be king, and a would-be king of Canada.

Charles III-to-be, it would seem, is his own interesting mixture, in his case of the fuzzy-headed Duke of Windsor and Charles's own dutiful mama. This does not necessarily mean he will be a bad king. Just the opposite. The fuzziness makes him seem more human than Elizabeth. I expect that many of the things people deride him for now – his "loony views" on architecture and farming, his affection for "holistic" solutions to everything from disease to inner-city poverty – will come back as great examples of his humanity.

Consider another interesting parallel, this one between Charles and his great-great grandfather, Edward VII. The two men even seem to have a genetic attachment to similar mistresses (Camilla Parker Bowles is a descendant of one of Edward's mistresses). There were many people convinced Edward VII would be a disaster as king. He had even been hauled into "the common courts" (actually, the Queen's Court) after an ugly society brawl. His personal habits were a source of vast concern amongst the more Protestant clergy of the established Church of England. He had to wait so long for the throne that people thought they were sick and tired of him and there was even talk (not much, but some) in the letter columns of the popular press of bypassing Edward for the newly emerging star of the Royal Family, Prince George (later George V). Yet Edward ruled well and is cited with dramatically improving the atmosphere between England and France, thus assisting in the signing of the famous Entente Cordiale after a royal visit to Paris. Like William Congreve's character Millamant in *The Way of the World*, people came to love him not only in spite of his foibles, but precisely for his foibles.

VI

Personal encounters with royalty are usually brief and, to the non-royal, invariably memorable, however banal the words or comical the situation (or comical the words and banal the situation). I first cast my eyes directly on the Queen in 1959 when my father spent a working summer in England and brought the family along. I was about to turn fifteen and my mother had brought me to stand outside the gates of Buckingham Palace to see the changing of the guard. A few minutes before the soldiers started marching down The Mall, one of the palace's side gates mysteriously opened by itself and out cruised an ancient black Daimler, complete with running boards, followed by another vehicle. There was a royal coat of arms emblazoned on a small shield just atop the spine of the Daimler's front windshield.

Inside was Herself and a woman I didn't recognize, presumably a lady-in-waiting. As the car turned a sharp left outside this north gate and headed in the direction of West Kensington, she looked directly into my eyes. *I swear it!* For 1.3 seconds. Right into my adolescent eyes. That was enough to hold me tight in the royalist camp for quite a few years, although in truth there was no need to be defensive about admiring the royal family in those days, especially since her newly appointed representative in Canada was the hero of my life, Governor General Georges Vanier.

Looking back on 1959, it still seems to me the apogee of the peaceable kingdom of Canada. Our never-ending linguistic wars were in a state of happy suspension and the Quiet Revolution was still a year or so away. John George Diefenbaker did not seem quite so mad as he later did, and mighty national projects, such as the building of the St. Lawrence Seaway, were still part of the Canadian story. And in General Vanier we had, without realizing it, a brilliant solution for a head of state: a heroic, selfless, and noble model figure who may have been the most perfect Canadian since Sir Wilfrid Laurier, representing a semi-mythical monarch across the seas. Uniting the two was a symbol – the Crown – whose cipher floated inconspicuously and freely above the courts, the post office, all provincial and federal legislation, immigration documents validating new Canadians, and death certificates burying old ones. The Crown then seemed totally benign: unhectoring, unobtrusive, hardly jingoistic, discreet, dignified, historic, romantic, practical, and – above all – *different* from anything else in North or South America. As for the saintly Georges Vanier, he went about his often tedious and humdrum duties with a majestic modesty that made you understand how potent symbolic leadership could be. And the semi-mythical creature in Buckingham Palace was somehow part of our story too, as a constitutional duenna to the formalistic and dull of mind, and as an imagined godmother to fanciful fourteen-year-olds. Plus this: she never stayed too long.

The semi-mythical status of the sovereign is mostly gone, of course, except for a few diehards like me. It was destroyed as much by constitutional revisionism and murkiness as by Prince Charles's cellphone call and the brutal onslaught of privacy-invading journalism. Notions of deference became increasingly repugnant, even to some Tory historians. And then, in the process of "Canadianizing" the office of governor general, successive prime ministers – perhaps resentful of the vast repository of integrity represented by Vincent Massey and Georges Vanier – started dipping into their poisonous patronage files and matter-of-factly handed the office to second-rate politicians. Thus did the occupants of Rideau Hall, who once ennobled public service and allowed politicians to function as politicians rather than as jumped-up, self-styled "public figures," dwindle into faceless time-servers (Ed Schreyer and Ray What's-his-name) or arrogant boobies (Jeanne, Duchess of Sauvé) or pleasant has-beens (the exhausted recent occupant, Romeo LeBlanc). Adrienne Clarkson looms as the most significant – and hopeful – break in this dreary parade, but as I write in the waning hours of 1999, it is still early days for her.

Schreyer holds a special place in this dreary pantheon. When he was appointed Governor General by Prime Minister Trudeau, he so clearly misunderstood the role and opportunity he had been handed, he joked with the press that instead of twiddling his thumbs, he planned to start reading the *Encyclopedia Britannica*. Implicit in his joke was not only contempt for the post he had just accepted but also a somewhat aggrandized view of his own reading skills. Among those who had tried to converse seriously with him, there was some doubt that he could get much beyond "aardvark."

A personal encounter with Mr. Ed or Ray What's-his-name was about as memorable as a meeting with the president of the Elks Club. But a meeting with royalty, as I said, was always fraught with a strong sense of history and the clash between myth and human reality. I am here dancing around a memorable moment in my own life that still causes me to wince in embarrassment. It's worth recounting simply because it shows how silly and unnatural – or too natural! – people can be in front of royalty and how forbearing the human beings who must play royal roles can be.

It was Centennial Year, 1967, and I was still an undergraduate student at Memorial University of Newfoundland in St. John's when the Queen Mother came to town aboard the royal yacht HMS *Britannia*. I learned early on during my four years in "Britain's Oldest Colony and Canada's Youngest Province" that Newfoundland was an exceptionally interesting spot to be in if you wanted to get the measure of the world. The butt of all those stupid Newfie jokes, poor by national standards, stuck out in the middle of the North Atlantic, a half-hour out of sync with the rest of North America: these sorts of things helped buttress, rather than hinder, the most distinctive English-speaking culture in North America.

There certainly was an undeniably Ruritanian quality to official life in St. John's in those days, however. Possibly it was all due to scale. I was a student journalist at the St. John's *Evening Telegram*, for example, who somehow got translated into a royal reporter. At the time, I was going out with a girl whose father was a minister in Joey Smallwood's Liberal cabinet and had "Honourable" stuck in front of his name. After *Britannia* sailed through the famous St. John's Narrows and the band of the Royal Marines on board played jaunty martial tunes, girlfriend, reporter, and cabinet minister all got wildly elevated for few days.

An embossed invitation to attend upon "Her Majesty Queen Elizabeth the Queen Mother" at a reception aboard *Britannia* for the provincial cabinet members and their spouses was about the most precious thing I had received since the coronation coin of

1953. The card was extra stiff and the embossed coat of arms was ... well, as you would expect, regal. I still have it carefully retained inside my set of *The Books of Newfoundland* (Vols. III & IV, edited with an introduction by the Honourable Joseph R. Smallwood, former premier of Newfoundland and Labrador, *soi-disant* "Father of Confederation," and possibly the biggest BSer of his era).

What a lucky day for the Queen Mum: she was going to get Joey, my girlfriend's papa, me, and – as it turned out – my girlfriend too, subbing for her ailing mother. There was only one small problem. The girlfriend and I had broken up acrimoniously the day before when she informed me that we were no longer a couple. She was about to announce her upcoming marriage to her real boy-friend, she said, who had been away at Dalhousie University during the two years we had gone out. That's when I discovered she had maintained the relationship all the time she'd been going out with me. Conveniently, when I went home to Toronto at Christmas, he would make his only visit of the year to St. John's. I never knew – or questioned – why she went so often to Halifax to see "her best friend." *Bitter memories!* I think my last comment to her, as I went down her front steps, was, "Well, T., I'm sure we'll all give you the benefit of the doubt for the first few months." Writing it out now, I regret having said it, but at the time – as I soon discovered – I had made a palpable hit. She was several months pregnant, and not by me, but when I found out it gave me no satisfaction, only additional pain.

Twenty hours after she hurled a telephone book at me for that comment, we found ourselves side by side at a railing aboard *Britannia* about ten feet from the Queen Mother. When I first caught sight of T. coming aboard with her father, I worked very hard to stay on the opposite side of the deck. That way I could try to ignore her irritating presence and savour the moment. The sun was going down brilliantly in the west, the harbour and city looked serene, *Britannia* gleamed as she floated on the dark-green water, officers of the Royal Navy in attendance were wearing their crisp dress whites, the band was playing Broadway show tunes, waiters with small silver trays brought drinks in crystal glasses and delicious tiny canapés, and from this privileged position on a perfect late afternoon it was not hard to believe that this was the best of all possible worlds at the best of all times, *tra la, tra la, tra la.*

I stepped back to turn around and look again over the ship's railing and there she was, right beside me as I inadvertently managed to step on her toe.

"Watch it," she said sharply.

"You watch it," I retorted.

"You watch it yourself," she snapped back.

It was at this precise moment that an equerry approached us and said the Queen Mother wanted to talk to "some young people." Behind him was a naval rating carrying a tray of fresh drinks. Like obedient children, we deposited our old glasses, picked up new ones and trotted along behind the equerry – carefully tracking each other out of the malevolent corners of our eyes – towards the centre of the deck where Herself was holding court.

Introductions were made and within seconds I realized I was talking too much, which I do often and twice as much when I'm nervous. I was in such a high babble I even heard myself solemnly referring to her husband, King George VI, as "His Late Majesty." I didn't learn that at school. I have no idea where it came from or what induced me to start talking like a fool. Was I a court recorder to King Richard III in a previous life? We may never know. In any event, my ex-girlfriend mercifully took over the conversation:

"I don't remember your last visit to Newfoundland, Your Majesty," she said, all shy and blonde and gorgeous and coquettish and duplicitous and utterly, utterly hateful.

"But how could you, my dear," said the Queen Mother kindly. "You would have been far too young. It was 1939, after all."

"So young, Ma'am," I chimed in helpfully, "that she wasn't born for another eight years."

The moment I said it, I knew it was a mistake.

"Excuse me, John," the ex said with menace in her every syllable. "Daddy took a lot of film of the visit . . ."

"Oh well then, I suppose that makes you an expert on the subject."

"Why don't you just get over it and leave me alone," she said, her eyes welling up.

"I'm sorry. I've never made a habit of just walking away from people."

Quietly and sweetly, the forgotten Third Personage in this little group, eyes twinkling with both concern and benign amusement, intervened:

"Children, children, this will all pass, believe me." She turned to me. "Tell me about your work. You seem very young to be holding down such a responsible job. . . ."

Me oh my! *Young indeed.* It still hurts to tell this tale, but the vivid memory of this warm, understanding grandmother compensates hugely.

VII

I n addition to nonsense like this, there is also such a thing as collective silliness of which the finest example I ever experienced came a year after that absurd rendezvous with the Queen Mother. After the death of General Vanier, in office, during the centennial year, Prime Minister Pearson appointed Roland Michener as the Queen's representative in Rideau Hall, and thus the former Speaker of the House of Commons and High Commissioner to India became our third Canadian-born governor general. The "deference" problem reared its head immediately, as Michener was married to the intellectually complicated and socially stuffy Norah Michener, whom the redoubtable Marion Pearson, wife of the prime minister, loathed. Shortly before the announcement, or shortly after (journalists don't really know everything), Mrs. Pearson told her husband she would never curtsy to Mrs. Michener, as custom prescribed, and Mr. Pearson – knowing only too well who ruled the domestic roost – so informed the nation. That was only the first shock for poor Mrs. Michener. The next was that her first big foray with His Excellency to the hinterland would be a tour of Newfoundland and Labrador.

Those of a sardonic, suspicious nature in St. John's simply assumed that Joey Smallwood's fiefdom had been chosen so that the Micheners could make all their beginners' faux pas unobserved by anyone who mattered. Whatever. I had already established my credentials as a peerless reporter of royalty the previous summer, so

vice-regality would be a snap and this tour was to include a cir-
cumnavigation of the island in a Canadian destroyer. Here was an
unequalled opportunity to see a lot more of the most exciting, surprising, and warm-hearted province in the country before I
departed to graduate school in England. I had fallen headlong in
love with Newfoundland three years before, so it seemed a wonderful assignment.

While lacking the noblesse of the Vaniers, the Micheners were
nevertheless an appropriately dignified couple, even if at this early
stage of the game they were a little unprepared for the curious
mixture of circus and circumstance, pomp and happenstance, that
crowd the official day of a vice-regal office-holder. By the time we
had made it up the eastern coast of the island to Twillingate on
New World Island, it was beginning to dawn on Mrs. Michener
that the unexpected was as likely – if not more likely – to happen
as not. The whole town had assembled to greet the Governor
General and his lady. Our party had arrived in some state on a
Canadian naval destroyer and it required a helicopter to fly us from
ship to shore, shore being an open field a mile or so outside the
town. Here was assembled a remarkable local cavalcade of "pre-
sentable" automobiles, led by a venerable and largely dilapidated
Chevrolet Bel Air convertible (circa 1954 or 1955) that was to
ferry Mr. and Mrs. Michener to the town centre.

As Mrs. Michener looked on in some dismay at her rusty con-
veyance, Esmond Butler, the official secretary to the Governor
General and chief bureaucrat at Rideau Hall, walked briskly over
to the driver and spoke a few words that left the man beaming.
Whatever it was that Butler said, I suspect the driver briefly joined
those many Canadians who thought the affable but always formal
Butler was the governor general and the other chap merely the

hired help (or in Michener's case, in the wicked words of Mordecai Richler, "the *maître d'* of the Palm Court Lounge"). From inside his attaché case Butler removed a small vice-regal flag standard attached to a metal mantle. He licked the suction cup at the base and slammed it down authoritatively on the hood of the Chevrolet. A piece of chrome trim on the side of the car immediately fell off from the impact.

"This is the coach, Your Excellency," he said to Mrs. Michener, who was still looking aghast as local fishermen crowded to get a closer look at the swells from the mainland. "And our driver assures me he knows how to keep out of all the potholes."

"All right, Esmond," said Mrs. Michener, "if you think it's safe."

Within a few minutes, the makeshift cavalcade had approached the town centre, where everyone was assembled. A loud public-address system was delivering a jaunty air that Butler, with his impeccable ability to anticipate problems, immediately noticed and recognized as the middle bars of "Marseillaise."

"Hmmm," he said, quickly scanning the order of the greeting ceremony. It called for the playing of the first half of the royal anthem the moment the Governor General alighted from his car. "This could prove interesting."

By the time the cavalcade had come to a full stop, the tune had shifted to "The Star-Spangled Banner," and it was clear the PA system was hooked up to a recording of national anthems from around the world. The mayor of Twillingate approached the Chevrolet. Mr. Michener got out. There was a terrific introductory drum roll over the PA system. Everyone stood to attention waiting for the familiar opening strains of "God Save the Queen" – everyone except Butler, that is, who had quietly moved behind the Governor General. When instead of "The

Queen" the assembled throng was treated to a particularly mili-
taristic version of "Deutschland, Deutschland über Alles," Butler
turned without a twitch to the mayor of Twillingate and said,
"What a fine day you have provided for Their Excellencies, Mayor
Manuel. Why don't we go and inspect the school first? We can do
the national anthems later, if you like."

"Excellent idea, Esmond," said the Governor General, turning
to Mrs. Michener, who was still fingering her program in utter
perplexity. "Come, my dear, we're going to the school now." A
loud scratch came from the loudspeakers and suddenly the dying
strains of "O Canada" could be heard.

Mayor Manuel smiled tightly in grim relief and prepared to
move off with the vice-regal party, but not before turning to a colleague and saying in a loud whisper, "We're going into the school.
Why don't you go over to Harold and pull his thumbnails out for
me?" Harold, I subsequently learned, was the Twillingate town
councillor who had not only secured the recording but was also
manning the PA system.

Despite her institutional tetchiness – there were times when
she could make the archly sardonic Mrs. Pearson seem like Sweet
Sister Sue – my heart occasionally went out to Mrs. Michener, as
we had bonded under unusual circumstances on this trip. It began
earlier in the week with an impromptu organ recital when she was
paying a visit to the Newfoundland (Anglican) Cathedral of Saint
John the Divine. The cathedral was also my own parish church
and the subdean and rector, seeing me in Mrs. Michener's
company, pointed out to her that her "reporter" sometimes played
the pipe organ.

So I played for her, silently cursing the subdean in his own
cathedral. She professed to enjoy it, which was flattering, and

every time we hit a church for the next ten days I was automatically obliged to play something. In Trinity on Conception Bay, we even got the Governor General himself to pump an old wheeze-box. So we bonded, the governor's lady and I, but not enough, alas, to prevent my enthusiastic and immature participation in the subsequent game of Sightings that diverted me, a Canadian press reporter and photographer, and a magazine writer from the Mainland, during the long and often tedious vice-regal tour of Newfoundland.

When I say tedious, I mean tedious. So also are royal tours. The visits are not in any way tedious to the people and communities honoured by a visit; they are only tedious to the reporters who have to cover such highlights as a tea party at an Orange Lodge clubhouse-cum-tourist information centre, or a tour of a fish plant, or the planting of a tree in Bowering Park, or the unveiling of a parking-lot plaque at the Grenfell Mission Hospital in St. Anthony, and so on. And no doubt they are especially tedious for the Royals themselves. Nevertheless, an enormous amount of effort has always gone in to the tours and events the Queen or the Governor General attends. Their presence is often the glorious culmination of years of fund-raising, community organization, and major service commitment. The visit brings honour and dignity to quiet but substantial achievement and volunteer efforts. The pride of accomplishment the local community takes in a royal or vice-regal visit is hard to quantify or otherwise describe in a news story, which is why you seldom read about them, but it is real nevertheless. The tedium is relevant only to the little court of fellow-travellers on the tour, and the comical snafus and sardonic jokes are the small rewards for keeping the show going.

Usually, the sardonic element isn't as subversive as our little game of Sightings. The tour of Newfoundland began with three days in St. John's followed by eight days aboard the destroyer touring the Newfoundland coast and stopping at over a dozen communities, with a dramatic side trip to Labrador. Before the morning of the second day was over, the journalists covering the tour realized that Mrs. Michener must have a condition, as they say, which required her to make discreet visits to every washroom that loomed on the horizon. On the second morning, when the vice-regal cavalcade made an unscheduled stop at a gas station en route to Mt. Pearl (a St. John's suburb), the idea of Sightings began to form. We did not speculate too much on poor Mrs. Michener's problems beyond supposing she had a weak bladder.

Any game must have rules, so each morning of the tour just before the beginning of the official day, the four accompanying journalists would sneakily assemble to put five dollars each into an envelope along with his guess of how many times we would catch sight of Mrs. Michener either entering or leaving a washroom. This was a "sighting." The sport of the game was that every sighting had to have two witnesses, so that if you alone saw her and the lady-in-waiting entering the washroom at Mack's Chicken Villa in Placentia, for example, you then had to scurry to find a colleague to witness the exiting. That observed visit thus became an official sighting. At the end of the day, all the sightings were totalled up and the person whose guess at the beginning of the day came closest won the daily pot of twenty dollars.

It was a cruel game, of course, but in self-defence I would have to say it enlivened the trip enormously and Mrs. Michener had no idea what we were up to. In a strange way too, all the glee with which we partook in the game made us feel a trifle guilty, making us marginally more sympathetic to the vice-regal couple in that we realized what an extra health burden they had while stoically going about their duties. And Mrs. Michener needed our sympathy. She could be terrifically haughty. Once on the trip, I was sitting in quarters next to the captain's dining room where he and his senior officers were dining with Mr. and Mrs. Michener. Only a badly drawn curtain separated our two spaces. The tight circumstances did not in any way cramp Mrs. Michener's devotion to the strict protocol due her lofty station in life. At a certain juncture, the captain stood up to propose a toast to the Queen. To our eavesdropping astonishment, we heard Mrs. Michener bark at him, "Sit down. It's not for you to propose the loyal toast in His Excellency's presence." She was not a "people's princess," that's for sure, and her brutal hauteur assuaged a bit of the guilt we felt for our sightings.

At Twillingate, however, the business literally exploded and we made a collective decision to stop the shenanigans. Besides, by this time there was a danger that members of the vice-regal party were starting to catch on. The business of finding a witness occasionally got farcical and Mrs. Michener must have started to wonder what was afoot because each time she emerged from a washroom she seemed to be attended by graciously smiling journalists in pairs, threes, and – often enough – fours. I'm sure the lady-in waiting had caught on to something by Twillingate, so perhaps it was all for the best what subsequently happened.

Still, the remembered laughter at the end of the day, as each sighting was retold, makes me chuckle even as I write this. In Brigus, where Mrs. Michener and her lady-in-waiting suddenly departed from the unveiling of a plaque to the nearby Anglican church, we discovered that there were two exits from the priest's vestry room (with interior washroom) into which the ladies had retreated. This necessitated the full resources of two reporters on each station. At this point, we were already at a count of seven and this sighting, if confirmed, would make eight. Two of our group had bet eight sightings that morning, one had bet ten, but a fourth colleague had bet seven and was about to lose the day's takings.

Before Mrs. Michener and her lady-in-waiting emerged from whichever exit, the likely loser left his exterior post and scurried into the church and down the nave to the interior exit I and another were guarding.

"What are you doing here?" we hissed at him. "Get back to your post."

He had a worried look on his face.

"I think Mr. Michener has had some sort of heart attack," he said bleakly.

We bolted down the aisle. *How stupid we were!* Playing this ridiculous game when real news was just outside where we should have been all along. But when we arrived back at the plaque unveiling, there was the jaunty Governor General – an early morning exercise nut – chatting up the locals and looking in the pink of good health. We turned around in confusion to see our colleague come sauntering out of the church.

"I thought you said the Governor General had a heart attack?" one of us said.

"Well," said the crafty fourth with a hint of a smile, "perhaps it was just indigestion."

Behind him, we saw Mrs. Michener emerge from the church door, with her official smile – which could freeze-dry peas in seconds – pasted onto her face.

"I believe," said our insidiously clever colleague, "that the count is still seven."

The sport ended gruesomely in Twillingate and the incident is still painfully etched in my mind. Following all the shenanigans with the national anthems, the Micheners were deposited back into their Chevrolet limousine and driven back the short distance to the field where the helicopter was waiting for the official party to take us back to our ship. As we rounded a corner, there was suddenly the most enormous sequence of explosions. The lead car was the RCMP escort. Then the vice-regal Chevy, followed by an ancient sedan bearing the lady-in-waiting and Esmond Butler. Then us, the grinning Fourth Estate.

The explosions were courtesy of a half-dozen swoilers – fishermen in the summer, sealers in the winter – each holding giant blunderbusses that were, I was later told, sometimes used to break up ice so ships could pass to new quarry. Their somewhat drunken vice-regal salute had not been on the official program, as evidenced by the RCMP escort, which tumbled out of the lead car and was all over the uncomprehending swoilers. Once we realized this was a comical diversion, rather than an attempted assassination, we chuckled a little until we saw the poor Governor General signalling frantically from the back of the Chevy convertible to the lady-in-waiting in the car behind. Slowly, we realized the problem. The surprise explosions had had a debilitating effect on Mrs. Michener, whose lap had to be covered in a blanket so that onlookers would not see the embarrassing results.

Later that same evening, in solemn convocation, we four journalists agreed to end the game of Sightings, as it was now too cruel even for our tastes. However, at the juncture of the impromptu swoilers' salute, the count had been at five (the figure chosen by the CP photographer), while his colleague, the CP reporter, had chosen six. There was a rancorous debate about whether the untoward events inside the Chevy constituted a legitimate sighting. On one hand, there were four witnesses; on the other, there was the gruesomeness of it all. The business could not be resolved. Finally, ever the peacemaker (after inventing the game), I got them to agree to split the pot. So to speak.

VIII

I valued the invitation. What royalist wouldn't? My friend Thomas Symons, the founding president of Trent University in Peterborough, Ontario, and a long-time member of the board of the United World Colleges, wondered if I would like to travel from London down to Wales and meet the Prince Thereof while he attended to his duties at Atlantic College.

What a perfectly ripping way to spend the weekend, I almost but didn't quite think to myself. I had already been posted by *The Globe and Mail* to its dreamy European bureau based in the United Kingdom for a couple of years by the time the invitation came and following the desiccated titled classes in England was an amusing anthropological diversion. I had feuded briefly with Sir Peregrine Worsthorne of *The Daily Telegraph*, weekended with the Master of Polwarth and his father, Lord Polwarth, in the Borders area west of Edinburgh, and lunched at the House of Lords dining room with

Lord Longford (the Earl of Longford, to be exact, and the premier earl of England, or "Lord Porn" as the tabloids called him for his advocacy of anti-pornographic legislation). Still working my way up *Burke's Peerage* but in no particular order, I had also inadvertently stepped backwards onto the bunion-troubled toes of the Duke of Marlborough at a reception held at the Reform Club on Pall Mall. Why shouldn't I then spend the weekend with the good old Prince of Wales? As I said, "Ripping!"

Thus endeth the stereotypes. It is one of the anomalies of monarchy that much of the world assumes its members live their lives according to the fixations of our own imaginings, while the more complicated reality of everyday royal life seems almost inconceivable. Whether we admire the monarchy or not, we seem to want its members to follow some sort of ancient gilded ritual and live their lives somehow apart from anything we ourselves know. The reality is that members of the royal family pretty well live exactly as we would live if we were handed their circumstances. Or, to put it another way, had Prince Charles and Princess Diana somehow been plopped down in Scarborough or West Vancouver they would in all probability have been this nice youngish couple down the street who had somehow screwed up their marriage ("She was aimless and difficult, you know, and I think he'd been having a fling"). The people whose lives actually tend to resemble the ones we think the royals lead are the very, very rich, who are not weighed down by public responsibilities and the rigours of political correctness. I was to see this for the first time during that ripping weekend in Wales.

The United World Colleges are a collection of senior high schools scattered about the globe. Pearson College on Vancouver Island is the Canadian member. Atlantic College is in Wales, where

I was headed. There were also colleges in India and Africa and plans for others all over the place. The organizing idea nearly four decades ago was to bring "mature" teenagers from all parts of the Commonwealth together for a couple of years in a rigorous but rewarding program of physical and mental challenges. It was the brainchild of the Prince of Wales' uncle and godfather, Lord Mountbatten of Burma, who by the time I went to Wales had already been blown up and killed in his sailboat by members of the Irish Republican Army. In Prince Charles's mind, it was easy to see, the colleges had become a kind of trust for him to nurse along their way as a living memorial to his beloved uncle and mentor.

I took the train from London to the nearest large station to the college, rented a car, and drove the pleasant final half-hour of the way. It was a glorious day, with spring wildflowers glowing in the fields after a gentle early-morning rain. One field was so pretty I stopped and walked a little way in. Clouds of butterflies flew up with every step. Was I in Eden? Nope. Just rural Glamorganshire, but I was in a heightened mood – anticipation of meeting royalty, no doubt – so the butterflies seemed premonitory. I believed I had read somewhere that he talks to butterflies, or was it to tulips?

Of all the worthies attending upon the annual meeting of the United World Colleges, the Prince was not the first to arrive. A Rolls-Royce slowly drove up the cinder driveway making a pleasing crunch every inch of the way, a crunch that seemed redolent of Jacobean country houses, Georgian sterling tea services, Victorian decanters of pre-dinner sherry and late-night port, and shooting parties on Edwardian hunting estates. I was ensconced in a reception room having some tea with my friend Tom Symons as the crunching came to a halt outside the adjoining front door. There was immediately an organized commotion and fluttering of staff as the words "Yes, my Lord" and "Straight away, Sir" floated in from the outside. Bertie Wooster could have been peering over his *Times* in the next chair.

We were given no time to exchange courtesies with Lord Crunch, for following on his baronial heels was something I had never witnessed before: the arrival of a billionaire mogul worried about his safety. This was the late "Dr." Armand Hammer, the legendary Russian-born oil entrepreneur whose fortune was largely earned being a middleman between the thugs who ran the old Soviet Union and the ones who bought and sold from them in the West. The human species doesn't get much more reptilian than "Dr." Hammer, but he had given many dollars and pounds to Prince Charles's favourite causes in an effort to ingratiate himself and so he had become a board member of the United World Colleges.

If memory serves me right, he arrived in a procession of two Mercedes stretch limousines preceded by two sedans and a large, ominous dark van with tinted windows. Behind these vehicles and the limos were another two sedans. The entire cavalcade came to a stop several yards from the reception room entranceway where Tom and I were formerly ensconced. There was no pleasing crunch, just the sound of low, rumbling motors and inchoate orders belched out from somewhere. Tom and I were up now and took all this in through a window as we gulped the dregs of our tea. Two big men got out of the lead car and came towards the reception area. When they came in, they saw us, nodded and paid us no further heed. I had never met them before, but they seemed to know exactly who Tom and I were. They then separated briefly, one checking out the adjoining room and the other going through a two-way door that led to a pantry servery. A third man came in and soon began mumbling to the one who had been in the servery. The other returned and a huddle by all three ensued. Being a journalist, of course, I wanted to be in the scrum, but they were awfully big. For once, I withstood the impulse.

Finally, some sort of agreement was clearly worked out and two of three went outside again. Within moments, another two men arrived carrying a flat, dramatically heavy object that at first I thought was a thick tabletop. It had been taken from the van, I learned later, which also housed paramedic gear. A man at either end, they were visibly straining as they brought this strange object into the tearoom and set it on the floor. The heavy tabletop was laid flat on the floor and only then did one of the men take off his jacket.

"Excuse us, gentlemen," he said to Tom and me. "This will just take a second and then Dr. Hammer can come in."

The two upended the tabletop and to my immense surprise I soon grasped that it was a four-part hinged screen made out of bullet-proof metal of some sort. It was set up like a W immediately inside the front doorway. After this elaborate exercise was concluded, one of the men moved an armchair directly in front of the screen, along with a small side table. From nowhere, tea emerged from the servery and suddenly there he was, "Dr." Hammer himself, a wizened old man who did not know how to smile, but politely said, "How d'you do?" to which we responded with similar politeness. It was certainly a relief to know that we could have a second cup of tea untroubled by any fear that machine-gun fire or telescoped rifles could penetrate "Dr." Hammer's bullet-proof screen.

Tom had obviously met this particular Wizard of Oz before and made the introductions. I believe, with no sense of chagrin, that my name went in one ear and out the other in a nanosecond, as befitted my status in Hammer's storied life. Before I had time to contemplate this, however, there was a terrific whirring noise outside. I felt like jumping for cover because the last time I had heard such an overhead clatter was when some Chinese army helicopters set off for a nasty little border skirmish with Vietnam late in 1978. I had just finished an extensive four-week tour of Vietnam and was on a train with my wife from Hanoi to Beijing along with the last people to cross the Sino-Vietnamese border before full-scale war broke out. With typical journalistic humility, I later assumed the helicopters were simply waiting for me to get safely back to China before doing their damage.

In Wales eight years later, it turned out not to be the People's Liberation Army (airborne division) at all, but simply Galen and Hilary Weston arriving from London for the board meeting. It was the first time I ever saw Mrs. Weston, who later became the lieutenant-governor of Ontario. As she emerged from the helicopter, her long blonde hair flowing in the wind, I had a momentary sensation that someone so beautiful could only have come straight from heaven. *Those Westons!* They can really make impressive travel connections.

In the distance, slowly proceeding up the laneway but making much less crunch than the Rolls, appeared a humble blue Ford Escort. It came to an unostentatious stop and out stepped a man with a quizzical look masked by a nice smile. I wanted to tell him he had come to the wrong place, that only people with outriders and escorts were allowed. On second glance, however, I could see that he did belong. It was the Prince of Wales.

The rest of the weekend failed to live up to the animation of the arrivals. The business meeting, reception, and dinner were unsurprising in all respects but one: I got an understanding, as I never had before, of the tedium that crowds the day and work of symbolic figures. It's a bit like being on a glamorous movie set for the first time. All your romantic illusions from hours of watching movies all your life are flattened by the humdrum reality of sitting around for hours on end, waiting for any sort of action. The royal movie isn't so slowly paced, but it isn't a hell of a lot more exciting. I did however acquire an admiration for Prince Charles and his professional sense of duty. He soldiers on quite valiantly despite all the terrible things that are said about him, despite the public mess and tragedy of his marriage, despite all the glum predictions about his worthiness to ascend the throne, indeed despite the speculation over whether there will even be a throne for him to ascend (I am talking England here, and not just Canada).

On this one occasion, which gave me the chance to watch him closely over two days, he was conscientious and kind to everyone he met. He delighted in seeing old friends such as the Westons and seemed genuinely stimulated to meet interesting new people. He is terrific at putting nervous people at ease, forbearing to well-meaning bores, and impatient with snobs. He has a self-deprecatory sense of humour and a natural grace that is nicely set off by those famous jug ears, for which he has not yet succumbed to corrective plastic surgery.

Will he be King one day? Maybe. Maybe not. One thing I know, if England and Canada retain the monarchy there will be no one better for the job. Like his mother in Canada, he will never overstay his welcome and he will enhance the constitutional and legislative journey we make in life, especially if Adrienne Clarkson lives up to the early promise of her spectacularly different posting as his Canadian representative. Mercifully for Canadians, there has been a wonderful model for many years. Not a model: an exemplar. This is General and Madame Vanier. Especially Madame Vanier.

On one level, I can explain precisely why the Vanier family springs so quickly to mind whenever I think of altruism and grace in leadership. First of all, Georges and Pauline Vanier were the epitome of altruism and grace when they lived at Rideau Hall, and because he was the first French Canadian to hold that office, he seemed somehow to personify all the positive things English Canadians of good heart wanted to cherish about that essential part of their country which they never fully understood but wanted to stay united with.

Many Quebecers and almost all francophones outside Quebec admired the Vaniers for their patrician dignity and grace that elevated their countrymen's own sense of themselves. It is true there were also francophones who would tell you that Vanier was such an anglified francophone as to be hardly a Quebecer at all and Pauline Vanier's maiden name, Archer, said it all. In fact, Madame Vanier's father, Judge Archer, was Irish (Catholic) Canadian – not exactly the dark heart of the Anglo-Canadian WASP establishment conspiracy. But there is no denying that General Vanier admired things British. How could he fail to? He was born in a particular era and to a particular ethos, when the Empire's dying embers were casting a rosy glow over many parts of the world. His beloved regiment, the legendary *Vingt-Deuxième*, was created and manned according to British military practice and wisdom, the general received all his commissions in the army from the kings and queen he served under (Edward VII, George V, Edward VIII, George VI, and finally Elizabeth II), and he was deeply attached to several governors general, notably Viscount Byng of Vimy and the Earl of Athlone and his wife, Princess Alice.

His French-Canadian sense of self was strong, but it was as a French Canadian in the British Empire that he truly identified his personal cause and if that seems strange today, the parallel stands still with French Canadians who identify with the Canadian federation. It is very difficult for Canadians under the age of, say, fifty to appreciate the degree to which identity with the "mother country" passed for patriotism in an earlier era. If, in 1930, a francophone had expressed dismay at the degree to which Anglo Canadians identified with the United Kingdom while expressing the belief that love of Canada itself should be sufficient as a dutiful expression of good citizenship, well there is no question that this francophone would have been marked off by many as a malcontent, a nationalist, and generally up to much mischief. This era is not that far away from our time.

But, of course, it was not General and Madame Vanier's ethnic or linguistic identification that makes them so special in the constitutional and social history of Canada. It was their natural ability to provide moral and symbolic leadership through their graceful bearing and lives of purposeful devotion to each other and their God. All this came together to create a unique couple in Canadian history. It is not for nothing that some people are working hard at creating both of them saints. A particular focus in the campaign within the Roman Catholic Church is to have them beatified together to show the church's strong support for loving, faithful marriages.

I saw the Vaniers together in office only twice, once as a teenager and the other time a few years later when I was a student journalist in St. John's. The earliest encounter was when I was a prodigal of Upper Canada College returning with a scowl to collect the book prize for "public speaking" from the Governor General the year after I had failed Grade XI and dropped out of the school. All memories of these sorts of events are notoriously hazy, but what I vividly recall was my nervousness at ascending the dais in the College's Prayer Hall and the warm, enveloping charm of his presence. I loved his drooping moustache and his snow-white hair. And this too: I remember him looking at my prize book, Rudyard Kipling's *Stalky and Co.*, and saying it was a good book but perhaps a little immature for such a fine older chap as myself, or some such thing. He was flattering my alleged intelligence, which had only lately been found so wanting by my old school. I grabbed the compliment with gratitude and floated on it for days.

It is only in retrospect that I think I can remember her. Madame Vanier, I mean. Of course, she would have been at his side; of course, she would have been covering for him at any given moment, when he got tired, or when his severed leg went numb, or when he was simply feeling defeated by everything that was expected of him. But this insight and the perception of having encountered her before I am sure only came much later, after I saw her with him during his last few months and on his last vice-regal tour (Newfoundland, again), and after I got to know her well in her miraculous retirement home in Toisly, France. She had gone there to be close to her eldest son, Jean Vanier, the founder of the worldwide L'Arche movement for the mentally handicapped. She made her peace with the world and the country she and her husband had served for so long, and in her eighth decade moved halfway across the world to be of service to people who were about as removed from the privileged life she had hitherto led as was possible to imagine.

I fell headlong in love with her on that last vice-regal trip. Several incidents that became talismans to their glory stay in my mind. The way they worked together was key. He was so old and frail and close to death that she watched his every movement like a hawk. I saw him visibly fade in a conversation with some St. John's worthies at a municipal reception in Bowering Park and so did she. Walking right into the middle of the group, she grabbed the conversation in order to give him respite. I shall never forget the beaming look of gratitude that was on his face, a mixture of huge relief and palpable love. There is an oil painting my wife and I bought in the southwest of France that now adorns the living room of our residence at Massey College. It's called *La tendresse* and depicts a small moment in an elderly couple's life in which the man leans over to the woman to give her a secret, gentle kiss. I got it ostensibly because of the vibrant colours, but deep down I know I wanted it because the couple look so much like the Vaniers. The painting captures a tiny fragment of their relationship that was such a joy to bask in, and every time I look at it, at any hour of the day, they are summoned – willy-nilly – into my grateful consciousness.

Earlier, at that 1966 Bowring Park reception in St. John's, Vanier had planted a tree with the usual silver shovel. A young and somewhat scruffy street boy who had insinuated himself to the front of the crowd of dignitaries soon attracted negative attention to himself. Scruffy boys were born to attract negative attention to themselves. An aide to the mayor of St. John's was in the process of firmly removing the miscreant, but before he could do so Madame Vanier, who must have been watching the whole exercise with her usual attentive eye, moved over to the boy even as her husband was turning the earth. She was tall and still held herself very erect in those days, so she towered over the boy, leaning dramatically forward so that they could be as close to eye contact as she could manage. I haven't a clue what was discussed, but at one point the boy smiled shyly and she then stood up, put her hand on his shoulder, and stayed by his side until the ceremony was finished.

It was a wisp of a moment, but silver nonetheless. In it, I discovered for the first time the practical management of symbolic leadership. Did the boy appreciate all this? I haven't a clue and it would be wrong to sentimentalize the incident. But the mayor's assistant probably still remembers it, and even if he doesn't I certainly do and my witness can be multiplied by thousands of Canadians who saw her as she did her duty throughout her nine decades on earth. But for her part, of course, it was done instinctively and that's the point. Such kindness was inherent in her person and how she saw her vocation in life.

In Troisly, with Jean, she was always in danger of verging into sainthood and it was the task of all who loved her – or so I claimed and it made her laugh – to keep her human by rehearsing before her the limitless measure of her human frailties and sins. Emotionally, she could sink into deep depression from time to time, almost to the point of a breakdown. It was her faith that sustained her through such dark days. As all her old friends died off, she craved the company of younger people with an intensity that was both understandable and wonderful to behold. Those of us in her orbit each had different functions. She had her "political Jesuit," as well as her "spiritual Jesuit." I held responsibilities in the subcategories of "media," "China," and "Canada" and was expected to make contributions on all fronts. She had large expectations of all her friends that were sometimes difficult to sustain, but she held a natural court to all who wanted to pay her deference. For my wife and me, her small sitting room in Troisly was Camelot enough.

Her death, as I learned of it, seemed appropriate. She was ill and was taken to hospital while Jean was far away and before any of her other children could get to her bedside. For several hours, she was abandoned on a gurney, naked under a sheet and utterly ignored by the staff. According to a friend from Troisly who eventually got there, she had had a final epiphany. The indignity of her abandonment, nakedness, and anonymity was shocking to her at first. Had she not knelt in prayer with several popes? Had she not dined at Buckingham Palace with the King and Queen? Had she not had tea with General De Gaulle at the Elysée? Had she not . . . had she . . . had . . . *had she not come naked into this world and would she not leave it naked?* Was she not now ready to leave behind the last of earthly vanities and return to the bosom of the Lord, letting the Lord cradle her and rock her through the final journey? As her son Jean was to say later at her state funeral in Quebec City, was she not just the same young girl at her end as she was when Georges Vanier first found her, a young girl full of hope and tenderness and longing to be loved?

And she was loved, a monarch of kindred spirits and kind hearts everywhere. She ruled with an ease and gentleness that was so great we did not know we were her subjects until she was no longer there. For me and for many Canadians, the memory of her reign and that of her gentle and loving husband lingers on.

IX

The Queen really can look glum, I guess. All the British media have reported on this at one time or another. Indeed she can look *extraordinarily* glum at times. At her glummest, media commentators usually trot out her "Hanoverian" genes to explain the royal pout. But why does she get so glum? Why should someone who lives in several palaces and castles and has *fleets* of servants and jewels beyond counting, why should such a person ever feel glum? I don't know exactly. Perhaps because she's a human being and has a family. Then again, perhaps it comes from contemplating the media, who knows for sure? She must realize by now, though, that at some point during her long reign, which is still unfolding, things changed, dramatically. Now the only lucky souls the media leave alone are media barons. They are the one who have apportioned unto themselves the deference that was once due the monarch. The multinational Rupert Murdoch (Australian-British-American-Wherever-a-buck-can-be-made-land) is the chief example. No one has persecuted, mocked, and humiliated members of the Royal Family more than Murdoch through his wretched newspapers, particularly *The News of the World* and the tabloid *Sun*, but not excluding the "up-market" *Times* and *Sunday Times*, which take a secondary feeding off the royals after the scum papers have had their first bites. Clever observers will have noticed, however, that when the great and mighty Murdoch abandoned his wife of many years and the mother of his children (the "breeder" in modern

parlance) for a young Asian beauty, there was precious little speculation in the opposition press and none whatsoever in his own. I
think the Queen might be grateful for just half the consideration
Murdoch gives his own circumstances. Half, did I say? I'm sure
she'd settle for a tenth.

Occasionally, then, the Queen may have a right to look a little
glum. I think we can give her that. I have seen her glum and
smiling, curious and argumentative, flirtatious and solemn. All at
public occasions. The only special access I had was a journalist's
identity card and, perhaps, the desire to observe. I admire her enormously, as much for the way she carries on regardless of all the BS
she is obliged to swallow. What truly amazes me is how little of the
time she actually seems glum, especially over the past few years.

When I was posted to London, I covered a half-dozen sched-
uled, protocol-saturated royal events and got some measure of her
approach to these affairs in her late middle-age, long after whatever
thrills attended upon her younger self when she became Queen
were overtaken by the dull monotony of duty, survival, and the
accommodation of betrayal. In Westminster Hall, shortly after the
Sunday Times had reported she was on a major collision course
with the British prime minister, Margaret Thatcher, over
Commonwealth sanctions against South Africa, I saw her and
Thatcher welcome the Commonwealth Parliamentary Association
biannual meeting. She wasn't glum at all on this occasion, she was
studiously cheerful, well aware that all the hacks were watching
and waiting for any sign – the merest flicker of an eyelash, say – to
prove she and Mrs. T were on the outs.

I went to an investiture of knights and dames and lesser fry in
the Throne Room at Buckingham Palace and covered the doomed
marriage of Prince Andrew and Fergie. And I also attended a

Commonwealth Day service at Westminster Abbey followed by a reception in Marlborough House on Pall Mall, the former London residence of both Queen Alexandra and Queen Mary and now the Commonwealth Secretariat. The only vivid reminder of the dowager empresses, incidentally, is the dog cemetery in a shady nook just off from the main grounds. My favourite final wee resting place is for Mr. Wiggins, "loyal to H.M. Queen Alexandra till the day he died." If I were a royal personage this century, I would say "Give me dogs over people anyday" too. Or at least that's what I think dear Mr. Wiggins represents.

I grant you most people don't have their own dog cemetery and I am not really trying to argue here that the House of Windsor is comprised of humble home folks. It is, instead, caught up in a remarkable time warp, one that drives some people to anger and frustration, and others – like me – to utter amazement because we regard the monarchy's survival under the levelling onslaught of the late twentieth century as a bit of a miracle. Let me explain. In theory, there should be no more kings and queens, princes and princesses, especially in an egalitarian age, especially in a country that is struggling with class divisions (Britain) or is trying to stand interdependently alone in the world (Canada). A hereditary monarchy simply makes no sense. I didn't vote it into office; you didn't vote it into office; our parents didn't and our grandchildren won't. In Canada, beyond the fact that our fractious constitutional wrangles mean that the issue of monarchy is almost the least of our worries, what possible argument could there be for retaining an English-German family based in London to provide our nominal head of state? None, right? That certainly is the growing conventional wisdom of many opinion makers in the country.

Long ago, I accepted that the old emotional, almost tribal basis of support for the monarchy in Canada – part of which, I must admit, spurs my own loyalty – doesn't turn a lot of old or new Canadians on any more. So of course the issue of monarchy is a real problem. At the same time, government and schools no longer play up the monarchical connection; mostly it is handled with whispers and severe embarrassment. Monarchist societies are marginalized and made to look silly by the national media if they are noticed at all. The Canadianization of the vice-regal offices in Ottawa and the provinces has continued apace and the royal connection is hardly a hiccup at an official event. The recently departed editor-in-chief of *The Globe and Mail* has called for the end of the monarchy when Queen Elizabeth dies and the elevation of the office of governor general to the status of full head of state – its occupants to be "elected" by the august membership of the Companions of the Order of Canada.

All of this makes a sort of sense, I suppose, but for me it seems blind-sided thinking, removed from any connection to our past and remarkably cavalier about our uncertain future. I used to say that when the English-Canadians and the French-Canadians figure out how to live together, then it will be time enough to dismiss the monarchy. This was a petty ruse on my part, knowing that this Canadian version of the New Jerusalem might not come until well into the third millennium. I don't say this any more, even in jest, because it seems such a negative defence, such a back-handed way of acknowledging that the monarchy has been a good thing for Canada even though it has so few champions any more. On the other hand, I resist saying what I really think because it is so negative about the small minds I see around me. In Canada, we have a convoluted and inconclusive history. We have not been revolutionaries and, *vide* William Lyon Mackenzie, we have not really been enraptured by rabble-rousers. We have been a careful, self-deprecating folk, and while our past has its own dark share of evil – for aboriginals and Asians, for example – it does not at all feature in the front or even secondary ranks of evil, as the last two centuries stand witness.

Yet we *lust* for tidiness. We keep wanting to revise our story to suit the political situation – the mood – of the moment. To do that it seems we must obliterate our past. Every five or six years we seem to rewrite the official record. Where once we were known for taming half of a vast continent, now it seems our highest achievement is universal medicare. Where once we were hardy and brave, now we are kinder and gentler. This is such vanity! There is so much good that Canada has done and stands for, despite everything, that this past should be constantly dredged to discover what secrets it still holds and rediscover the truths our parents and grandparents took for granted. They knew things we have forgotten or have never learned: this is a country that tries to make amends for past mistakes; this is a country that has always welcomed immigrants and allows them new lives; this is a country that has conquered winter through literature and central heating; this is a country where every element of our society, from aboriginals to the latest refugees from Kosovo, have had to deal directly with some sort of defeat (or else their ancestors did) and where defeat can be transformed into triumph; this is a country of possibilities; and, above all, this is a country where courage and endurance have been inseparable and where we are defined by the peaceful struggle – rather than the vainglory – of remaining united.

This is also a place that has embraced the notion of monarchy and monarchical symbolism since the sixteenth century and now it is proposed that we simply dispense with it once the old lady of Windsor is dead upon her throne. I suspect she will have the last laugh yet. Her mother, a century to the good, is still with us. It may well be that all those reading this book will be dead or grandparents by the time this sovereign decides to give up the ghost. By then, of course, we will have solved all our little internal problems (we might even first try to figure out a way to include non-natives and daughters into our national anthem) and will be able to deal with the issue of monarchy on a sensible and logical basis. Right.

Until that famous day, let me tell you about the day Her Majesty flirted with Don Jamieson. Well, I say "flirted," but that's not strictly accurate. Let us say she talked to him in a jolly nice way and only at the end thought to ask the whereabouts of Mrs. Jamieson. It was at the reception in Marlborough House on Commonwealth Day. Most of the high bureaucrats of the Commonwealth Secretariat were out in force, along with the high commissioners or their representatives, and a few journalists – some gushy ("Aye, aye and ready, Sir, Ma'am") and some cynical. At one point I found myself standing beside Mrs. Jamieson, whom I really liked. She was from The Bay in Newfoundland, but had travelled extensively and shared the life of Don Jamieson, both as a colonial campaigner for Confederation, as a provincial media bigwig, as a federal cabinet minister, and finally as his consort in the plushy London high commissioner's residence in Grosvenor Square.

I had heard through the grapevine that Mr. Jamieson had become a favourite of the Queen's thanks to his undoubted gift of the gab. He can yatter on entertainingly almost without a break, and everyone of a certain age in Newfoundland will tell you this is true. Once, in the lead-up to provincial election-night coverage in the 1960s, a featured guest failed to turn up for the CJON-TV two-hour election preview. No problem! In stepped Jamieson, the camera stayed focused on his massive head, varying not an angle for most of the two hours, and on and on he yakked until the first results started trickling in. I was watching the spectacle at the Kingsbridge Tourist Home in St. John's, along with a motley crowd of other long-term renters. Mr. Bridle, a scrappy little caretaker, would come back and forth during this unique marathon, stay for a few minutes, and shake his head in wonder: "Tis sumpting splendid to watch old Don spoutin' like dat. Not a man nor devil can stop 'im!"

Nor Her Majesty, one suspects, nor would she want to, evidently. I was chatting amiably to Mrs. Jamieson at the Commonwealth gathering at Marlborough House, as the high commissioner was talking to someone else just beside us. Suddenly, I heard the familiar voice.

"Ah, there you are, High Commissioner, I was wondering where you were."

I can't remember what he said, but I could tell none of this fazed Mrs. Jamieson. She knew her performer well.

"You're coming tomorrow night, I believe," she said, whatever tomorrow night was.

"Yes, Ma'am, with all flags flying."

She smiled. "I want you to tell that story again. Do you mind? About the little fisherman. No one else will have heard it but me."

Jamieson beamed. The Queen looked around, probably for her lady-in-waiting as this encounter took place on her way out to her limousine-in-waiting.

"Where's Mrs. Jamieson?" asked the Queen, almost absent-mindedly.

"Why right here, Your Majesty. Right at my side. Where else would you have her?" Don replied.

The Queen chuckled again, said a tidy hello to Mrs. Jamieson, and then left for the main entrance. Mr. Jamieson turned to me with a twinkle in his eye. "Now I just have to remember which damn fisherman story she was talking about."

For a shy woman, and she was intensely shy when her reign started, the Queen has worked on her social skills sufficiently well to work a room with a modest amount of, shall we say, structured informality. She still commands inordinate admiration and even veneration from most ordinary people, but she eschews any embarrassing displays of royal fervour. Dignified respect is all she has ever asked for her office and in return she has steadfastly adhered to her coronation oath and promise "to serve and defend" the people of the Commonwealth until her dying day.

Earlier that same day, I watched her at Westminster Abbey, where she had gone to preside over the annual Commonwealth Day service. African drums had greeted her at the main doors, a reminder of the days of Empire and the lingering spell of the changing Commonwealth, but she did what she has often done in her very own cathedral church – the font and throne-keeper of monarchy. She simply processed down the main aisle, through the nave, around the choir, and took her seat of honour in the sanctuary as head of the church, head of state, and head of the Commonwealth. A small woman with a penetrating look, she gazed carefully and directly into all eyes as she passed them during this familiar progress, straight into all the eyes that were staring so intently on her. The message, it seemed to me, was very simple: *I am a symbol of what we are as a people, I am a symbol of justice, I am a symbol of humanity that aspires above the ordinary, I am a symbol for ordinary people to share their humanity, I am a symbol of service and duty . . . I am nothing more but nothing less than what you want to make of me.*

X

There is no question in my mind where it all began, this notion of monarchy and Canada. I have already cited tribal chiefs and French sovereigns and the reign of King George II, but I would rather stick to a Victorian lady's diary. In my universe, it started in the fastness of Georgian Bay and not too far from Manitoulin Island, a moment in the imagination in which the grandeur of the northern geography matched the mind's ability to translate a scrap of faraway news into the panoply of humanity's purpose on earth. The year was 1837 and the author of this end piece is the redoubtable Anna Brownell Jameson, wife of the attorney general of Upper Canada. The Jamesons, together with their small party, were travelling by sailboat towards Manitoulin Island for a rendezvous with both British and Indian authorities.

For sure, they passed along part of the route Samuel de Champlain travelled two centuries earlier. Probably they went right past what is now Adrienne Clarkson and John Ralston Saul's small property. It is only my own fanciful mind that one of the

stop-overs she writes about in the passage that follows was where
nearly two centuries later Canada's first governor general of Asian
ancestry picks her blueberries and raspberries and looks out on the
primordial splendour of the place. In Madam Clarkson's first
address to her countrymen as governor general she evoked the
place with passion. It haunts her as it haunts Mrs. Jameson's
amazing journey, as it haunted the Mohawks and Iroquois, Tom
Thomson and the Group of Seven, and the poet Douglas LePan,
as it haunts every human being great and small who has ever set
eyes upon it. Mrs. Jameson's journey to Manitoulin is a journey
not just into the Canadian wilderness, but into a concept of place
that had its own inherent majesty, into a tangible but somehow
mythological demi-paradise where the symbolism of kingship
seems as natural as the clearing view through the morning mist.
The following passage (edited for length) is from Mrs. Jameson's
famous book, *Winter Studies and Summer Rambles in Canada*, first
published in 1838, and we join her after she and the Attorney-
General's party have already been underway for two days:

> The next morning was beautiful: the sun shone brightly
> though the lake was yet heaving and swelling from the recent
> storm, – altogether it was like the laughing eyes and pouting
> lips of the half-appeased beauty. About nine o'clock we ran
> down into a lovely bay, and landed to breakfast on a little lawn
> surrounded by high trees and a thick wood, abounding in rat-
> tlesnakes and squirrels. Luckily for us, the storm had dispersed
> the mosquitoes. . . .
>
> We breakfasted in much mirth, and then we set off again.
> The channel widened, the sky became overcast, the wind
> freshened, and at length blew hard. Though this part of the

lake is protected by St. Joseph's and the chain of islands from the swell of the main lake, still the waves rose high, the wind increased, we were obliged to take in a reef or two of our sail, and scudded with an almost fearful rapidity before the wind. In crossing a wide, open expanse of about twenty miles, we became all at once very silent, then very grave, then very pathetic, and at last extremely sick.

On arriving among the channels of the Rattlesnake Islands, the swell of course subsided; we landed on a most beautiful mass of rock, and lighted our fire under a group of pines and sycamores; but we were too sick to eat. Mr. MacMurray heated some port wine and water, into which we broke biscuit, and drank it most picturesquely out of a slop basin – too thankful to get it! Thus recruited, we proceeded. The wind continued fresh and fair, the day kept up fine, and our sail was most delightful and rapid. . . .

[The next day] we made eighteen miles before breakfast; and then pursued our way through Aird's bay, and among countless islands of all shapes and sizes; I cannot describe their beauty, nor their harmonious variety: at last we perceived in the east the high ridge called the mountains of La Cloche. They are really respectable hills in this level country, but hardly mountains: they are all of limestone, and partially clothed in wood. All this coast is very rocky and barren; but it is said to be rich in mineral productions. At about five in the evening we landed at La Cloche.

Here we found the first and only signs of civilised society during our voyage. The north-west Company have an important station here; and two of their principal clerks, Mr. MacBean and Mr. Bethune, were on the spot. We were received with much kindness, and pressed to spend the night, but there was yet so much daylight, and time was so valuable, that we declined. The factory consists of a large log house, an extensive store to contain the goods bartered with the Indians, and huts inhabited by work people, hunters, voyageurs, and others; a small village, in short; and a number of boats and canoes of all sizes were lying in the bay. It is not merely the love of gain which induces well-educated men – gentlemen – to pass twenty years of their lives in such a place as this; you must add to the prospective acquirement of a large fortune, two possessions which men are most wont to covet – power and freedom. The table was laid in their hall for supper, and we carried off, with their good-will, a large mess of broiled fish, dish and all, and a can of milk, which delicious viands we discussed in our boat with great satisfaction. . . .

Daylight was just creeping up the sky, and some few stars yet out, when we bestirred ourselves, and in a very few minutes we were again afloat: we were now steering towards the south-east, where the Great Manitoolin Island was dimly discerned. There was deep slumberous calm all around, as if nature had not yet awoke from her night's rest: then the atmosphere began to kindle with gradual light; it grew brighter and brighter: towards the east, the lake and sky were intermingling in radiance; and *then* just there, where they seemed flowing and glowing together like a bath of fire, we saw what seemed to us the huge black hull of a vessel, with masts and spars rising against the sky – but we knew not what to think or believe! As we kept on rowing in that direction, it grew more distinct, but lessened in size: it proved to be a great heavy-built schooner, painted black, which was going up against the lake against wind and current. One man was standing in her bows with an immense oar, which he slowly pulled, walking backwards and forwards; but vain seemed all his toil, for still the vessel lay like a black log, and moved not: we rode up to the side and hailed him – "What news?"

And the answer was that William the Fourth was dead, and that Queen Victoria reigned in his place! We sat silent, looking at each other, and even in that very moment the orb of the sun rose out of the lake, and poured its beams full in our dazzled eyes.

We asked if the governor were at the Manitoolin Island? No; he was not there; but the chief officer of the Indian department had come to represent him, and the presents were to be given out to the assembled Indians this morning. We urged the men to take their oars with spirit, and held out course due east down by the woody shores of this immense island; among fields and reeds and rushes, and almost under the shadow of the towering forests.

Meantime many thoughts came into my mind – some tears too into my eyes – not certainly for that dead king who in ripe age and in all honour was gathered to the tomb – but for that living queen, so young and fair –

"As many hopes hang on that noble head
As there hang blossoms on the boughs in May!"

And what will become of *them* – of *her!* The idea that even here, in this new world of woods and waters, amid these remote wilds, to her so utterly unknown, her power reaches and her sovereignty is acknowledged, filled me with compassionate awe.

I say *compassionate*, for if she feel in the whole extent the liabilities of her position, alas for her! And if she feel them not! – O worse and worse!

I tried to recall her childish figure and features. I thought over all I had heard concerning her. I thought she was not such a thing as they could make a mere pageant of; for *that* there is too much within – too little without. And what *will* they make of her? For at eighteen she will hardly make anything of them – I mean of the men and women round her. It is of a woman I think, more than of the queen; for as part of the state machinery she will do quite as well as another – better, perhaps; so far her youth and sex are absolutely in her favour, or rather in *our* favour. If she be but simple-minded, and true-hearted, and straightforward, with the common portion of intellect – if a royal education have not blunted in her the quick perceptions and pure kind instincts of the woman – if she has only had fair play, and carries into business plain and distinct notions of right and wrong – and the fine moral sense that is not to be confounded by diplomatic verbiage and expediency – she will do better for us than a whole cabinet full of cut and dried officials, with Talleyrand at the head of them. And what a fair heritage is this which has fallen to her! A land young like herself – a land of hopes – and fair, most fair! Does she know – does she care anything about it? – while hearts are beating warm for her, and voices bless her – and hands are stretched out towards her, even from these wild lake shores!

These thoughts were in my mind, or something like to these, as with the aid of sail and oar we were gliding across the bay of Manitoolin.

And this thought has long been in my mind: if, as a people, we become so foolish as to let the monarchy disappear, the moment of its demise will also mark the end of our imagination and our ability to transcend our past, rather than merely obliterate it.

In the early days after the appointment of Adrienne Clarkson, it seemed that there would, after all, be another chance. Why is it that a refugee child from China, who came here when the British aristocracy still held sway at Rideau Hall, should be the one chosen to take up the vice-regal challenge when the office of governor general seemed to be on its deathbed? I don't think there are answers for that sort of thing. They belong in the "Who'd-have-thought-it?" school of philosophy which permits unexpected things to come along and change the wisdom of sages and fools alike. And how did it happen that Ottawa school teachers in the 1940s and Toronto academics in 1950s, who did not know that by the standards of the 1990s they were woefully ignorant of racial and women's oppression, would nevertheless help inspire in the refugee child such a confident vision of Canada – bilingual, multicultural, egalitarian, and altruistic? It was a vision that had the power to inspire us even after my fellow journalists made sure we knew everything about her mortal life, her character flaws, her quick marriage to John Ralston Saul by an Anglican bishop, her failures, her this, her that, her . . . her . . . her humanity. The only difficulty we had in accepting her was acknowledging that she had come from our midst. But, in the end, if you will forgive me, we can at last say: *She is Adrienne Clarkson, and so are all of us.*

So here the story rests for the moment at an interesting conjunction. It's one I pondered deeply as I looked on the front pages of the somewhat anti-royalist *Globe and Mail* and the more-or-less-royalist *National Post* and saw Adrienne and John with Elizabeth II. It seemed a fit. Indeed, I expect someone from the House of Windsor to paddle past the Champlain Monument in Georgian Bay any fine old summer day now.

Dictionary of Canadian Biography, Volume XIII (1901 to 1910). Published in 1994 by the University of Toronto Press.

The Imperial Canadian: Vincent Massey in Office, by Claude Bissell. Published in 1986 by the University of Toronto Press.

The Private Capital: Ambition and Love in the Age of Macdonald and Laurier, by Sandra Gwyn. Published in 1984 by McClelland & Stewart.

The Queen: A Biography of Queen Elizabeth II, by Ben Plimpton. Published in 1996 by HarperCollins.

Queen Victoria, by Lytton Strachey. Published in 1921 by Harcourt, Brace and Co.

Queen Victoria: Born to Succeed, by Elizabeth Longford. Published in 1964 by Harper & Row.

Vanier: Soldier, Diplomat and Governor General, by Robert Speaight. Published in 1970 by Collins.

What's Past is Prologue: The Memoirs of Vincent Massey. Published in 1963 by Macmillan of Canada.

Afterword
An Inconvenient Past

They were there, all together in the Canadian Room at the Royal York Hotel on a hot summer evening in 1997: The sovereign, the bishop, the prime minister, and the editor-in-chief. The bishop said the grace, the prime minister was the host and welcomed the sovereign. The sovereign graciously replied. The editor-in-chief was supposed to be in the crowd somewhere (his name was on the guest list, but it is not certain if he was there in the flesh, although his minions from the newsroom were).

Toronto was celebrating its bicentennial, and this vast gathering (the Canadian Room at the Royal York Hotel can seat well over a thousand), which gave me so many ideas of how to stitch this book together, was something of a triumph of historical perseverance over tortuous reality. I mean, consider the situation. The editor-in-chief was less than two years away from being catapulted from the top to the bottom of his masthead, and deservedly so as he had left his newspaper far too vulnerable to external attack. The bishop was still trying to shake the monkey of Father Ferry's case off his back, perhaps deservedly so since the problem with which he was grappling – the role gay people are to be allowed in life – was being solved by society and not by the church. As for the sovereign, she had many jolts still to absorb in the ensuing months.

The only way in which she deserved the lashes she and the House of Windsor were being stung with, however, was as a symbolic whipping post. The imagined grievances that were coming at her from all sorts of bizarre sources – the media's absurd faith in its ability to discern the future (it can shape it, but not often in the manner it supposes); the generation gap, via Diana's crowd; post-colonial neuroses (which vary from ex-colony to ex-colony); and so on – would have tried even the saintliest soul.

Only the prime minister was getting a fairly comfortable ride, but his moment will come sooner or later. It always does in politics. Or perhaps it won't come for him if only because the degree to which he is already despised by Quebec nationalists, English-Canadian editorialists, Western chauvinists, and so on – everyone in the country except for a mysterious, persistently large majority – means that for all his days he will feel under-appreciated. Or perhaps his moment will come after he leaves office. Whatever. The whiff of failure hovers above all of them, or it will soon enough.

If it had ever been possible to get John Strachan, George Brown, Wilfrid Laurier, and Victoria together, I'm not sure they would have different tales to tell about the vicissitudes of life and the nature of fame and glory. It's only the passage of time that wipes away the tears. Victoria's grief at Albert's death is practically a joke now, but it left her prostrate for years while her reign almost collapsed. The sense of despair Laurier felt at the end seems to bear no relationship to the gleaming role he now plays in Canada's story. John Strachan's debts were so crippling he feared dying for what he would be bequeathing his heirs. It overwhelmed his creaking frame. George Brown's personal affairs were also frequently in a mess as a result of overextending himself in cattle farming, and he soured badly on politics. And yet who can say that, despite their failings, these four did not make a difference? Who can say that they did not directly and indirectly affect the lives of all Canadians today in ways both great and small? We can see it with the forebears so much more clearly than with our own crowd, and yet they are us in so many ways that we should pause before we dismiss them.

How will history treat today's establishment leaders? We haven't a clue, really. History is very surprising. Who would have ever thought many of the events of the last few years would happen – the fall of communism, say, or Diana's death and Clinton's zipper, and even a new Canadian national newspaper – but when it happened, how quickly we absorbed it all.

Canada has been cursed for too long – at least a quarter of a century and maybe more – with a history that we keep finding inconvenient. We view our past, which defines so much of our present and points to so many things in the future, as embarrassing, politically incorrect, or simply too boring for words. The easiest thing to do has been to bury it, with the predictable result that no one knows nothing, as Jack Benny's co-star Eddie "Rochester" Anderson used to say. The media loves reporting the random ignorance of Canadians about their country and its past. I don't know how many stories I've read about the results of quizzes of one sort of another which establish that Canadian young people can hardly name their current leaders let alone a leader from a generation ago or any of the founding figures. (The prime minister himself isn't a lot better at history, it turns out). This is a miserable state of affairs, but recently it seems to be changing, partly because good people are sounding the right alarms and partly because there has been a genuine revival of interest in how we got to where we are.

What I learned from the exercise that resulted in this book is basic, but it struck me with force: Everyone has to go through a struggle. The restlessness within the human spirit unites past and present. You can see it in John Strachan's thrusting desire to expand his church's influence and all the trouble that got him into. You can see it in Terence Finlay's heart's desire to extend God's kingdom to the poor and disadvantaged and figure out what on earth was God's purpose in making some people gay. It's there in Laurier's desire to forge a sense of Canadian unity out of a recognition of the good fortune we share on this continent. You can see the heartbreak of nearly all Canadian leaders who tried and still try to hold this country together, not the least Jean Chrétien. George Brown set out to persuade a doubting population on the advantages of Confederation. He succeeded, but it never translated into real power for him, and after enough politics the dumb beasts of the field seemed to him to be a kindlier audience. William Thorsell often looked out upon his newsroom as if he were regarding dumb beasts in the field, but he also had a strong vision and a great intelligence which he tried as best he could to harness for the benefit of Canada. He also showed the same sort of courage George Brown did when espousing unpopular causes, and in this regard the two men gave public evidence that an editor works best when he is true to himself.

What does it all add up to? The only thing that is readily apparent is that we build on our past and, if we are lucky, we will get a chance to do something positive ourselves, something to which succeeding generations can contribute. It sounds modest enough put this way, but for those in positions of great trust, it has been life itself.

Acknowledgements

I had a wonderful time wondering about, researching, and writing this book over three busy years while I was occupied primarily with administering a graduate residential college in Toronto, as well as writing a weekly newspaper column. Except during the summers, I worked in stolen snatches of time, and for all the averted eyes at such moments I must thank everyone at Massey College.

The manuscript was late, so my gratitude to a patient and encouraging publisher is particularly heartfelt. At McClelland & Stewart, both Avie Bennett, chairman, and Douglas Gibson, publisher, are the great standard-bearers for Canadians trying to keep independent book publishing alive in this country. My admiration for them parallels my affection. Ditto for my agent, Bruce Westwood of Westwood Creative Artists. Dinah Forbes, my editor at M&S, brought her own brand of patience to her tasks, along with her impeccably crisp style and skills as a guru of structure. And Heather Sangster, my copy editor, was my saviour more than once. I thank you all.

A few anecdotes in *Eminent Canadians* were first published in a different form in various newspaper columns I have written over the years for *Saturday Night, The Toronto Star,* and *The Globe and*

Mail. They are stories that bear repeating, I think, and in the book they are set in quite different contexts.

Many people helped me in the research and writing of this book and I would like to thank especially the following people: Katherine Ashenburg, Ann Brumell, Douglas Chambers, James Fleming, Richard Gidney, Sandra Gwyn, David Harris, Francess Halpenny, Marie Korey, Patricia Kennedy, Richard Landon, Peter Lewis, Anna Luengo, Douglas Stoute, and Indira Stewart. Any others I have inadvertently omitted, please accept my apologies and thanks.

In my family, my generous stepmother, Mary Fraser, again did me the favour of proofing the galleys. My three beautiful teenaged daughters – Jessie, Kate, and Clara – ensured that my life remained hilariously eventful rather than monotonous and lonely during the writing of this book, while their mother, Elizabeth MacCallum, protected and encouraged me as usual with her loyalty, courage, and love.

Massey College
Toronto
December 1999